THE HUEY P. NEWTON READER

THE HUEY P. NEWTON READER

Edited by
David Hilliard and Donald Weise
Foreword by
Fredrika Newton
Introduction by
David Hilliard

SEVEN STORIES PRESS
New York • Oakland

Seven Stories Press
140 Watts Street
New York, NY 10013
www.sevenstories.com

Library of Congress Cataloging-in-Publication Data
Newton, Huey P.
The Huey P. Newton reader / Huey P. Newton ; edited by David Hilliard and Donald Weise.— A Seven Stories Press 1st ed.
p.   cm.
Includes bibliographical references.
ISBN 978-1-58322-466-3 — ISBN 978-1-58322-467-0 (pbk.)
1. Newton, Huey P.—Archives. 2. Black Panther Party—Archives.
3. African American political activists—Archives.
4. African Americans—Politics and government—20th century—Sources.
5. Black power—United States—History—20th century—Sources.
6. Radicalism—United States—History—20th century—Sources.
7. United States—Race relations—Sources. 8. United States—Politics and government—1945–1989--Sources.
I. Hilliard, David. II. Weise, Donald. III. Title.
E185.97.N48 A28 2002
322.4'2'092--dc21
2002001885

9 8 7 6 5

College professors may order examination copies of Seven Stories Press titles for free. To order, visit www.sevenstories.com/textbook, or fax on school letterhead to (212) 226-1411.

Book design by Adam Simon

Printed in the U.S.A.

Contents

Part III: The Second Wave

Part IV: The Last Empire

Foreword

HUEY P. NEWTON and the Black Panther Party he created have passed out of existence, as all things do. Like all things, they leave behind memories, those private sensory recollections sadly destined to be weaned out of history with each new generation. Like some, they leave behind certain tangible references to lives lived and life works. But, in kinship with those rare few whose footprints remain in defiance of time, they leave a legacy, a humane legacy that is a beacon from the past for those of us searching still to cross the abyss of human barbarity that seems written into eternity.

I came to know and embrace the best of Huey Newton, first as a Black Panther Party youth member and later as his wife during the last five years of his life. In that, I am a witness to the enlightened dreams as well as the torture of the dreamer. I came to know that he was the truest revolutionary, seeking always to bring harmony between the nature of things and the state of things, to transform dark into light, to challenge fear and hate with courage and love.

The Huey P. Newton Reader is the first summation of this revolutionary life told in Huey's own words. From this definitive collection of writings, readers will discover, perhaps for the first time, the astonishing breadth of Huey's thoughts and actions. For history is a witness to the fact that he acted on his vision by inventing an instrument for freedom and enlightenment called the Black Panther Party. This was his essence and his life's work, left behind as his personal legacy. As such, the Black Panther Party has left a living legacy, a work begun, but left undone, a foundation laid, a seed sown whose flowers brighten the barren fields today.

Fredrika Newton, President
The Dr. Huey P. Newton Foundation

A people who have suffered so much for so long at the hands of a racist society must draw the line somewhere.
—Huey P. Newton, from *Executive Mandate No. 1*, 1967

introduction

It has been twelve years since the death of Black Panther Party founder Huey P. Newton. Yet I still struggle with the memory of his life and the message of his legacy. Huey was a complicated man who resists easy categorization, even by lifelong comrades such as myself. He refused to be trapped by ideological or identity labels, considering himself to be, quite literally, a work-in-progress. Nevertheless, there is a tendency on the part of supporters and detractors alike to fix Huey in place. He is either the revolutionary savior of African Americans or public enemy number one. Hero worship and vilification, however, obscure more than they illuminate. For these often fanciful recollections, in spite of their divergent intentions, fail to help us understand that beneath the mythology lived an intrepid man with dreams, fears, and vulnerabilities—in short, an ordinary man whose extraordinary courage changed the world in ways we are still coming to terms with today.

To me a useful starting point for interpreting Huey's life and legacy is October 28, 1967, when the twenty-five-year-old Black Panther leader was charged with the shooting-death of Oakland policeman John Frey. Huey's armed confrontations with law enforcement officials had headlined San Francisco Bay Area newspapers since the Party's inception the previous fall. But he had not been patrolling police in the early hours of October 28th when an officer signaled him to the curb. "Well, well, well, what do we have here? The great, *great* Huey P. Newton," Frey is remembered to have said to the driver, who had been looking for parking. Experienced in routine police intimidation procedure, Huey patiently awaited release. Without provocation Frey suddenly ordered the unarmed Panther from his car. Protests that the officer was detaining him illegally were met with an unexpected blow to the face, knocking Huey to the ground. When he attempted to rise, the policeman fired once, wounding him in the stomach. Then a series of gunshots rang out in the morning darkness, and Officer Frey dropped over dead. Establishing the identity of the unknown trigger-man became the national focal point for the press over the next three years, with journalists arriving from as far away as London to report on what quickly became the cause célèbre of the New Left and a turning point in Black Panther history.

This incident raises many of the issues relevant to, if not also the misperceptions that preclude, a clear understanding of Huey's formative contributions to liberation politics in America. The vast movement to "Free Huey" that evolved in the wake of his arrest launched the Black Panthers—an organization I had joined in 1966 as a founding member and its chief of staff—from the periphery of the declining civil rights struggle of the late 1960s and into the vanguard position of the black liberation movement. On a separate level, the events of October 28th also function symbolically to underscore the challenges inherent in any attempt to reclaim a man from the myths that overwhelm all vestiges of the native son. When the man in question is an African-American revolutionary leader identified with the open display of firearms and, more importantly, his willingness to employ those weapons in self-defense as no civil rights leader had done before or since, the task becomes especially strenuous. Indeed, despite his acquittal in the killing of Officer Frey over thirty years ago, Huey's memory remains figuratively "on trial," often mired in the salacious details of disgruntled critics who have purposefully taken up the myth on behalf of political conservatism under various names. The historical record, however, speaks from a more sophisticated perspective, reminding us that the man in full can be appreciated only once the mythology has been laid to rest.

The Huey P. Newton Reader performs this role in several ways. Firstly, the book restores Huey's voice as the Party's founder and theoretician. It is therefore the benchmark for Black Panther ideology. This is also the first comprehensive volume of Huey's writings, speeches, and dialogues ever published. The unprecedented scope of the project com-

bines classic texts ranging in topic from the creation of the Black Panthers to African Americans and self-defense, Eldridge Cleaver's controversial defection from the Party, FBI infiltration of civil rights
groups, the Vietnam War, and the burgeoning feminist and gay liberation movements, along with never-before-published writings,
including articles on President Richard Nixon, prison martyr George
Jackson, Pan-Africanism, and affirmative action. When approached
collectively, this body of work assists the process of revisiting and revi-
talizing the intellectual legacy of African Americans whose political
innovations shook the foundations of popular notions of socially
acceptable forms of protest. One needs only to look to the resurrected
historical standing of the long-maligned Malcolm X to understand that
although old myths die hard, they do ultimately surrender to the
scrutiny of time. As such, *The Huey P. Newton Reader* attests to the
perennial relevance of Huey's vision, inviting a new generation of
activists to adapt his ideas to serve the present-day struggle against
repression and as a model for youth toward meeting today's challenges.

If the deconstruction of Huey's "outlaw" status is one point of entry
to this collection, then the impact of Malcolm X on the Black Panthers is also worthy of comment. "Malcolm X was the first political
person in this country that I really identified with," Huey writes of the
Party's origins. "We continue to believe that the Black Panther Party
exists in the spirit of Malcolm . . . the Party is a living testament to
his life and work." Although Huey and co-founder Bobby Seale did
not aspire to replicate Malcolm's Organization of Afro-American
Unity, the fledgling political entity whose fruition was cut short by his
murder in February 1965, Malcolm's teachings were nevertheless fundamental in structuring the Black Panther Party for Self-Defense, as
the group was originally named in October 1966. This new call for
self-defense, however, furthered Malcolm's ideology, rejecting his black
nationalism while incorporating a class-based political analysis that
owed much to the writings of Frantz Fanon, Che Guevara, and Mao
Tse-tung. Huey's innovation lay in arguing for the necessity of armed
resistance while at the same time realizing that oppression would not
be resolved through armed struggle alone. Rather, the Party's corner-
stone Ten Point Program approached self-defense in terms of political empowerment, encompassing protection against joblessness and the

circumstances that excluded blacks from equal employment opportunities; against predatory business practices intended to exploit the needs of the poor; against homelessness and inferior housing conditions; against educational systems that denigrate and miscast the histories of oppressed peoples; against a prejudiced judiciary that convicts African Americans and other people of color by all-white juries; and, finally, against the lawlessness of law enforcement agencies that harass, abuse, and murder blacks with impunity.

Still, it was the police patrols and not our work on behalf of jobs and housing that won the Black Panthers immediate notoriety. It bears mentioning here that anyone who wished to carry a loaded, unconcealed weapon at the time was legally entitled to do so, as white militant groups like the Minutemen, the Rangers, and the Ku Klux Klan had done with limited intervention from the establishment. Among African Americans, especially activists schooled in the tenets of nonviolent resistance, armed self-defense was contentious to say the least. "We had seen Watts rise up," Huey recalls. "We had seen Martin Luther King come to Watts in an effort to calm the people, and we had seen his philosophy of nonviolence rejected. Black people had been taught nonviolence; it was deep in us. What good, however, was nonviolence when the police were determined to rule by force?" The press therefore delighted in our public displays of weaponry, disregarding in the process the law-abiding basis at the foundation of the Party's operations. "We wanted to show that we didn't have to tolerate police abuse, that the black community would provide its own security, following the local laws and ordinances and the California Penal Code." We were not, however, a security force but a community model for legally protesting police misconduct. Even highly publicized actions such as the Black Panther demonstration at the California State capitol in Sacramento, wherein twenty-nine armed African-American men and women entered the congressional floor to challenge pending legislation aimed at depriving blacks of their constitutional right to carry weapons, was administered by Huey in strict accordance with state laws. The Mulford Bill, or "Panther Bill," as the legislation was alternately known when it was passed in July 1967, in effect criminalized all open displays of loaded firearms. "We knew how the system operated. If we used the laws in our own interest and against theirs, then the power structure would simply change the laws." Nonetheless, we abided by the new legislation, ending our patrols overnight.

In spite of this momentary setback, the Black Panthers had left an indelible impression on the political landscape in a matter of months. According to Huey, "Our newspaper [*The Black Panther*] was reaching the people; the Sacramento stance had received tremendous support; new chapters were springing up in many cities; we were exploring new ways to raise the consciousness of Black people. Everything was working well." Included in the rush of events was the addition of newly appointed Black Panther Party Minister of Information Eldridge Cleaver, a former-convict-turned-journalist who had won acclaim with the release of his controversial bestseller *Soul on Ice,* in 1966. Like Huey, Eldridge was a committed proponent of Malcolm's teachings. Significantly, Huey and Eldridge parted over ideological differences. "When Eldridge joined the Party it was after the police confrontation, which left him fixated with the 'either/or' attitude. This was that either the community picked up the gun with the Party or else they were cowards and there was no place for them." Eldridge ultimately dismissed the Party's broad self-defense package, defining the black liberation battle exclusively in terms of armed struggle. But these differences were not wholly apparent to anyone, including myself, in 1967. At that moment, Eldridge was an articulate Black Panther spokesperson, a position that assumed critical importance with Huey's arrest in the death of Officer Frey that fall.

It is perhaps impossible today for anyone who did not witness the proceedings at the Alameda County Courthouse in Oakland to fully appreciate the political magnitude of Huey's trial. On the court's opening day in July 1968 over 5,000 demonstrators and 450 Black Panthers crowded the streets to protest the injustice of the case, while messages of solidarity were received by the Party from around the world. There had, of course, been solidarity movements to free American political prisoners in the early part of the twentieth century. The call to "Free Huey," however, was louder and larger than any other. Simply put, there had never before been a movement of this magnitude because never before had there been an African-American political prisoner of this caliber. Principally, this was due to the fact that there had never been a U.S. protest group that posed a greater threat to the racial status quo than the Black Panther Party. For Huey's trial was in reality another form of state-sponsored political retaliation against the Panthers. Much as the ruling establishment had employed the Mulford Bill in a failed attempt to shut down the Party, monied interests now made use of the courts to accomplish what the legislature had been unable to do. Even a side glance at the details later involved in the state's attempts to prosecute other African-American activists, including Angela Davis and Black Panther leaders Bobby Seale, Ericka Huggins, George Jackson, Geronimo Pratt, and, more recently, Mumia Abu-Jamal, illustrate a pattern of politically motivated repression against black dissidents that has continued for years. Indeed, Huey's defense movement is the progenitor of the modern American prison movement, and echoes from the call to "Free Huey" can now be heard in the public outcry to "Free Mumia."

While the immense groundswell of support for Huey positioned us at the forefront of the struggle for social justice, this sudden prestige also incurred severe political backlash. According to FBI Director J. Edgar Hoover in October 1968, the Panthers were "the greatest threat to the internal security of the country," and field agents were instructed "to exploit all avenues of creating . . . dissension within the ranks of the BPP." Further, an FBI memorandum dated the following month orders agents to develop "hard-hitting counterintelligence measures aimed at crippling the BPP." COINTELPRO, an acronym for the Bureau's "counterintelligence program," became the FBI vehicle of choice in Hoover's "war" against the Panthers. Of particular usefulness was the special COINTELPRO "Black Nationalist" division, whose specific purpose, in the FBI's own words, was to "expose, disrupt, misdirect, discredit, or otherwise neutralize the activities of the Black nationalists." Hoover was determined to prevent the rise of a black "Messiah" who might "unify and electrify" African Americans. With Malcolm X and Martin Luther King, Jr., dead, Hoover predicted that Huey would fill this "messianic" role. The fanfare surrounding the "Free Huey" movement undoubtedly exacerbated Hoover's hysteria, leading in turn to a campaign of military-style attacks new to the Bureau's long, disgraceful history in combating activists. Wiretaps, burglaries, forgeries, as well as the use of undercover agent provocateurs and FBI-orchestrated killings of Black Panthers, were all put to use in the Bureau's mission to splinter and destroy the Party. Therefore, when I speak of Hoover's "war" against the Panthers, I mean precisely that: a declaration of war by the U.S. government against the Black Panther Party.

Perhaps the most unlikely target of FBI backlash was the Party's free community service programs. As mentioned earlier, our Ten Point platform for self-defense included pragmatic concerns of social welfare alongside issues of armed resistance. To this end the Party, in late 1968, initiated a series of Survival Programs, or grassroots outreach programs, which provided free groceries, clothing, medical care, legal assistance, and other basic necessities to thousands of people nationwide. "We called them 'survival programs pending transformation of society,' since we needed long-term programs and a disciplined organization to carry them out," Huey writes of this pioneering work. "They were designed to help the people survive until their consciousness is raised, which is only the first step in the revolution to build a new America." Among the most successful of these offerings was the Breakfast for Children Program, which provided free hot meals to schoolchildren. Our programs were also enormously effective in communicating the Party's teachings to the people, and law enforcement agencies accordingly took dramatic, if unsuccessful, measures to sabotage operations. Police raided the Breakfast for Children Program, ransacked food storage facilities, destroyed kitchen equipment, and attempted to disrupt relations between the Black Panthers and local business owners and community advocates, whose contributions made the programs possible. "The ostensible reason for this was that children participating in the program were being propagandized, which simply meant that they were being taught how to think, not what to think," Huey comments. Nevertheless, the Survival Programs endured, growing to address issues of employment, housing, prisoner aid, and senior safety as well as other concerns in the 1970s.

Compounding the state's frustrated attempts to end the Survival Programs was its concurrent failure to convict Huey in the murder of Officer Frey. Freed in July 1970, Huey returned to the streets to resume the leadership he had administered indirectly from his prison cell during the past three years. Unbeknownst to him, however, the landmark trial had exalted his image among the people to heights beyond his control. No longer Oakland's native son nor even the renowned Black Panther charged with killing a policeman, Huey had become a symbol. "There was now an element of hero worship that had not existed before I got busted," he writes of this unwelcome dynamic that separated him from the movement that had steadfastly protested his innocence and, in effect, freed him from prison. "Too many so-called leaders of the movement have been made into celebrities and their revolutionary fervor destroyed by mass media.... The task is to transform society; only the people can do that—not heroes, not celebrities, not stars." Resisting idolatry, Huey set to work on "life-and-death issues," most visibly defending political prisoners Bobby Seale, Ericka Huggins, and the Soledad Brothers. Huey also prioritized launching the Ideological Institute, a Black Panther education and leadership training center established in 1971. "I did not want to be, could not be, the only one developing ideas," he observes of his role as the Party's chief theoretician. "Given the opportunity, other comrades would be able to come up with fresh solutions as they encountered changing conditions."

Central to the Party's longevity was Huey's ongoing commitment to adapting Black Panther ideology to changing times, especially as these changes pertained to world affairs. Starting with Marx's concept of "dialectical materialism" as his basis (that is, the struggle of opposites based upon their unity, contradiction being the ruling principle of the universe), Huey formulated an analysis in which he argued that the U.S. was not a nation but an empire. Indeed, foreign governments of any size could no longer claim complete independence from American interests, as Huey's meetings with world leaders such as Yasser Arafat, Chinese premier Chou En-lai, and Mozambique president Samora Moises Machel made clear during his travels abroad in 1971. Instead, what had once been a series of separate nations now functioned collectively as a network of U.S.-controlled "communities." Huey's philosophy of "Intercommunalism," one of the earliest recorded premonitions of present-day "globalism," became the guiding intellectual current of the Party, infusing the Panthers with a global perspective that flew in the face of nationalism. "As one country becomes free, it makes each country stronger because it develops a base of liberated territory so that we'll be in a better position to liberate our communities," Huey asserts, underscoring the possibility for worldwide solidarity wherever opposition to U.S. dominance exists. "We will slowly strangle imperialism by freeing one country after another. This is why we support the brothers and sisters in southern and northern Africa as well as those in Asia and Latin American who are struggling against the U.S. empire."

Huey's intellectual currency was further enhanced with the 1972 publication of *To Die for the People*, his first collection of writings and speeches made available to the general reading public. With Toni Morrison as the book's editor, the project was instrumental in disseminating Black Panther ideology beyond the movement. In addition to highlighting seminal writings reprinted from the Black Panther newspaper, Huey addresses topics such as black capitalism, the relevance of the African-American church, and the Party's role in mediating events after the Attica prison uprising. Following the success of *To Die for the People* he published a more intimate articulation of Party history in his autobiography, *Revolutionary Suicide*. When the book came out in 1973, Huey's private life, particularly his formative years predating the Black Panthers, was still widely underreported and therefore unknown to most readers. Further, the book helped demystify the Party in the popular imagination. Attacked by the FBI and slandered throughout the press as "cop killers" and suicidal thugs, we were victims of outrageous accusations, which even the book's title seeks to rectify. "Revolutionary suicide does not mean that I and my comrades have a death wish; it means just the opposite. We have such a strong desire to live with hope and dignity that existence without them is impossible . . . . Above all, it demands that the revolutionary see his death and life as one piece." Appearing the same year as his autobiography was *In Search of Common Ground*, a book-length conversation with famed psychoanalyst Erik T. Erikson, in which Huey presents his most in-depth rendering of Intercommunalism up to that moment.

By the mid-1970s, the Party had reached its pinnacle of influence. Huey was the preeminent African-American leader for social justice in the world, with the Panthers counting over forty chapters domestically, as well as chapters in England, Israel, Australia, and India. In addition to political coalitions with liberation movements overseas were unions established among Asian Americans, Latinos, white peace activists, feminists, and lesbians and gay men in the U.S. Fundamental to our work of this period was Huey's renewed call for institution building. Although this feature had been central to the ideological platform laid in the Ten Point Program in 1966, we had strayed from our original purpose. Eldridge Cleaver, for example, had alienated the Black Panthers from many in the community who did not relate to his "either/or" philosophy of "revolution now." Moreover, Eldridge had abandoned the Survival Programs during Huey's absence while he was incarcerated, leading to further breaches in support where those ties were most essential: namely, between the Party and people living in local communities where we were active. Reclaiming the politics of empowerment as our keystone, the Black Panthers now exercised considerable strength to transform the American establishment, lobbying on behalf of the poor to secure thousands of jobs, low-cost housing, and public funding to operate the free community programs. Through this influence we helped elect progressive political candidates, including Party members, who now sat on public-school boards and other positions of regional and national authority. As a result, critics soon charged Huey with selling out the movement to the very "system" from which the Panthers had previously demanded independence. In reply, Huey invoked Intercommunalism by way of an explanation. "I contend that no one is outside the system. The world is so close now, because of technology, that we are like a series of dispersed communities, but we're all under siege by the one empire-state authority, the reactionary inner circle of the United States."

From its beginnings the chief ambition of the Black Panther Party had been to change the U.S. government by exhausting all legal means, and we had done so to an astounding degree by the late 1970s. The undeniably racist tenor of American culture and politics persisted, of course. Obliterating that reality altogether had never been our objective. However, African Americans and other oppressed peoples had in fact made tremendous advances through the work of the Black Panthers: Our police patrols had taken the initial steps toward establishing both the first community-based police review boards and the first wave of African-American officer recruitment; the Survival Programs provided revolutionary models for social service, which public agencies and, remarkably enough, the federal government adopted to feed children, clothe families, and offer medical necessities; the Party's groundbreaking inroads into electoral politics brought the first black mayor to Oakland, laying in part the foundation for today's political power base among black congressional leaders; and perhaps most notable of all, we raised the political consciousness of African Americans everywhere. I should add for purposes of clarity that, contrary to popular belief, Huey did not intend for the Party to "make" revolution. We realized at a very early point in our development that only the people are the makers of revolution. "The main function of the Party is to awaken the people and teach them the strategic method of resisting a power structure," Huey remarks of the Party's purpose. "The people make revolution; the oppressors, by their brutal actions, cause resistance by the people. The vanguard party only teaches the correct methods of resistance." And that is precisely what those of us in the Black Panther Party did for almost fifteen years.

Dialectical materialism assures us that all things ultimately reach a point of negation wherein there is a new stage of development. Around 1980 the Party took on new characteristics, realizing its slogan "Power to the People." With progressive political representatives in authority and government agencies performing tasks previously operated by the Panthers, our revolutionary self-defense platform had by then been largely integrated into the political mainstream. Furthermore, Huey was exhausted by Hoover's COINTELPRO campaign. The FBI's relentless attacks, which had grown in sophistication with the Party's own political maturity, now included charges of income tax fraud and misappropriation of funds. Complicating matters was Huey's drug addiction, which I speak to prominently in my memoir, *This Side of Glory*. One of the saddest ironies in Huey's iconoclastic life was that he died in 1989 at the hands of a drug dealer just a few blocks from where Officer Frey had been killed. Even in death, however, Huey remains a necessary source of political inspiration, as this collection of writings and speeches attests. For his is a living history. The work of the Black Panther Party remains an unfinished agenda. Huey states that revolution is a process—not a conclusion. Contradictions are the ruling principles of the universe. "I will fight until I die, however that may come. But whether I'm around or not to see it happen, I know that the transformation of society inevitably will manifest the true meaning of 'all power to the people.'"

David Hilliard, Executive Director
The Dr. Huey P. Newton Foundation

Part One
The First Steps

HUEY P. NEWTON was born the last of seven children in Monroe, Louisiana, in 1942. The family migrated three years later to Oakland, California, where his father served as a Baptist minister. Despite Huey's religious upbringing and close family ties, he was a troubled student involved in petty criminal activity and subject to constant expulsion from school throughout his adolescence. In part, this resulted from his being unable to read until age sixteen. Embarrassed by his illiteracy and determined to keep up with his older siblings' academic strides, he taught himself to read with the assistance of an older brother. By 1959 Huey had advanced himself to college-level comprehension, entering Oakland City College that same year. Here he discovered the influential writings of W.E.B. Du Bois, Mao Tsetung, and Malcolm X, which shaped his fledgling intellect.

As his political consciousness became radicalized, Huey put his learning into action by taking part in black student activism. Unfortunately, the many self-described campus "radicals" focused on student issues alone, neglecting the concerns of the black community at large. Having grown up among poor African Americans, Huey understood that in spite of the newly granted legislative victories, blacks still lacked equality under the law. The Voter Rights Act of 1964 and the Civil Rights Act of 1965 were breakthroughs for African Americans but did not create urgently needed jobs and other basic necessities such as health care. Huey thus realized at this early point in his political development that only a liberation movement whose program addressed survival issues would bring about the revolutionary agenda he had begun to envision.

Although campus organizing had been a disappointing experience, this work was nevertheless instrumental in bringing Huey together with classmate and future Black Panther Party co-founder Bobby Seale. The following excerpts from Huey's autobiography, *Revolutionary Suicide*, chronicle this formative period, including the Party's founding in 1966, its turbulent first year on the streets, Huey's historic encounter with Officer Frey, and the overnight rise of the Black Panthers to international prominence.

scoring

first studied law to become a better burglar. Figuring I might get busted at any time and wanting to be ready when it happened, I bought some books on criminal law and burglary and felony and looked up as much as possible. I tried to find out what kind of evidence they needed, what things were actually considered violations of the law, what the loopholes were, and what you could do to avoid being charged at all. They had a law for everything. I studied the California penal code and books like *California Criminal Evidence* and *California Criminal Law* by Fricke and Alarcon, concentrating on those areas that were somewhat vague. The California penal code says that any law which is vague to the ordinary citizen—the average reasonable man who lives in California and who is exposed to the state's rules, regulations, and culture—does not qualify as a statute.

Later on, law enforcement courses helped me to know how to deal with the police. Before I took Criminal Evidence in school, I had no idea what my rights really were. I did not know, for instance, that police can be arrested. My studying helped, because every time I got arrested I was released with no charge. Until I went to prison for something I was innocent of, I had no convictions against me; yet I had done a little of everything. The court would convict you if it could, but if you knew the law and were articulate, then the judges figured you were not too bad because your very manner of speaking indicated that you had been "indoctrinated" into their way of thinking.

I was doing a lot of things that were technically unlawful. Sometimes my friends and I received stolen blank checks from a company, which we would then make out for $150 to $200, never more than an amount consistent with a weekly paycheck. Sometimes we stole the checks ourselves; other times we bought them from guys who had stolen them. You had to do this fast, before the companies distributed check numbers to banks and stores.

We burglarized homes in the Oakland and Berkeley hills in broad daylight. Sometimes we borrowed a pickup truck and put a lawn mower and garden tools in it. Then we drove up to a house that appeared empty and rang the bell. If no one answered, we rolled the lawn mower around to the back, as if we planned to cut the grass and trim the hedges. Then, swiftly, we broke into the house and took what we wanted.

Often I went car prowling by myself. I would walk the streets until I saw a good prospect, then break into the car and take what was on the seat or in the glove compartment. Many people left their cars unlocked, which made it easier.

We scored best, however, with the credit game or short-change games. We stole or bought stolen credit cards and then purchased as much as possible with them before their numbers were distributed. You could either sell the booty or use it yourself.

A very profitable credit game went like this: we would pay $20 or $30 to someone who owned a small business to say that we had worked for him five years or so. This established a work record good enough for credit in one of the big stores. Then we would charge about $150 worth of merchandise and pay $20 down. Of course, we used an assumed name and a phony address, but we let them check the address, because we gave them a location and telephone number where one of our friends lived. We made payments for a couple of months. Then we would charge over the $150 limit. If you were making payments, they raised your credit. We would buy a big order, and then stop making payments. If they called our "place of work," they were told we had just quit. If they called our alleged address, they learned we had "moved over a month ago." The store was left hanging. They did not really lose, because they were actually robbing the community blind. They just wrote off the amount and continued their robbing. The lesson: you can survive through petty crime and hurt those who hurt you.

Once into petty crime, I stopped fighting. I had transferred the conflict, the aggression, and hostility from the brothers in the community to the Establishment.

The most successful game I ran was the short-change game. Short-changing was an art I developed so well that I could make $50 to $60 a day. I ran it everywhere, in small and large stores, and even on bank tellers. In the short-change game I would go into a store with five one-dollar bills, ask the clerk for change, and walk out with a ten-dollar bill. This was the $5-to-$10 short-change. You could also do a $10-to-$20 short-change by walking into the store with ten one-dollar bills and coming out with a twenty-dollar bill.

The $5-to-$10 short-change worked this way: you folded up four of the bills into a small tight wad. Then you bought something like candy or gum with the other bill so that the clerk had to open the cash register to give you change. I always stood a little distance from the register so that the clerk had to come to me to give me the change. You have to get the cash register open and get the clerk to move away from it so that his mind is taken off what he has in the register.

When he brought my change from the candy, I handed him the wad of four one-dollar bills and said, "Here are *five* singles. Will you give me a five-dollar bill for them?" He would then hand me the five-dollar bill before he realized that there were only four singles in the wad. He has the register open, and I am prepared for him to discover the error. When he did, I would then hand him another single, but also the five-dollar bill he had given me and say, "Well, here's six more; give me a ten." He would do it, and I would take the $10 and be gone before he realized what had happened. Most of the time they never understood. It happened so fast they would simply go on to another customer. By the time things began to click in their minds, they could never be sure that something had in fact gone wrong until the end of the day when they tallied up the register. By that time I was just a vague memory. Of course, if the clerk was quick and sensed that something was not right, then I pretended to be confused and would say I had made a mistake and give him the right amount. It was a pretty safe game, and it worked for me many times.

The brother who introduced me to short-changing eventually became a Muslim, but before that he taught me to burglarize cars parked by the emergency entrances of hospitals. People would come to the hospital in a rush and leave their cars unlocked, with valuables in the open. I never scored on Blacks under any condition, but scoring on whites was a strike against injustice.

Whenever I had liberated enough cash to give me a stretch of free time, I stayed home reading, books like Dostoevsky's *Crime and Punishment, The Devils,* and *The House of the Dead; The Trial* by Franz Kafka; and Thomas Wolfe's *Look Homeward, Angel.* I read and reread *Les Miserables* by Victor Hugo, the story of Jean Valjean, a Frenchman who spent thirty years in prison for stealing a loaf of bread to feed his hungry family. This really reached me, because I identified with Valjean, and I often thought of my father being in a kind of social prison because he wanted to feed his family. Albert Camus's *The Stranger* and *The Myth of Sisyphus* made me feel even more justified in my pattern of liberating property from the oppressor as an antidote to social suicide.

I felt that white people were criminals because they plundered the world. It was more, however, than a simple antiwhite feeling, because I never wanted to hurt poor whites, even though I had met some in school who called me "nigger" and other names. I fought them, but I never took their lunches or money because I knew that they had nothing to start with. With those who had money it was a different story. I still equated having money with whiteness, and to take what was mine and what the white criminals called theirs gave me a feeling of real freedom.

I even bragged to my friends how good I felt about the whole matter. When they were at my apartment during times when there wasn't any food to eat, I told them that even though I starved, my time was my own and I could do anything I wanted with it. I didn't have a car then, because most of my money was spent on the apartment, food, and clothes. When friends asked me why I did not get a car, I told them it was because I did not want bills and that a car was not my main goal or desire. My purpose was to have as much leisure time as possible. I could have pulled bigger jobs and gotten more, but I did not want any status symbols. I wanted most of all to be free from the life of a servant forced to take those low-paying jobs and looked at with scorn by white bosses.

Eventually, I got caught, and more than once, but by then I had developed a fairly good working knowledge of the law, and I decided to defend myself. Although no skilled legal technician, I could make a good defense. If you are an existentialist, defending yourself is another manifestation of freedom. When you are brought into the courts of the Establishment, you can show your contempt for them. Most defendants want to get high-priced counsel or use the state to speak for them through the Public Defender. If you speak for yourself, you can say exactly what you want, or at least not say what you do not want to. Or you can laugh at them. As Elaine Brown, a member of the Black Panther Party, says in her song, "The End of Silence," "You laugh at laws passed by a silly lot that tell you to give thanks for what you've already got." The laws exist to defend those who possess property. They protect the possessors who should share but who do not. By defending myself, I showed my contempt for that structure.

It gave me real pleasure to defend myself. I never thought in terms of conviction or acquittal, although it was an added treat to escape their net. But even a conviction would not have dismayed me, because at least I had the opportunity to laugh at them and show my contempt. They would see that I was not intimidated enough to raise the money to get counsel—money that I did not have in the first place—or to accept a Public Defender.

I especially liked traffic violations. For a while, I paid a lot of traffic tickets. When I became my own defender, I never paid another one. Of the three major cases in which I defended myself, the only one I lost was the one in which I was innocent.

Once, I was indicted on sixteen counts of burglary through trickery as a result of the short-change game, and I beat the cases during the pretrial period because the police could not establish the *corpus delicti* or the elements of the case. Each law had a body of elements, and each element has to be violated in order for a crime to have been committed. That's what they call the *corpus delicti*. People think that term means the physical body, but it really means the body of elements. For example, according to California law, in order to commit armed robbery you have to be armed, and you must expropriate through fear or force related to weapons; you can have armed robbery without any bullets in the gun. The elements of the case relate to fear and force in connection with weapons.

In the short-change or "bunko" case I was accused of running my game in sixteen stores. However, they could get only a few people to say they were short in their registers. I was really saved from being convicted because the police tried to get a young woman teller from a bank to say that I had short-changed her. A lot of people will not admit they have been short-changed. In the pretrial, in which they were trying to get a federal case, they asked me whether I had gone into the bank. I refused to admit it. I knew that the young woman whom they wanted to testify against me had not shown up at court. When I bailed out, I went to her bank and asked her if the police had been there. She said they had and that they were trying to persuade her that I had short-changed her. She said she would not testify because she knew it had not happened. I invited her to court to testify on my behalf. She came and explained to the judge that the police had tried to persuade her to testify, but she would not comply.

My argument was that the police had invented the short-change rap against me. I pointed out that clerks who were short-changed would have missed the money either when I was in the store or at the end of the day. None of these people had notified the police. The police had sought them out and by suggesting that they had been short-changed were really offering the clerks a chance to make five or ten extra dollars—a sort of pay-off for testifying. Most people, I said, are not as honest as the young girl bank teller.

Another argument I put forth in my defense was that if someone else had gotten change after I had been in the store before inventory of the register, it was quite possible, even probable, that the money had been lost at some other time. I got a dismissal on the grounds of insufficient evidence.

In the second major case, I was accused of having stolen some books from a store near the school and of having burglarized the car of another student and taken his books. He reported to the bookstore that his books had been stolen. They were on the lookout for books with the marking he had described. I had not stolen the books, even though they were in my possession. I was doing a lot of gambling at the time, and some students who owed me money gave me the books instead. We used books for money, because if a book was required in a course, we could sell it to the bookstore. Even though I did not know where the books came from, I suspected that they were stolen.

I figured there was about $60 worth of books in the stack. When I needed money, I sent my cousin to the bookstore to cash them in. The scoring

bookstore took them away from her, claiming that they were stolen. They would not give her any money, nor would they return the books. I went down to the store and told them they could not confiscate my books without due process of law. They knew I was a student at the college and that they could call the police on me any time they wanted. I told them that either they return the books right then or I would take as many books as I thought would equal the amount they had stolen from me. They gave me the books, and I went on to class.

Apparently the bookstore notified the Dean of Students, who called the police. While I was in class, the Oakland police came and escorted me with the books to the campus police, who took me to the Dean's office. No one could arrest me, because there was no warrant. The bookstore wanted to wait until the man who had reported the books stolen returned from the Army to identify them. So they took me to the Dean's office, and the Dean said he would give me a receipt, keeping the books until the owner came back. I told him that he would not give me a receipt, because they were my books and he could not confiscate my property without due process of law; to do so would be a violation of my constitutional rights. I added, "Furthermore, if you try to confiscate my property, I will ask the police over there to have you arrested." The police stood looking stupid, not knowing what to do. The Dean said the man would not be back for about a week, but he wanted the books. I took the books off his desk and said, "I'm enrolled here, and when you want to talk to me, I'll be around." Then I walked out of the office. They did not know how to deal with a poor oppressed Black man who knew their law and had dignity.

When I was charged and brought to trial, I defended myself again. The case revolved around identifying the books. The man knew that his books had been stolen; the bookstore knew they had lost some books. Identification had not been made, but I was charged with a theft. I had stashed the books away so that nobody could locate them, and when I came to court, I left them behind. They brought me to trial without any factual evidence against me, and I beat the case with the defense I conducted, particularly my cross-examination.

The woman who owned the bookstore took the stand. The previous year, on Christmas Eve, she had invited me to her home, and I had seen her off and on after that. When I was unwilling to continue a relationship with her, she became angry. I wanted to bring this out, but when I began this line of questioning, the judge was outraged and stopped it. By this time, however, she had broken down in tears on the stand, and it was apparent to the jury by the questions I asked and her reaction to them that she had personal reasons for testifying against me.

When the Dean testified, I really went to work. Although no books were entered into evidence, he said that I had in my possession some books identical to those on the list the day the police brought me to his office. I asked him, "Well, if the police were right there, why didn't you put me under arrest?" He said, "I wasn't sure of my rights." This was the opening I needed. I said, "You mean to say that I attend your school, and you're teaching me my rights without even knowing your own? You're giving me knowledge, and you don't know your basic civil rights?" Then I turned to the jury and argued that this was strange indeed. The judge was furious and almost cited me for contempt of court. I was in contempt, all right, and not only of the court. I was contemptuous of the whole system of exploitation, which I was coming to understand better and better.

I knew what the jury was thinking, and when the Dean said that he did not know his rights, I used his ignorance to my advantage. People automatically think, "You mean you're a college professor and you don't know something that basic and simple?" Once I planted this idea in the minds of the jurors, it completely negated the Dean's testimony.

I told the jury that I collected books, which I did, traded and sold them, and that I had some volumes similar to those named in the indictment—same names, authors, and so forth. When they wanted to view the books, I asked the judge if I could go home and get them. The judge said that he could not stop a trial in the middle (it was a misdemeanor case) to let me go home. My strategy worked, however, and I ended up with a hung jury.

Then came the second trial. This time I had the books in court, but nobody could identify them. I had acquired some different books— same authors and same names—and put some similar markings in them. The man who claimed his car had been burglarized, the Dean, and the owner of the bookstore could not positively identify them. They kept saying that the books were either similar or the same, but they were not sure.

I emphasized this uncertainty, saying that all I knew was I had purchased the books from another person. I told the jury that I had not in fact stolen the books and that by bringing them to court I was trying to find out if they belonged to those who had brought the charges. I got another hung jury.

They tried me a third time, with the same result. When they brought the case up a fourth time, the judge dismissed it. Off and on, with continuances and mistrials, the case dragged over a period of nine months. It was simple harassment, as far as I was concerned, because I had not stolen the books. They might also have been trying to test new prosecutors; I had a different one every time, every chump in Alameda County, and still they got nowhere. I looked them straight in the eye and advanced.

The third case came out of a party I attended with Melvin at the home of a probation officer who had gone to San Jose State College with him. Melvin had known some of the people at the party quite a while, and most of them were related to each other in some way, either by blood or by marriage. Melvin and I were outsiders. As usual, I started a discussion. A party was good or bad for me depending on whether I could start a rap session. I taught that way for the Afro-American Association and recruited a lot of the lumpens.

Some of these sessions ended in fights. It was almost like the dozens again, although, here, ideas, not mothers, were at issue. The guy who could ask the most penetrating questions and give the smartest answers "capped," or topped, all the others. Sometimes after a guy was defeated, or "shot down," if he wanted to fight, I would accommodate him. It was all the same. If I could get into a good rap and a good fight, too, the night was complete.

At the party, while we were talking, someone called Odell Lee came up and entered the conversation. I did not know him, had only seen him dancing earlier in the evening, but I had gone to school with his wife, Margo, who was there. Odell Lee walked up and said, "You must be an Afro-American." I replied, "I don't know what you mean. Are you asking me if I am of African descent, or are you asking me if I'm a member of Donald Warden's Afro-American Association? If the latter, then I am not. But if you're asking me if I'm of African ancestry, then I am an Afro-American, just as you are." He said some words in

Chinese and I came back in Swahili. Then he asked me, "Well, how do you know that I'm an Afro-American?" I replied, "Well, I have twenty-twenty vision, and I can see your hair is just as kinky as mine, and your face just as black, so I conclude that you must be exactly what I am, an Afro-American."

Saying that, I turned my back and began to cut my steak. I was the only one in the room with a steak knife. All the others had plastic utensils, but since the steak was kind of tough, I had gone into the kitchen for a regular steak knife. Having made my point, my move, so to speak, I turned my back on Lee in a kind of put-down. To him it was a provocative act.

Odell had a scar on his face from about the ear to just below his chin. This was a very significant point, because on the block you run into plenty of guys with scars like that, which usually means that the person has seen a lot of action with knives. This is not always the case, but when you are trying to survive on the block, you learn to be hip to the cues.

So I turned my back and began cutting steak with the knife I had in my right hand. He grabbed my left arm with his right and turned me around abruptly. When he did, my knife was pointed right at him in ready position. Lee said, "Don't turn your back on me when I'm talking to you." I pushed his hand off my arm. "Don't you ever put your hands on me again," I said, and turned around once more to my steak.

Ordinarily I would not have turned my back a second time, because he had all the signs of a tush hog. But somehow the conditions did not add up. Most people there were professionals—or training to become professionals—and this man with the scar did not seem to fit. We were not on the block, so I thought perhaps the scar meant nothing. All of a sudden, however, he was acting like a bully, and now he wanted everyone to know he was not finished with me. When I turned my back on him a second time, this would have ended the whole argument for the Black bourgeoisie, but the tush hog responded in his way.

He turned me around again, and the tempo picked up. "You must not know who you're talking to," he said, moving his left hand to his left hip pocket. I figured I had better hurry up. Since the best defense is a good offense, my steak knife was again in a ready position, instinctively. I said to him, "Don't draw a knife on me," and I thrust my knife forward, stabbing him several times before he could come up with his left hand. He held on to me with his right hand and tried to advance, but I pushed him away. I still do not know what he was doing with his left, but I was expecting to be hurt any time and determined to beat him to the punch.

Melvin grabbed Lee's right arm and pushed him into a corner, where he fell, bleeding heavily. He got up and charged me again, and I continued to hold my knife ready. Then Melvin jumped between us, and Lee fainted in his arms. As Melvin took the knife from me, we turned to the rest of the people, and somebody asked, "Why did you cut him?" Melvin said, "He cut him because he should have cut him," and we backed out of the room. Melvin wanted me to press charges against the man, but I would never go to the police.

About two weeks later, Odell Lee swore out charges against me. I don't know why he delayed so long, perhaps because he was in the hospital for a few days. Maybe he was hesitant. He had been talking about getting me, I know, but I also heard that his wife had urged him to press charges instead. To me, he was not the kind of character who would go to the police. I saw him as a guy who would rather look for me himself and deal right there. When he sent word that he was after me, I started packing a gun. Instead, I was arrested at my house on a warrant and indicted for assault with a deadly weapon. After I pleaded not guilty, it went to a jury trial. I defended myself again.

I was found guilty as charged, but only because I lacked a jury of my peers. My defense was based on the grounds that I was not guilty, either by white law or by the culture of the Black community. I did not deny that I stabbed Odell Lee—I admitted it—but the law says that when one sees or feels he is in imminent danger of great bodily harm or death, he may use whatever force necessary to defend himself. If he kills his assailant, the homicide is justified. This section of the California penal code is almost impossible for a man to defend himself under unless he is a part of the oppressor class. The oppressed have no chance, for people who sit on juries always think you could have picked another means of defense. They cannot see or understand the danger.

A jury of my peers would have understood the situation and exonerated me. But the jurors in Alameda County come out of big houses in the hills to pass judgment on the people whom they feel threaten their "peace." When these people see a scar on the face of a man on the block, they have no understanding of its symbolism. Odell Lee got on the stand and said that his scar resulted from an automobile accident. It may well have. But taking everything in context—his behavior at the party, the move toward his left hip, and his scar—my peers would never have convicted me.

Bobby Seale explains it brilliantly in *Seize the Time:* you may go to a party and step on someone's shoes and apologize, and if the person accepts the apology, then nothing happens. If you hear something like "An apology won't shine my shoes," then you know he is really saying, "I'm going to fight you." So you defend yourself, and in that case striking first would be a defensive act, not an offensive one. You are trying to get an advantage over an opponent who has already declared war.

It is all a matter of life styles that spills over into the problem of getting a jury of one's peers. If a truck driver is the defendant, should there be only truck drivers on the jury, or all white racists on the jury if a white racist is on trial? I say no. There is, nevertheless, an internal contradiction in a jury system that totally divides the accused and his jury. Different cultures and life styles in America use the same words with different shades of meaning. All belong to one society yet live in different worlds.

I was found guilty of a felony, assault with a deadly weapon, and faced a long jail sentence for the first time. Before and during the trial, I had been out on bail for several months. I came to court each time I was supposed to, but when I was convicted, the judge decided to revoke my bail immediately and place me in the custody of the bailiff while he considered what sentence to impose. Wanting none of this, I demanded to be sentenced right then. The judge said that if he sentenced me then, I would be sent to the state penitentiary. I told him to send me there immediately so that I could start serving my time. He refused, asking me, "Do you realize what you're saying?" I said, "I know what I'm saying, that you found me guilty. But I am not guilty, and now I don't want to wait around a month serving dead time while you think about it." No time was dead to me. It was all live time, life. I felt that if the judge wanted to think about it for thirty days, he should let me stay out on bail while he did so. But he would not. He had me confined to the Alameda County jail, a place I would get to know well—very well.

While I was waiting, my family hired a lawyer to represent me at the sentencing. The judge was a man named Leonard Dieden, who did not give lawyers, much less defendants, any respect. He has sent so many people to the penitentiary that a section of San Quentin is called "Dieden's Row." I was against my family hiring a lawyer because I felt it was useless. Nevertheless, they did, and he charged them $1,500 to go to court one time. When I arrived for sentencing, he was there, and he worked his "white magic": the judge sentenced me to six months in the county jail. Even though I had been convicted of a felony, the time they gave me was for a misdemeanor. This was to become a critical issue in my later capital trial, because the law says you can reduce a felony to a misdemeanor by serving less time. The penalty for a felony is no less than a year in the state penitentiary and no more than a life sentence or death. For a misdemeanor the maximum is one year in the county jail.

freedom

Jail is an odd place to find freedom, but that was the place I first found mine: in the Alameda County Jail in Oakland in 1964. This jail is located on the tenth floor of the Alameda County Court House, the huge, white building we call "Moby Dick." When I was falsely convicted of the assault against Odell Lee, Judge Dieden sent me there to await sentencing. Shortly after I arrived, I was made a trusty, which gave me an opportunity to move about freely. Conditions were not good; in fact, the place blew up a few weeks later, when the inmates refused to go on eating starches and split-pea soup at almost every meal, and went on a food strike. I joined them. When we were brought our split-pea soup, we hurled it back through the bars, all over the walls, and refused to lock up in our cells.

I was the only trusty who took part in the strike, and because I could move between cell blocks, they charged me with organizing it. True, I had carried a few messages back and forth, but I was not an organizer then, not that it mattered to the jail administration. Trusties were supposed to go along with the Establishment in everything, and since I could not do that, I was slapped with the organizing label and put in the "hole"—what Black prisoners call the "soul breaker."

I was twenty-two years old, and I had been in jail before on various beefs, mostly burglary and petty larceny. My parents were pretty sick of me in my late teens and the years following; so I had to depend on Sonny Man to come up from Los Angeles, or wherever he was, to bail me out. Since I had been "given" to him, he came whenever he could. But sometimes I could not find him. At any rate, I was no stranger to jail by 1964, although I had never been in extreme solitary confinement.

Within jail, there are four levels of confinement: the main line, segregation, isolation, and solitary—the "soul breaker." You can be in jail in jail, but the soul breaker is your "last" end of the world. In 1964, there were two of these deprivation cells at the Alameda County Court House; each was four and a half feet wide, by six feet long, by ten feet high. The floor was dark red rubber tile, and the walls were black. If the guards wanted to, they could turn on a light in the ceiling, but I was always kept in the dark, and nude. That is part of the deprivation, why the soul breaker is called a strip cell. Sometimes the prisoner in the other cell would get a blanket, but they never gave me one. He sometimes got toilet paper, too—the limit was two squares—and when he begged for more, he was told no, that is part of the punishment. There was no bunk, no washbasin, no toilet, nothing but bare floors, bare walls, a solid steel door, and a round hole four inches in diameter and six inches deep in the middle of the floor. The prisoner was supposed to urinate and defecate in this hole.

A half-gallon milk carton filled with water was my liquid for the week. Twice a day and always at night the guards brought a little cup of cold split-pea soup, right out of the can. Sometimes during the day they brought "fruit loaf," a patty of cooked vegetables mashed together into a little ball. When I first went in there, I wanted to eat and stay healthy, but soon I realized that was another trick, because when I ate I had to defecate. At night no light came in under the door. I could not even find the hole if I had wanted to. If I was desperate, I had to search with my hand; when I found it, the hole was always slimy with the filth that had gone in before. I was just like a mole looking for the sun; I hated finding it when I did. After a few days the hole filled up and overflowed, so that I could not lie down without wallowing in my own waste. Once every week or two the guard ran a hose into the cell and washed out the urine and defecation. This cleared the air for a while and made it all right to take a deep breath. I had been told I would break before the fifteen days were up. Most men did. After two or three days they would begin to scream and beg for someone to come and take them out, and the captain would pay a visit and say, "We don't want to treat you this way. Just come out now and abide by the rules and don't be so arrogant. We'll treat you fairly. The doors here arc large." To tell the truth, after two or three days I was in bad shape. Why I did not break I do not know. Stubbornness, probably. I did not want to beg. Certainly my resistance was not connected to any kind of ideology or program. That came later. Anyway, I did not scream and beg; I learned the secrets of survival.

One secret was the same that Mahatma Gandhi learned—to take little sips of nourishment, just enough to keep up one's strength, but never enough to have to defecate until the fifteen days were up. That way I kept the air somewhat clean and did not have the overflow. I did the same with water, taking little sips every few hours. My body absorbed all of it, and I did not have to urinate.

There was another, more important secret, one that took longer to learn. During the day a little light showed in the two-inch crack at the bottom of the steel door. At night, as the sun went down and the lights clicked off one by one, I heard all the cells closing, and all the locks. I held my hands up in front of my face, and soon I could not see them. For me, that was the testing time, the time when I had to save myself or break.

Outside jail, the brain is always being bombarded by external stimuli. These ordinary sights and sounds of life help to keep our mental processes in order, rational. In deprivation, you have to somehow replace the stimuli, provide an interior environment for yourself. Ever since I was a little boy I have been able to overcome stress by calling up pleasant thoughts. So very soon I began to reflect on the most soothing parts of my past, not to keep out any evil thoughts, but to reinforce myself in some kind of rewarding experience. Here I learned something. This was different.

When I had a pleasant memory, what was I to do with it? Should I throw it out and get another or try to keep it to entertain myself as long as possible? If you are not disciplined, a strange thing happens. The pleasant thought comes, and then another and another, like quick cuts flashing vividly across a movie screen. At first they are organized. Then they start to pick up speed, pushing in on top of one another going faster, faster, faster, faster. The pleasant thoughts are not so pleasant now; they are horrible and grotesque caricatures, whirling around in your head. Stop! I heard myself say, stop, stop, stop. I did not scream. I was able to stop them. Now what do I do?

I started to exercise, especially when I heard the jangle of keys as the guards came with the split-pea soup and fruit loaf. I would not scream; I would not apologize, even though they came every day, saying they would let me out if I gave in. When they were coming, I would get up and start my calisthenics, and when they went away, I would start the pleasant thoughts again. If I was too tired to stand, I would lie down and find myself on my back. Later, I learned that my position, with my back arched and only my shoulders and tight buttocks touching the floor, was a Zen Buddhist posture. I did not know it then, of course; I just found myself on my back. When the thoughts started coming again, to entertain me, and when the same thing happened with the speed-up, faster, faster, I would say stop! and start again.

Over a span of time—I do not know how long it took—I mastered my thoughts. I could start them and stop them; I could slow them down and speed them up. It was a very conscious exercise. For a while, I feared I would lose control. I could not think; I could not stop thinking. Only later did I learn through practice to go at the speed I wanted. I call them film clips, but they are really thought patterns, the most vivid pictures of my family, girls, good times. Soon I could lie with my back arched for hours on end, and I placed no importance on the passage of time. Control. I learned to control my food, my body, and my mind through a deliberate act of will.

After fifteen days the guards pulled me out and sent me back to a regular cell for twenty-four hours, where I took a shower and saw a medical doctor and a psychiatrist. They were worried that prisoners would become mentally disorganized in such deprivation. Then, because I had not repented, they sent me back to the hole. By then it held no fears for me. I had won my freedom.

Soul breakers exist because the authorities know that such conditions would drive them to the breaking point, but when I resolved that they would not conquer my will, I became stronger than they were. I understood them better than they understood me. No longer dependent on the things of the world, I felt really free for the first time in my life. In the past I had been like my jailers; I had pursued the goals of capitalistic America. Now I had a higher freedom.

Most people who know me do not realize that I have been in and out of jail for the past twelve years. They know only of my eleven months in solitary in 1967, waiting for the murder trial to begin, and the twenty-two months at the Penal Colony after that. But 1967 would not have been possible without 1964. I could not have handled the Penal Colony solitary without the soul breaker behind me. Therefore, I cannot tell inexperienced young comrades to go into jail and into solitary, that that is the way to defy the authorities and exercise their freedom. I know what solitary can do to a man.

The strip cell has been outlawed throughout the United States. Prisoners I talk to in California tell me it is no longer in use on the West Coast. That was the work of Charles Garry, the lawyer who defended me in 1968, when he fought the case of Warren Wells, a Black Panther accused of shooting a policeman. The Superior Court of California said it was an outrage to human decency to put any man through such extreme deprivation. Of course prisons have their ways, and out there right now, somewhere, prisoners without lawyers are probably lying in their own filth in the soul breaker.

I was in the hole for a month. My sentence, when it came, was for six months on the county farm at Santa Rita, about fifty miles south of Oakland. This is an honor camp with no walls, and the inmates are not locked up. There is a barbed-wire fence, but anyone can easily walk off during the daytime. The inmates work at tending livestock, harvesting crops, and doing other farm work.

I was not in the honor camp long. A few days after I arrived, I had a fight with a fat Black inmate named Bojack, who served in the mess hall. Bojack was a diligent enforcer of small helpings, and I was a "dipper." Whenever Bojack turned away, I would dip for more with my spoon. One day he tried to prevent me from dipping, and I called him for protecting the oppressor's interests and smashed him with a steel tray. When they pulled me off him, I was hustled next door to Graystone, the maximum security prison at Santa Rita.

Here, prisoners are locked up all day inside a stone building. Not only that, I was put in solitary confinement for the remaining months of my sentence. Because of my experience in the hole, I could survive. Still, I did not submit willingly. The food was as bad in Graystone as it had been in Alameda, and I constantly protested about that and the lack of heat in my cell. Half the time we had no heat at all.

Wherever you go in prison there are disturbed inmates. One on my block at Santa Rita screamed night and day as loudly as he could; his vocal cords seemed made of iron. From time to time, the guards came into his cell and threw buckets of cold water on him. Gradually, as the inmate wore down, the scream became a croak and then a squeak and then a whisper. Long after he gave out, the sound lingered in my head.

The Santa Rita administration finally got disgusted with my continual complaints and protests and shipped me back to the jail in Oakland, where I spent the rest of my time in solitary. By then I was used to the cold. Even now, I do not like any heat at all wherever I stay, no matter what the outside temperature. Even so, the way I was treated told me a lot about those who devised such punishment. I know them well.

Bobby Seale

Out of jail and back on the street in 1965, I again took up with Bobby Seale. We had a lot to talk about; I had not seen him in more than a year.

Bobby and I had not always agreed. In fact, we disagreed the first time we met, during the Cuban missile crisis several years before. That was the time President Kennedy was about to blow humanity off the face of the earth because Russian ships were on their way to liberated territory with arms for the people of Cuba. The Progressive Labor Party was holding a rally outside Oakland City College to encourage support for Fidel Castro, and I was there because I agreed with their views. There were a number of speakers and one of them, Donald Warden, launched into a lengthy praise of Fidel. He did this in his usual opportunistic way, tooting his own horn. Warden was about halfway through his routine, criticizing civil rights organizations and asking why we put our money into that kind of thing, when Bobby challenged him, expressing opposition to Warden and strong support for the position of the National Association for the Advancement of Colored People. He felt that the NAACP was the hope of Black people and because of this, he supported the government and its moves against Cuba. I explained to him afterward that he was wrong to support the government and the civil rights organizations. Too much money had already been put into legal actions. There were enough laws on the books to permit Black people to deal with all their problems, but the laws were not enforced. Therefore, trying to get more laws was only a meaningless diversion from the real issues. This was an argument I had heard in the Afro-American Association and in Oakland by Malcolm X, who made the point over and over again. Bobby began to think about this and later came over to my point of view.

Whatever our early disagreements, Bobby and I were close by 1965. Later, I recruited him into the Afro-American Association, but when I left it, he continued to stick with Warden. At that time I was still going through my identity crisis, looking for some understanding of myself in relation to society. While I took a back seat in the Association and refused to make a stand on any position, Bobby threw all his energy into it, even after I left.

Still, we did not establish close contact until I got out of the hole in 1965. At that point, Bobby was planning to get married, and he needed a bed for his new apartment. I was breaking up with my girl friend and had a bed I no longer wanted. I sold it to him, and we hauled it to his home. That afternoon we began to talk; he told me that he also had left the Afro-American Association to hook up with Ken Freeman and his group, the Revolutionary Action Movement (RAM). Most of the brothers in this group attended Oakland City College, but the organization was a sort of underground, off-campus operation. They also had a front group called Soul Students Advisory Council, which was a recognized campus organization. The RAM group was more intellectual than active. They did a lot of talking about the revolution and also some writing. Writing was almost a requirement for membership, in fact, but Bobby was no writer. At the time I got out of jail, Bobby had been involved in an argument with the members and had been suspended for a time. Still angry about this, he told me he intended to break with them. Like me, like thousands of us, Bobby was looking for something and not finding it.

Bobby and I entered a period of intense exploration, trying to solve some of the ideological problems of the Black movement; partly, we needed to explain to our own satisfaction why no Black political organization had succeeded. The only one we thought had promised long-term success was the Organization of Afro-American Unity started by Malcolm X, but Malcolm had died too soon to pull his program together. Malcolm's slogan had been "Freedom by any means necessary," but nothing we saw was taking us there. We still had only a vague conception of what freedom ought to mean to Black people, except in abstract terms borrowed from politicians, and that did not help the people on the block at all. Those lofty words were meant for intellectuals and the bourgeoisie, who were already fairly comfortable.

Much of our conversation revolved around groups in the San Francisco, Oakland, and Berkeley areas. Knowing the people who belonged to them, we could evaluate both positive and negative aspects of their characters and the nature of their organizations. While we respected many of the moves these brothers had made, we felt that the negative aspects of their movements overshadowed the positive ones.

We started throwing around ideas. None of the groups were able to recruit and involve the very people they professed to represent— the poor people in the community who never went to college, probably were not even able to finish high school. Yet these were our people; they were the vast majority of the Black population in the area. Any group talking about Blacks was in fact talking about those low on the ladder in terms of well-being, self-respect, and the amount of concern the government had for them. All of us were talking, and nobody was reaching them.

Bobby had a talent that could help us. He was beginning to make a name for himself in local productions as an actor and comedian. I had seen him act in several plays written by brothers, and he was terrific. I had never liked comedians, and I would not go out of my way to hear one. If a person presents his material in a serious way and uses humor to get his points across, he will have me laughing with all the rest, but stand-up, wisecracking comedians leave me cold. Still, I recognized Bobby's talent and I thought he could use it to relate to people and persuade them in an incisive way. Often, when we were rapping about our frustrations with particular people or groups, Bobby would act out their madness. He could do expert imitations of President Kennedy, Martin Luther King, James Cagney, Humphrey Bogart, and Chester of "Gunsmoke." He could also imitate down to the last detail some of the brothers around us. I would crack my sides laughing, not only because his imitations were so good, but because he could convey certain attitudes and characteristics so sharply. He caught all their shortcomings, the way their ideas failed to meet the needs of the people.

We planned to work through the Soul Students Advisory Council. Although SSAC was just a front for RAM, it had one large advantage—it was not an intellectual organization, and for that reason it would appeal to many lower-class brothers at City College. If these brothers belonged to a group that gave them feelings of strength and respect, they could become effective participants. It was important to give them something relevant to do, something not degrading. Soul Students was normally an ineffective and transitory group without a real program. Only if something big was happening did their meetings attract a lot of people. In the quiet times only two or three would show up.

Just then, however, Soul Students had a hot issue—the establishment of a program of Afro-American history and culture in the college's regular curriculum. Although it was a relevant program, the authorities were resisting it tooth and nail. Every time we proposed a new course, they countered with reasons why it could not be; at the same time, ironically, they encouraged us to be "concerned." This was simple trickery; they were dragging their feet.

Bobby and I saw this as an opportunity to move Soul Students a step further by adopting a program of armed self-defense. We approached them, proposing a rally in front of the college in support of the Afro-American history program. We pointed out that this would be a different kind of rally—the Soul Student members would strap on guns and march on the sidewalk in front of the school. Partly, the rally would express our opposition to police brutality, but it would also intimidate the authorities at City College who were resisting our program. We were looking for a way to emphasize both college and community, to draw them in together. The police and the school authorities needed a strong jolt from Blacks, and we knew this kind of action would make them realize that the brothers meant business. Carrying guns for self-defense was perfectly legal at the time.

We explained all this to Soul Students and showed them that we did not intend to break any laws but were concerned that the organization start dealing with reality rather than sit around intellectualizing and writing essays about the white man. We wanted them to dedicate themselves to armed self-defense with the full understanding that this was defense for the survival of Black people in general and in particular for the cultural program we were trying to establish. As we saw it, Blacks were getting ripped off everywhere. The police had given us no choice but to defend ourselves against their brutality. On the campus we were being miseducated; we had no courses dealing with our real needs and problems, courses that taught us how to survive. Our program was designed to lead the brothers into self-defense before we were completely wiped out physically and mentally.

The weapons were a recruiting device. I felt we could recruit Oakland City College students from the grass roots, people who did not relate to campus organizations that were all too intellectual and offered no effective program of action. Street people would relate to Soul Students if they followed our plan; if the Black community has learned to respect anything, it has learned to respect the gun.

We underestimated the difficulty of bringing the brothers around. Soul Students completely rejected our program. Those brothers had been so intimidated by police firepower they would not give any serious consideration to strapping on a gun, legal or not. After that setback we went to the Revolutionary Action Movement. They did not have many members, just a few guys from the college campus who talked a lot. We explained that by wearing and displaying weapons the street brothers would relate to RAM's example of leadership. We also talked about a new idea, patrolling the police, since the police were the main perpetrators of violence against the community. We went no further than those two tactics: armed self-defense and police patrol. A more complete program was sure to get bogged down on minor points. I just wanted them to adopt a program of self-defense, and after that was worked out, we could then develop it more fully. We were not aiming then at party organization; there were too many organizations already. Our job was to make one of them relevant; that would be contribution enough. However, we were having a lot of trouble breaking through. RAM rejected the plan, too. They thought it was "suicidal," that we could not survive a single day patrolling the police.

This left us where we had been all along: nowhere.

the founding of the
Black Panther Party

All during this time, Bobby and I had no thought of the Black Panther Party, no plan to head up any organization, and the ten point program was still in the future. We had seen Watts rise up the previous year. We had seen how the police attacked the Watts community after causing the trouble in the first place. We had seen Martin Luther King come to Watts in an effort to calm the people, and we had seen his philosophy of nonviolence rejected. Black people had been taught nonviolence; it was deep in us. What good, however, was nonviolence when the police were determined to rule by force? We had seen the Oakland police and the California Highway Patrol begin to carry their shotguns in full view as another way of striking fear into the community. We had seen all this, and we recognized that the rising consciousness of Black people was almost at the point of explosion. One must relate to the history of one's community and to its future. Everything we had seen convinced us that our time had come.

Out of this need sprang the Black Panther Party. Bobby and I finally had no choice but to form an organization that would involve the lower-class brothers.

We worked it out in conversations and discussions. Most of the talk was casual. Bobby lived near the campus, and his living room became a kind of headquarters. Although we were still involved with Soul Students, we attended few meetings, and when we did go, our presence was mostly disruptive; we raised questions that upset people. Our conversations with each other became the important thing. Brothers who had a free hour between classes and others who just hung around the campus drifted in and out of Bobby's house. We drank beer and wine

49

and chewed over the political situation, our social problems, and the merits and shortcomings of the other groups. We also discussed the Black achievements of the past, particularly as they helped us to understand current events.

In a sense, these sessions at Bobby's house were our political education classes, and the Party sort of grew out of them. Even after we formally organized we continued the discussions in our office. By then we had moved on to include not only problems but possible solutions.

We also read. The literature of oppressed people and their struggles for liberation in other countries is very large, and we pored over these books to see how their experiences might help us to understand our plight. We read the work of Frantz Fanon, particularly *The Wretched of the Earth*, the four volumes of Chairman Mao Tse-tung, and Che Guevara's *Guerrilla Warfare*. Che and Mao were veterans of people's wars, and they had worked out successful strategies for liberating their people. We read these men's works because we saw them as kinsmen; the oppressor who had controlled them was controlling us, both directly and indirectly. We believed it was necessary to know how they gained their freedom in order to go about getting ours. However, we did not want merely to import ideas and strategies; we had to transform what we learned into principles and methods acceptable to the brothers on the block.

Mao and Fanon and Guevara all saw clearly that the people had been stripped of their birthright and their dignity, not by any philosophy or mere words, but at gunpoint. They had suffered a holdup by gangsters, and rape; for them, the only way to win freedom was to meet force with force. At bottom, this is a form of self-defense. Although that defense might at times take on characteristics of aggression, in the final analysis the people do not initiate; they simply respond to what has been inflicted upon them. People respect the expression of strength and dignity displayed by men who refuse to bow to the weapons of oppression. Though it may mean death, these men will fight, because death with dignity is preferable to ignominy. Then, too, there is always the chance that the oppressor will be overwhelmed.

Fanon made a statement during the Algerian war that impressed me; he said it was the "Year of the Boomerang," which is the third phase of violence. At that point, the violence of the aggressor turns on him and strikes a killing blow. Yet the oppressor does not understand the process; he knows no more than he did in the first phase when he launched the violence. The oppressed are always defensive; the oppressor is always aggressive and surprised when the people turn back on him the force he has used against them.

Negroes with Guns by Robert Williams had a great influence on the kind of party we developed. Williams had been active in Monroe, North Carolina, with a program of armed self-defense that had enlisted many in the community. However, I did not like the way he had called on the federal government for assistance; we viewed the government as an enemy, the agency of a ruling clique that controls the country. We also had some literature about the Deacons for Defense and Justice in Louisiana, the state where I was born. One of their leaders had come through the Bay Area on a speaking and fund-raising tour, and we liked what he said. The Deacons had done a good job of defending civil rights marchers in their area, but they also had a habit of calling upon the federal government to carry out this defense or at least to assist them in defending the people who were upholding the law. The Deacons even went so far as to enlist local sheriffs and police to defend the marchers, with the threat that if law enforcement agencies would not defend them, the Deacons would. We also viewed the local police, the National Guard, and the regular military as one huge armed group that opposed the will of the people. In a boundary situation people have no real defense except what they provide for themselves.

We read also the works of the freedom fighters who had done so much for Black communities in the United States. Bobby had collected all of Malcolm X's speeches and ideas from papers like *The Militant* and *Muhammad Speaks*. These we studied carefully. Although Malcolm's program for the Organization of Afro-American Unity was never put into operation, he has made it clear that Blacks ought to arm. Malcolm's influence was ever-present. We continue to believe that the Black Panther Party exists in the spirit of Malcolm. Often it is difficult to say exactly how an action or a program has been determined or influenced in a spiritual way. Such intangibles are hard to describe, although they can be more significant than any precise influence. Therefore, the words on this page cannot convey the effect that Malcolm has had on the Black Panther Party, although, as far as I am concerned, the Party is a living testament to his life work. I do not claim that the Party has done what Malcolm would have done. Many others say that their programs are Malcolm's programs. We do not say this, but Malcolm's spirit is in us.

From all of these things—the books, Malcolm's writings and spirit, our analysis of the local situation—the idea of an organization was forming. One day, quite suddenly, almost by chance, we found a name. I had read a pamphlet about voter registration in Mississippi, how the people in Lowndes County had armed themselves against Establishment violence. Their political group, called the Lowndes County Freedom Organization, had a black panther for its symbol. A few days later, while Bobby and I were rapping, I suggested that we use the panther as our symbol and call our political vehicle the Black Panther Party. The panther is a fierce animal, but he will not attack until he is backed into a corner; then he will strike out. The image seemed appropriate, and Bobby agreed without discussion. At this point, we knew it was time to stop talking and begin organizing. Although we had always wanted to get away from the intellectualizing and rhetoric characteristic of other groups, at times we were as inactive as they were. The time had come for action.

patrolling

It was the spring of 1966. Still without a definite program, we were at the stage of testing ideas that would capture the imagination of the community. We began, as always, by checking around with the street brothers. We asked them if they would be interested in forming the Black Panther Party for Self-Defense, which would be based upon defending the community against the aggression of the power structure, including the military and the armed might of the police. We informed the brothers of their right to possess weapons; most of them were interested. Then we talked about how the people are constantly intimidated by arrogant, belligerent police officers and exactly what we could do about it. We went to pool halls and bars, all the places where brothers congregate and talk.

I was prepared to give them legal advice. From my law courses at Oakland City College and San Francisco Law School I was familiar with the California penal code and well versed in the laws relating to weapons. I also had something very important at my disposal—the law library of the North Oakland Service Center, a community-center poverty program where Bobby was working. The Center gave legal advice, and there were many lawbooks on the shelves. Unfortunately, most of them dealt with civil law, since the antipoverty program was not supposed to advise poor people about criminal law. However, I made good use of the books they had to run down the full legal situation to the brothers on the street. We were doing what the poverty program claimed to be doing but never had—giving help and counsel to poor people about the things that crucially affected their lives.

All that summer we circulated in the Black communities of Richmond, Berkeley, Oakland, and San Francisco. Wherever brothers gathered, we talked with them about their right to arm. In general, they were

interested but skeptical about the weapons idea. They could not see anyone walking around with a gun in full view. To recruit any sizable number of street brothers, we would obviously have to do more than talk.
We needed to give practical applications of our theory, show them that
we were not afraid of weapons and not afraid of death. The way we finally
won the brothers over was by patrolling the police with arms.

Before we began the patrols, however, Bobby and I set down in writing a practical course of action. We could go no further without a program, and we resolved to drop everything else, even though it might
take a while to come up with something viable. One day, we went to
the North Oakland Service Center to work it out. The Center was an
ideal place because of the books and the fact that we could work undis-
turbed. First, we pulled together all the books we had been reading and
dozens we had only heard about. We discussed Mao's program, Cuba's
program, and all the others, but concluded that we could not follow
any of them. Our unique situation required a unique program. Although
the relationship between the oppressor and the oppressed is universal,
forms of oppression vary. The ideas that mobilized the people of Cuba
and China sprang from their own history and political structures The
practical parts of those programs could be carried out only under a certain kind of oppression. Our program had to deal with America.

I started rapping off the essential points for the survival of Black
and oppressed people in the United States. Bobby wrote them down,
and then we separated those ideas into two sections, "What We Want"
and "What We Believe." We split them up because the ideas fell naturally into two distinct categories. It was necessary to explain why we
wanted certain things. At the same time, our goals were based on
beliefs, and we set those out, too. In the section on beliefs, we made
it clear that all the objective conditions necessary for attaining our goals
were already in existence, but that a number of societal factors stood
in our way. This was to help the people understand what was working against them.

All in all, our ten-point program took about twenty minutes to write.
Thinking it would take days, we were prepared for a long session, but
we never got to the small mountain of books piled up around us. We
had come to an important realization: books could only point in a general direction; the rest was up to us. This is the program we wrote down:

OCTOBER 1966
BLACK PANTHER PARTY PLATFORM AND PROGRAM
WHAT WE WANT / WHAT WE BELIEVE

1. We want freedom. We want power to determine the destiny of our Black Community.

We believe that Black people will not be free until we are able to determine our destiny.

2. We want full employment for our people.

We believe that the federal government is responsible and obligated to give every man employment or a guaranteed income. We believe that if the white American businessmen will not give full employment, then the means of production should be taken from the businessmen and placed in the community so that the people of the community can organize and employ all of its people and give a high standard of living.

3. We want an end to the robbery by the capitalist of our Black community.

We believe that this racist government has robbed us and now we are demanding the overdue debt of forty acres and two mules. Forty acres and two mules were promised 100 years ago as restitution for slave labor and mass murder of Black people. We will accept the payment in currency which will be distributed to our many communities. The Germans are now aiding the Jews in Israel for the genocide of the Jewish people. The Germans murdered six million Jews. The American racist has taken part in the slaughter of millions of Black people; therefore, we feel that this is a modest demand that we make.

4. We want decent housing, fit for shelter of human beings.

We believe that if the white landlords will not give decent housing to our Black community, then the housing and the land should be made into cooperatives so that our community, with government aid, can build and make decent housing for its people.

5. We want education for our people that exposes the true nature of this decadent American society. We want education that teaches us our true history and our role in the present-day society.

We believe in an educational system that will give to our people a knowledge of self. If a man does not have knowledge of himself and his position in society and the world, then he has little chance to relate to anything else.

6. We want all Black men to be exempt from military service.

We believe that Black people should not be forced to fight in the military service to defend a racist government that does not protect us. We will not fight and kill other people of color in the world who, like Black people, are being victimized by the white racist government of America. We will protect ourselves from the force and violence of the racist police and the racist military, by whatever means necessary.

7. We want an immediate end to POLICE BRUTALITY and MURDER of Black people.

We believe we can end police brutality in our Black community by organizing Black self-defense groups that are dedicated to defending our Black community from racist police oppression and brutality. The Second Amendment to the Constitution of the United States gives a right to bear arms. We therefore believe that all Black people should arm themselves for self-defense.

8. We want freedom for all Black men held in federal, state, county, and city prisons and jails.

We believe that all Black people should be released from the many jails and prisons because they have not received a fair and impartial trial.

9. We want all Black people when brought to trial to be tried in court by a jury of their peer group or people from their Black communities, as defined by the Constitution of the United States.

We believe that the courts should follow the United States Constitution so that Black people will receive fair trials. The Fourteenth Amendment of the U.S. Constitution gives a man a right to be tried by his peer group. A peer is a person from a similar economic, social, religious, geographical, environmental, historical, and racial background. To do this the court will be forced to select a jury from the Black community from which the Black defendant came. We have been and are being tried by all-white juries that have no understanding of the "average reasoning man" of the Black community.

10. We want land, bread, housing, education, clothing, justice, and peace. And as our major political objective, a United Nations–supervised plebiscite to be held throughout the Black colony in which only Black colonial subjects will be allowed to participate, for the purpose of determining the will of Black people as to their national destiny.

When, in the course of human events, it becomes necessary for one people to dissolve the political bands which have connected them with another, and to assume, among the powers of the earth, the separate and equal station to which the laws of nature and nature's God entitle them, a decent respect to the opinions of mankind requires that they should declare the causes which impel them to the separation.

We hold these truths to be self-evident, that all men are created equal; that they are endowed by their Creator with certain unalienable rights; that among these are life, liberty, and the pursuit of happiness. *That, to secure these rights, governments are instituted among men, deriving their just powers from the consent of the governed; that, whenever any form of government becomes destructive of these ends, it is the right of the people to alter or to abolish it, and to institute a new government, laying its foundation on such principles, and organizing its powers in such form, as to them shall seem most likely to effect their safety and happiness.* Prudence, indeed, will dictate that governments long established should not be changed for light and transient causes; and, accordingly, all experience hath shown, that mankind are more disposed to suffer, while evils are sufferable, than to right themselves by abolishing the forms to which they are accustomed. *But, when a long train of abuses and usurpations, pursuing invariably the same object, evinces a design to reduce them under absolute despotism, it is their right, it is their duty, to throw off such government, and to provide new guards for their future security.*

With the program on paper, we set up the structure of our organization. Bobby became Chairman, and I chose the position of Minister of Defense. I was very happy with this arrangement; I do not like to lead formally, and the Chairman has to conduct meetings and be involved in administration. We also discussed having an advisory cabinet as an information arm of the Party. We wanted this cabinet to do research on each of the ten points and their relation to the community and to advise the people on how to implement them. It seemed best to weight the political wing of the Party with street brothers and the advisory cabinet with middle-class Blacks who had the necessary knowledge and skills. We were also seeking a functional unity between middle-class Blacks and the street brothers. I asked my brother Melvin to approach a few friends about serving on the advisory cabinet, but when our plan became clear, they all refused, and the cabinet was deferred.

The first member of the Black Panther Party, after Bobby and myself, was Little Bobby Hutton. Little Bobby had met Bobby Seale at the North Oakland Service Center, where both were working, and he immediately became enthusiastic about the nascent organization. Even though he was only about fifteen years old then, he was a responsible and mature person, determined to help the cause of Black people. He became the Party's first treasurer. Little Bobby was the youngest of seven children; his family had come to Oakland from Arkansas when he was three years old. His parents were good, hard-working people, but Bobby had endured the same hardships and humiliations to which so many young Blacks in poor communities are subjected. Like many of the brothers, he had been kicked out of school. Then he had gotten an apartment and a job at the Service Center. After work he used to come around to Bobby Seale's house to talk and learn to read. At the time of his murder, he was reading *Black Reconstruction in America* by W. E. B. DuBois.

Bobby was a serious revolutionary, but there was nothing grim about him. He had an infectious smile and a disarming quality that made people love him. He died courageously, the first Black Panther to make the supreme sacrifice for the people. We all attempt to carry on the work he began.

We started now to implement our ten-point program. Interested primarily in educating and revolutionizing the community, we needed to get their attention and give them something to identify with. This is why the seventh point—police action—was the first program we emphasized. Point 7 stated: "We want an immediate end to police brutality and murder of Black people." This is a major issue in every Black community. The police have never been our protectors. Instead, they act as the military arm of our oppressors and continually brutalize us. Many communities have tried and failed to get civilian review boards to supervise the behavior of the police. In some places, organized citizen patrols have followed the police and observed them in their community dealings. They take pictures and make tape recordings of the encounters and report misbehavior to the authorities. However, the authorities responsible for overseeing the police are policemen themselves and usually side against the citizens. We recognized that it was ridiculous to report the police to the police, but we hoped that by raising encounters to a higher level, by patrolling the police with arms, we would see a change in their behavior. Further, the community would notice this and become interested in the Party. Thus our armed patrols were also a means of recruiting.

At first, the patrols were a total success. Frightened and confused, the police did not know how to respond, because they had never encountered patrols like this before. They were familiar with the community alert patrols in other cities, but never before had guns been an integral part of any patrol program. With weapons in our hands, we were no longer their subjects but their equals.

Out on patrol, we stopped whenever we saw the police questioning a brother or a sister. We would walk over with our weapons and observe them from a "safe" distance so that the police could not say we were interfering with the performance of their duty. We would ask the community members if they were being abused. Most of the time, when a policeman saw us coming, he slipped his book back into his pocket, got into his car, and left in a hurry. The citizens who had been stopped were as amazed as the police at our sudden appearance.

I always carried lawbooks in my car. Sometimes, when a policeman was harassing a citizen, I would stand off a little and read the relevant portions of the penal code in a loud voice to all within hearing distance. In doing this, we were helping to educate those who gathered to observe these incidents. If the policeman arrested the citizen and took him to the station, we would follow and immediately post bail. Many community people could not believe at first that we had only their interest at heart. Nobody had ever given them any support or assistance when the police harassed them, but here we were, proud Black men, armed with guns and a knowledge of the law. Many citizens came right out of jail and into the Party, and the statistics of murder and brutality by policemen in our communities fell sharply.

Each day we went out on our watch. Sometimes we got on a policeman's tail and followed him with our weapons in full view. If he darted around the block or made a U-turn trying to follow us, we let him do it until he got tired of that. Then, we would follow him again. Either way, we took up a good bit of police time that otherwise would have been spent in harassment.

As our forces built up, we doubled the patrols, then tripled them; we began to patrol everywhere—Oakland, Richmond, Berkeley, and San Francisco. Most patrols were a part of our normal movement around the community. We kept them random, however, so that the police could not set a network to anticipate us. They never knew when or where we were going to show up. It might be late at night or early in the morning; some brothers would go on patrol the same time every day, but never in a specific pattern or in the same geographical area. The chief purpose of the patrols was to teach the community security against the police, and we did not need a regular schedule for that. We knew that no particular area could be totally defended; only the community could effectively defend and eventually liberate itself. Our aim was simply to teach them how to go about it. We passed out our literature and ten-point program to the citizens who gathered, discussed community defense, and educated them about their rights concerning weapons. All along, the number of members grew.

The Black Panthers were and are always required to keep their activities within legal bounds. This was emphasized repeatedly in our political education classes and also when we taught weapons care. If we overstepped legal bounds, the police would easily gain the upper hand and be able to continue their intimidation. We also knew the community was somewhat fearful of the gun and of the policeman who had it. So, we studied the law about weapons and kept within our rights. To be arrested for having weapons would be a setback to our program of teaching the people their constitutional right to bear arms. As long as we kept everything legal, the police could do nothing, and the people would see that armed defense was a legitimate, constitutional right. In this way, they would lose their doubts and fears and be able to move against their oppressor.

It was not all observation and penal code reading on those patrols. The police, invariably shocked to meet a cadre of disciplined and armed Black men coming to the support of the community, reacted in strange and unpredictable ways. In their fright, some of them became children, cursing and insulting us. We responded in kind, calling them swine and pigs, but never cursing; this could be cause for arrest—and we took care not to be arrested with our weapons. But we demonstrated their cowardice to the community with our "shock-a-buku." It was sometimes hilarious to see their reaction; they had always been cocky and sure of themselves as long as they had weapons to intimidate the unarmed community. When we equalized the situation, their real cowardice was exposed.

Soon they began to retaliate. We expected this—they had to get back at us in some way—and were prepared. The fact that we had conquered our fear of death made it possible to face them under any circumstances. The police began to keep a record of Black Panther vehicles; whenever they spotted one, it would be stopped and investigated for possible violations. This was a childish ploy, but it was the police way. We always made sure our vehicles were clean, without violations, and the police were usually hard-pressed to find any justification for stopping us.

Since we were within the law, they soon resorted to illegal tactics. I was stopped and questioned forty or fifty times by police without being arrested or even getting a ticket in most instances. The few times I did end up on the blotter it merely proved how far they were willing to go. A policeman once stopped me and examined my license and the car for any violation of the Motor Vehicle Code. He spent about half an hour going over the vehicle, checking lights, horn, tires, everything. Finally, he shook the rear license plate, and a bolt dropped off, so he wrote out a ticket for a faulty license plate.

Some encounters with the police were more dramatic. At times they drew their guns and we drew ours, until we reached a sort of stand-off. This happened frequently to me. I often felt that someday one of the police would go crazy and pull the trigger. Some of them were so nervous that they looked as if they might shake a bullet out of their pistols. I would rather have a brave man pull a gun on me, since he is less likely to panic; but we were prepared for anything. Sometimes they threatened to shoot, thinking I would lose courage, but I remembered the lessons of solitary confinement and assigned every silly action its proper significance: they were afraid of us. It was as simple as that. Each day we went forth fully aware that we might not come home or see each other ever again. There is no closeness to equal that.

In front of our first Black Panther office, on Fifty-eighth Street in Oakland, a policeman once drew his gun and pointed it at me while I sat in my car. When people gathered to observe, the police told them to clear the area. I ignored the gun, got out of the car, and asked the people to go into the Party office. They had a right to observe the police. Then I called the policeman an ignorant Georgia cracker who had come West to get away from sharecropping. After that, I walked around the car and spoke to the citizens about the police and about every man's right to be armed. I took a chance there, but I figured the policeman would not shoot me with all those eyes on him. He was willing to shoot me without cause, I am sure, but not before so many witnesses.

Another policeman admitted as much during an incident in Richmond. I had stopped to watch a motorcycle cop question a citizen. He was clearly edgy at my presence, but I stood off quietly at a reasonable distance with my shotgun in hand. After writing up the citizen, he rode his motorcycle over to me and asked if I wanted to press charges for police brutality. About a dozen people were standing around watching us. "Are you paranoid?" I replied. "Do you think you're important? Do you think I would waste my time, going down to the police station to make a report on you? No. You're just a coward anyway." With that, I got into my car. When he tried to hold my door open, I slammed it shut and told him to get his hands off. By now people were laughing at the cop, and rather than suffer further humiliation, he drove off, steaming mad. About halfway down the street, he turned around and came back; he wanted to do something, and he was about fifty shades of red. Pulling up beside me, he stuck his head close and said, "If it was night, you wouldn't do this." "You're right," I replied, "I sure wouldn't, but you're threatening me now, aren't you?" He got a little redder and kicked his machine into gear, and took off.

The police wanted me badly, but they needed to do their dirty work out of view of the community. When a citizen was unarmed, they brutalized him anytime, almost casually, but when he was prepared to defend himself, the police became little more than criminals, working at night.

On another occasion I stopped by the Black Panther office after paying some bills for my father. Since I was taking care of family business, I had not carried my shotgun with me—it was at home—but I did have a dagger, fully sheathed, in my belt. In the office were two comrades, Warren Tucker, a captain in the Party, and another member. As we talked, an eleven-year-old boy burst into the office and said, "The police are at my friend's house, and they're tearing up the place." This house was only about three blocks away, so the two Black Panthers and I hurried to the scene. Warren Tucker had a .45 pistol strapped to his hip in full view, but the other two of us had no weapons. We never kept weapons in the office, since we were there only periodically.

When we arrived, we found three policemen in the house, turning over couches and chairs, searching and pushing a little boy around and shouting, "Where's the shotgun?" The boy kept saying, "I don't have a shotgun," but the police went right on looking. I asked the policeman who seemed to be in charge if he had a search warrant, and he answered that he did not need one because he was in "hot pursuit."

Then he told me to leave the house. The little boy asked me to stay, so I continued to question the police, telling them they had no right to be there. The policeman finally turned on me. "You're going to get out of here," he said. "No," I said, "you leave if you don't have a search warrant."

In the middle of this argument the boy's father arrived and also asked the police for a search warrant. When the police admitted they did not have one, he ordered them out. As they started to leave, one of the policemen stopped in the doorway and said to the father, "Why are you telling us to get out? Why don't you get rid of these Panthers? They're the troublemakers." The father replied, "Before this I didn't like the Panthers. I had heard bad things about them, but in the last few minutes I've changed my mind, because they helped my son when you pushed him around."

The police became even more outraged at this. All their hostility now turned toward us. As the whole group went down the steps and out into the yard, more policemen arrived on the scene. The house was directly across the street from Oakland City College, and the dozen or so police cars had attracted a crowd that was milling about. The policeman who had been ordered out of the house took new courage at the sight of reinforcements. Walking over to me in the yard, he came close, saying, "You are always making trouble for us." Coming closer still, he growled at me in a low voice that could not be overheard, "You motherfucker." This was a regular police routine, a transparent strategy. He wanted me to curse him before witnesses; then he could arrest me. But I had learned to be cautious. After he called me a motherfucker, he stood waiting for the explosion, but it did not come in the way he expected. Instead, I called him a swine, a pig, a slimy snake— everything I could think of without using profanity.

By now he was almost apoplectic. "You're talking to me like that and you have a weapon. You're displaying a weapon in a rude and threatening fashion." Then he turned to Warren Tucker—Warren's gun was still in its holster—and said, "And so are you." As if on signal, the fifteen policemen who had been standing around uncertainly stormed the three of us and threw on handcuffs. They did not say they were placing us under arrest. If they had, we would gladly have taken the arrest under the circumstances without any resistance. From the way we went hurtling off in the paddy wagon, with its siren wailing and police cars ahead and behind, you might have thought they had bagged a Mafia capo. After we were booked they searched us and found a penknife in Warren Tucker's pocket, the kind Boy Scouts use. So, they dropped the charge of "displaying a weapon in a rude and threatening manner," and charged him simply with carrying a concealed weapon. Even that charge was eventually dropped.

This was the kind of harassment we went through over and over again, simply because we chose to exercise our constitutional rights to self-defense and stand up for the community. In spite of the fact that we followed the law to the letter, we were arrested and convicted of all sorts of minor trumped-up charges. They sought to frighten us and turn the community against us, but what they did had the opposite effect. For instance, after this encounter, we gained a number of new members from City College students who had watched the incident and had seen how things really were. They had been skeptical about us earlier because of the bad treatment we had received in the press, but seeing is believing.

The policeman who started this particular incident testified against me in 1968 in my trial for killing a policeman. When my attorney, Charles Garry, questioned him under cross-examination, he admitted his fear of the Black Panthers. He is six feet tall and weighs 250 pounds; I am five feet, ten and a half inches, and weigh 150 pounds, yet he said that I "surrounded" him. Straying further from the facts, he testified that he had not said anything to me, that, on the contrary, he was too frightened to open his mouth. The Black Panthers allegedly frightened him by shaking high-powered rifles in his face, calling him a pig, and threatening to kill him. He was fearful, he said, that I would kill him with the dagger, though it was sheathed. He stated that I had come right up to him, that I was "in his face," and, as he put it, "He was all around me." So much for police testimony.

In addition to our patrols and confrontations with the police, I did a lot of recruiting in pool halls and bars, sometimes working twelve to sixteen hours a day. I passed out leaflets with our ten-point program, explaining each point to all who would listen. Going deep into the community like this, I invariably became involved in whatever was happening; this day-to-day contact became an important part of our organizing effort. There is a bar-restaurant in North Oakland known as the Bosn's Locker; I used to call it my office because I would sometimes sit in there for twenty hours straight talking with the people who came in. Most of the time, I had my shotgun with me; if the owners of the establishment did not object. If they did, I left it in my car.

At other times I would go to City College or to the Oakland Skills Center—anywhere people gathered. It was hard work, but not in the sense of working at an ordinary job, with its deadly routine and sense of futility in performing empty labor. It was work that had profound significance for me; the very meaning of my life was in it, and it brought me closer to the people

This recruiting had an interesting ramification in that I tried to transform many of the so-called criminal activities going on in the street into something political, although this had to be done gradually. Instead of trying to eliminate these activities—numbers, hot goods, drugs—I attempted to channel them into significant community actions. Black consciousness had generally reached a point where a man felt guilty about exploiting the Black community. However, if his daily activities for survival could be integrated with actions that undermined the established order, he felt good about it. It gave him a feeling of justification and strengthened his own sense of personal worth. Many of the brothers who were burglarizing and participating in similar pursuits began to contribute weapons and material to community defense. In order to survive they still had to sell their hot goods, but at the same time they would pass some of the cash on to us. That way, ripping off became more than just an individual thing.

Gradually the Black Panthers came to be accepted in the Bay Area community. We had provided a needed example of strength and dignity by showing people how to defend themselves. More important, we lived among them. They could see every day that with us the people came first.

Sacramento and the "Panther Bill"

Bobby and I look back on the early days of the Black Panthers with nostalgia. It was a time of discovery and enthusiasm; we had hit on something unique. By standing up to the police as equals, even holding them off, and yet remaining within the law, we had demonstrated Black pride to the community in a concrete way. Everywhere we went we caused traffic jams. People constantly stopped us to say how much they respected our courage. The idea of armed self-defense as a community policy was still new and a little intimidating to them; but it also made them think. More important, it created a feeling of solidarity. When we saw how Black citizens reacted to our movement, we were greatly encouraged. Despite the ever-present danger of retaliation, the risks were more than worth it. At that time, however, our activities were confined to a small area, and we wanted Black people throughout the country to know the Oakland story.

In April, 1967, we were invited to appear on a radio talk show in Oakland, the kind where people phone in questions and make comments. Early in the program we explained our ten-point program, why we were focusing on Point 7, and why it was necessary for Black men to arm themselves. We also made it clear that we were within our constitutional rights. Hundreds of calls poured in—the lines were jammed. Some people agreed with us; others disputed our points. We welcomed the discussion, because criticism helped us to find weaknesses in our program and to sharpen our position.

One of the callers was Donald Mulford, a conservative Republican state assemblyman from Piedmont, one of the wealthy, white sections of Oakland. Mulford was so close to Oakland's power structure that his call could only mean he saw political profit in attacking the Black Panthers. He told us that he planned to introduce a bill into the state legislature to make it illegal for us to patrol with our weapons. It was a bill, he said, that would "get" the Black Panthers. Mulford's call was a logical response of the system. We knew how the system operated. If we used the laws in our own interest and against theirs, then the power structure would simply change the laws. Mulford was more than willing to be the agent of change.

A few days later, the paper carried a story about Mulford's "Panther bill." In its particulars it was what we had expected—a bill intended to suppress the people's constitutional right to bear arms. Until then, white men had owned and carried weapons with impunity. Groups like the Minutemen and the Rangers in Richmond were known to have arsenals, but nobody introduced bills against them. Mulford had been asked by the Oakland police to introduce this bill because some "young Black toughs," as they called us, were walking around with guns. The bill was further evidence of this country's vicious double standard against Blacks. The usual pattern of white racism was gradually being put into effect. They would escalate the killing of Blacks, but this time the police would do the job that the Ku Klux Klan had done in the past.

The Black Panthers have never viewed such paramilitary groups as the Ku Klux Klan or the Minutemen as particularly dangerous. The real danger comes from highly organized Establishment forces—the local police, the National Guard, and the United States military. They were the ones who devastated Watts and killed innocent people. In comparison to them the paramilitary groups are insignificant. In fact, these groups are hardly organized at all. It is the uniformed men who are dangerous and who come into our communities every day to commit violence against us, knowing that the laws will protect them.

Bobby Seale and I discussed the Mulford bill against *this* background. Sheriff Younger had suggested, facetiously, that the Dowell family attempt to get their case heard at the state capitol. The Dowell family only wanted some good to come out of all the grief inflicted on them. We knew that the Dowells would get no better consideration in Sacramento than they had received from Younger.

The legislators would probably tell them to go to the governor, and the governor would point to Washington.

Institutions work this way. A son is murdered by the police, and nothing is done. The institutions send the victim's family on a merry-go-round, going from one agency to another, until they wear out and give up. This is a very effective way to beat down poor and oppressed people, who do not have the time to prosecute their cases. Time is money to poor people. To go to Sacramento means loss of a day's pay—often loss of a job. If this is a democracy, obviously it is a bourgeois democracy limited to the middle and upper classes. Only they can afford to participate in it.

Knowing all this, we nonetheless made plans to go to Sacramento. That we would not change any laws was irrelevant, and all of us—Black Panthers and Dowells—realized that from the start. Since we were resigned to a runaround in Sacramento, we decided to raise the encounter to a higher level in the hope of warning people about the dangers in the Mulford bill and the ideas behind it. A national outcry would help the Dowell family by showing them that some good had come from their tragedy; also, it might mobilize our community even more.

Dozens of reporters and photographers haunt the capitol waiting for a story. This made it the perfect forum for our proclamation. If the legislators got the message, too, well and good. But our primary purpose was to deliver it to the people. Actually, several groups went: four or five members of the Dowell family; a group of brothers from East Oakland, recruited by Mark Comfort, and the Black Panthers. The Black Panthers and Comfort's cadre were armed.

The Party agreed that I ought not to make the trip for two reasons. First, I was on probation from the Odell Lee case, and they did not want to jeopardize my freedom. Second, if any arrests were made in Sacramento, someone should be available to raise bail money and do whatever else was necessary.

Before they left, I prepared Executive Mandate Number One, which was to be our message to the Black communities. It read:

> The Black Panther Party for Self-Defense calls upon the American people in general, and Black people in particular, to take careful note of the racist California Legislature now considering legislation aimed at keeping Black people disarmed and powerless while racist

police agencies throughout the country intensify the terror, brutality, murder, and repression of Black people.

At the same time that the American Government is waging a racist war of genocide in Vietnam the concentration camps in which Japanese-Americans were interned during World War II are being renovated and expanded. Since America has historically reserved its most barbaric treatment for nonwhite people, we are forced to conclude that these concentration camps are being prepared for Black people who are determined to gain their freedom by any means necessary. The enslavement of Black people at the very founding of this country, the genocide practiced on the American Indians and the confinement of the survivors on reservations, the savage lynching of thousands of Black men and women, the dropping of atomic bombs on Hiroshima and Nagasaki, and now the cowardly massacre in Vietnam all testify to the fact that toward people of color the racist power structure of America has but one policy: repression, genocide, terror, and the big stick.

Black people have begged, prayed, petitioned and demonstrated, among other things, to get the racist power structure of America to right the wrongs which have historically been perpetrated against Black people. All of these efforts have been answered by more repression, deceit, and hypocrisy. As the aggression of the racist American Government escalates in Vietnam, the police agencies of America escalate the repression of Black people throughout the ghettos of America. Vicious police dogs, cattle prods, and increased patrols have become familiar sights in Black communities. City Hall turns a deaf ear to the pleas of Black people for relief from this increasing terror.

The Black Panther Party for Self-Defense believes that the time has come for Black people to arm themselves against this terror before it is too late. The pending Mulford Act brings the hour of doom one step nearer. A people who have suffered so much for so long at the hands of a racist society must draw the line somewhere. We believe that the Black communities of America must rise up as one man to halt the progression of a trend that leads inevitably to their total destruction.

When I gave Bobby his instructions, I impressed upon him that our main purpose was to deliver the message to the people. If he was fired upon, he should return the fire. If a gun was drawn on him and it was his interpretation that the gun was drawn in anger, he was to use whatever means necessary to defend himself. His instructions were not to fire or take the offensive unless in imminent danger. If they attempted to arrest him, he was to take the arrest as long as he had delivered the message. The main thing was to deliver the message. In stressing these points, I told him that if he was invited in or allowed inside the legislature, he was to read the message inside, but if it was against the rules to enter the legislature, or if measures were taken to block him, then he was not to enter, but to read the message from the capitol steps.

The Black Panther troops rolled out for Sacramento early on the morning of May 2. As soon as they left, I went to my mother's house. I had promised to mow her lawn that day. But I took a portable radio along and put it on the front step to listen for news; in the house I turned the television set on and asked my mother to keep an eye on it. Then I started mowing.

About noon a bulletin interrupted the radio program. It told of brothers at the capitol with weapons. My mother called out to me that all channels were showing the event. I ran into the house, and there was Bobby reading the mandate. The message was definitely going out. Bobby read it twice, but the press and the people assembled were so amazed at the Black Panthers' presence, and particularly the weapons, that few appeared to hear the important thing. They were concentrating on the weapons. We had hoped that after the weapons gained their attention they would listen to the message.

Later, another bulletin came on saying that the brothers had been arrested, Bobby for carrying a concealed weapon—although he was wearing his gun openly on his hip. Some of the other brothers were charged with failing to remove the rounds from the chambers of their guns when they put their weapons back in the car. I got on the phone and finally made contact with one of the Black Panther women who had gone along. She told me what had happened, and I began to initiate the next phase of our plan—raising bail money. That night I went to a local radio station, where a talk show was on. People calling in to discuss the incident had been told that I was in jail, and I decided the best way to deal with that was by confrontation. So I went in there, as Malcolm would have done, and asked for equal air time. One of the startled program directors looked at me and said, "Well, you're sort of in jail." I said, "Yes, I am in jail, but let me have equal time anyway."

On the air I explained the Sacramento ploy. My explanation was not very effective, I felt, because people who call these shows are always more interested in themselves than in issues, and you have to fight through that first. But I was able to make an appeal for money. We were faced with $50,000 bail in Sacramento, and within twenty-four hours I had raised the $50,000 needed to get the troops back on the streets. Our plans had worked exactly as we hoped.

Looking back, I think our tactic at Sacramento was correct at that time, but it was also a mistake in a way. It was the first time in our brief existence that an armed group of Black Panthers had been arrested, and it was a turning point in police perceptions. We took the arrests because we had a higher purpose. But it was not until then that the police started attempting to disarm the Party. They leveled shotguns on the brothers, handcuffed them, and generally pushed them around. I had given orders not to fire unless fired upon. Maybe the order should have been to fire on everybody in there; then they would have realized we were serious. But our purpose was not to kill; it was to inform, to let the nation know where the Party stood. The police, however, took it to mean that the Party was only a front with weapons, that we would not defend ourselves. This attitude caused a number of problems for us, and it took some time to restore caution to the police after Sacramento. Now, everything is as it used to be, because they know they will have a fight on their hands if they try to attack us.

Sacramento was certainly a success, however, in attracting national attention; even those who did not hear the complete message saw the arms, and this conveyed enough to Black people. The Bay Area became more aware of the Party, and soon we had more members than we could handle. From all across the country calls came to us about establishing chapters and branches; we could hardly keep track of the requests. In a matter of months we went from a small Bay Area group to a national organization, and we began moving to implement our ten point program.

crisis: October 28, 1967

When I was convicted of assaulting Odell Lee in 1964, the court sentenced me to three years' probation under condition that I first serve six months in the county jail. After release I reported regularly to my probation officer, all through the months that we founded the Black Panther Party and began our work in the community. The probation officer was better than average, really a pretty nice guy, intelligent and fair, and we got along well. Nonetheless, I was relieved when he told me early in October 1967, that my probation would end on October 27 and parole would begin. One of the requirements of parole was that I avoid some parts of Berkeley; in any case, no more reporting. October 27 was going to be a very special day, and my girl friend, LaVerne Williams, and I agreed that we would celebrate the occasion. On the afternoon of October 27, I was scheduled to speak at a forum on "The Future of the Black Liberation Movement," sponsored by the Black Students Union of San Francisco State College. Requests for speaking engagements had been coming in frequently since the end of the summer. The Sacramento publicity prompted a number of college groups to ask for an explanation of our approach to the problems of Blacks. They were also interested in hearing why we opposed spontaneous rebellions in Black communities and how we viewed the recent riots in Newark and Detroit. Bobby was in jail, and I was filling as many of these requests as possible, even though I am not very good at talking to large groups; nor do I enjoy it. Abstract and theoretical ideas interest me most, but they lack the rhetorical fire to hold audiences. I went to San Francisco State, anyway, because I was eager to increase our contacts with Black college students. Sharing the platform with me that afternoon was Dr. Harry Edwards, the sociology professor from San Jose State College, who was organizing the Olympic boycott by Black athletes.

That session was particularly challenging because it offered the opportunity for a lively discussion with people who disagreed with my ideas. (This was in 1967, just after one of the longest, hottest summers in American history. Student consciousness had never been higher.) I talked about the necessity for Black people to gain control of the institutions in their own communities, eventually transforming them into cooperatives, and of one day working with other ethnic groups to change the system. When I had finished speaking, an informal dialogue began; almost all the students' questions and criticisms were directed at the Black Panthers' willingness to work in coalition with white groups. We maintained this was possible as long as we controlled the programs, but the students were opposed to working with white groups, or, for that matter, almost anyone but Blacks. While this viewpoint was understandable to me, it failed to take into consideration the limitations of our power. We needed allies, and we believed that alliances with young whites—students and workers— were worth the risk.

I pointed out that many young whites had suddenly discovered hypocrisy; their fathers and forefathers had written and talked brotherhood and democracy while practicing greed, imperialism, and racism. While speaking of the rights of mankind and equality for all, of "free enterprise," the "profit system," of "individualism," and "healthy competition," they had plundered the wealth of the world and enslaved Blacks in the United States. White youths now saw through this hypocrisy and were trying to bring about changes through traditional electoral politics. But reality is impervious to idealism. These youngsters were discovering what Blacks knew in their bones—that the military-industrial complex was practically invincible and had in fact created a police state, which rendered idealism powerless to change anything. This led to disillusionment with their parents and the American power structure. At that point of disillusionment they began to identify with the oppressed people of the world.

When the Black Panthers saw this trend developing, we understood that their dissatisfaction could help our cause. In a few years' time, almost half of the American population would be composed of young people; if we developed strong and meaningful alliances with white youth, they would support our goals and work against the Establishment.

Everywhere I went in 1967 I was vehemently attacked by Black students for this position; few could present opposing objective evidence to support their criticisms. The reaction was emotional: all white people were devils; they wanted nothing to do with them. I agreed that some white people could act like devils, but we could not blind ourselves to a common humanity. More important was how to control the situation to our advantage. These questions would not be answered overnight, or in a decade, and time and again the students and I went for hours, getting nowhere. We talked right past each other. The racism that dominated their lives had come between us, and rational analysis was the victim. When I left San Francisco that afternoon, I reflected that many of the students who were supposedly learning how to analyze and understand phenomena were in fact caught up in the same predicament as the prisoners in Plato's cave allegory. Even though they were in college, they were still prisoners in the cave of exploitation and racism that Black people have been subjected to for centuries. Far from preparing them to deal with reality, college kept their intellects in chains. That afternoon I felt even more strongly that the Party would have to develop a program to implement Point 5 of our program, a true education for our people.

When I returned home around 6:30, I had a happy, righteous dinner of mustard greens and corn bread with my family. We discussed the college students and their attitudes and how difficult it had been to get through to them. That was our last meal together as a family for thirty-three months. But I had no premonition of this when I left the house and set out on foot for LaVerne's. The friends with me at San Francisco State had taken the car after driving me home. On the way, I planned our evening together, and thought about some of the things I might do now that I no longer had to report to my probation officer. At LaVerne's house, I found to my disappointment that she was ill and did not feel like going out. Although I wanted to stay with her, she insisted that I take her car and celebrate. She knew how much it meant to me that probation was over. By this time it was getting late, close to ten, so I decided to visit a few of my favorite places.

Nothing about my movements that evening was out of the ordinary. I went first to the Bosn's Locker, the bar where I had started recruiting. Most of the people there were close or casual friends, and

I talked, discussing my new freedom and celebrating with a liberation drink, Cuba libre, a rum and Coke. From there I went to a nearby church where a social was in full swing. Every Wednesday night this church held an Afro-history class, and on Friday nights a well-attended social with dancing and punch. I had one more place to go—a party being given by friends on San Pablo Street in Oakland. About 2:00 A.M., when the social was ending, I set out for the party with Gene McKinney, a friend I had known since grammar school. By now it was October 28; I was officially a free man and feeling great. Even though the food was gone by the time we got to San Pablo Street, I did not mind. It was good to mingle with the people and talk about the Black Panthers and answer their questions. We stayed until the very end, 4:00 A.M.

Then Gene McKinney and I headed for Seventh Street, the center of the action for West Oakland. There are a number of bars and soul-food restaurants on the street, a few nightclubs, and at almost any hour you can find something going on. Some of the restaurants serve up barbecue that is really saying something. Gene and I were hungry, and Seventh Street is the place to get righteous soul food.

As I turned into Seventh Street, looking for a parking place, I saw the red light of a police car in my rear-view mirror. I had not realized that I was being trailed by a policeman, and my initial reaction was here we go again, more harassment. But, having been stopped so many times before, I was ready. The police had a list of the licenses on cars Black Panthers frequently used, so we always expected this. I kept my lawbook between the bucket seats, and I knew that once I began to read the law to the "law enforcer" he would have to let me go. I wondered what his excuse would be this time; I had obeyed all the traffic regulations.

I pulled the car over to the curb, and the police officer stopped behind me, remaining in his car for a minute or so. Then he got out and came up to my window. When he got a good look at me, he stuck his head in the window within six inches of my face and said very sarcastically, "Well, well, well, what do we have here? The great, *great* Huey P. Newton." I made no reply but merely looked him in the eye. He acted like a fisherman who had just landed a prize catch he had never dreamed of landing. Then he asked for my driver's license, which

I gave to him. "Who does the car belong to?" he asked. I told him, "It belongs to Miss LaVerne Williams," and showed him the registration. After comparing it with the license, he gave me the license back and went to his car with the registration. While I sat in the car waiting for him to finish, another police officer pulled up behind the first one. This was not unusual, and I attached little significance to it. The second officer walked up to the first officer's car, and they talked for a moment. Then the second officer came to my window and said, "Mr. Williams, do you have any further identification?" I said, "What do you mean 'Mr. Williams'? My name is Huey P. Newton, and I have already shown my driver's license to the first officer." He just looked at me, nodding his head, and said, "Yes, I know who you are." I knew they both recognized me, because my picture and name were known to every officer in Oakland, as were Bobby's and most of the other Black Panthers'.

The first officer then came back to my car, opened the door, and ordered me out, while the second officer walked around to the passenger side and told Gene McKinney to get out. He then walked Gene to the street side of the car. Meanwhile, I picked up my lawbook from between the seats and started to get out. I thought it was my criminal evidence book, which covers laws dealing with reasonable cause for arrest and the search and seizure laws. If necessary, I intended to read the law to this policeman, as I had done so many times in the past. However, I had mistakenly picked up my criminal lawbook, which looks exactly like the other one.

I got out of the car with the book in my right hand and asked the officer if I was under arrest. He said, "No, you're not under arrest; just lean on the car." I leaned on the top of the car—a Volkswagen—with both hands on the lawbook while the officer searched me. He did it in a manner intended to be degrading, pulling out my shirttail, running his hand over my body, and then he pat-searched my legs, bringing his hands up into my genital area. He was both disgusting and thorough. All this time the four of us were in the street, the second officer with Gene McKinney; I could not see what they were doing.

The officer then told me to go back to his car because he wanted to talk to me. Taking my left arm in his right hand, he began walking, or rather pushing me toward his car. But when we reached it, he kept going until we had reached the back door of the second police car, where he brought me to an abrupt halt. At this I opened my law-book and said, "You have no reasonable cause to arrest me." The officer was to my left, just slightly behind me. As I was opening the book, he snarled, "You can take that book and shove it up your ass, nigger." With that, he stepped slightly in front of me and brought his left hand up into my face, hooking me with a smear that was not a direct blow, but more like a solid straight-arm. This momentarily dazed me, and I stumbled back four or five feet and went down on one knee, still holding on to my book. As I started to rise, I saw the officer draw his service revolver, point it at me, and fire. My stomach seemed to explode, as if someone had poured a pot of boiling soup all over me, and the world went hazy.

There were some shots, a rapid volley, but I have no idea where they came from. They seemed to be all around me. I vaguely remember being on my hands and knees on the ground, disoriented, with everything spinning. I also had the sensation of being moved or propelled. After that, I remember nothing.

trial

The morning my trial began, on July 15, 1968, in the Alameda County Court House, 5,000 demonstrators and about 450 Black Panthers gathered outside to show their support. Busloads of demonstrators came from out of town and joined the throng that crowded the streets and sidewalks outside the courthouse. Across the street from the building a formation of Black Panthers stood, lined up two deep, and stretching for a solid block. At the entrance to the building a unit of sisters from the Party chanted "Free Huey" and "Set Our Warrior Free." In front of them, on both sides of the courthouse door, two Party members held aloft the blue Black Panther banner with FREE HUEY emblazoned on it. Black Panther security patrols with walkie-talkie radio sets ringed the courthouse.

The building was under heavy guard. At every entrance and patrolling every floor, armed deputies from the sheriff's office prowled up and down, and plainclothes men were assigned positions throughout the building. On that first day nearly fifty helmeted Oakland police stood inside the main entrance, and on the rooftop more cops with high-powered rifles stared down into the street. The trial was conducted in the seventh-floor courtroom, a small depressing room kept ice cold throughout the trial. Security was so tight that the courtroom was carefully inspected before every session; everyone, even my parents, was searched before entering. The spectators' section had only about sixty seats: two rows were reserved for my family; the press had twenty-five or so seats; and the rest was for the general public. Every morning around dawn people began lining up outside for the few remaining places.

Presiding was Superior Court Judge Monroe Friedman, seventy-two years old, dour and humorless. Of course, no one admits prejudice, but Judge Friedman betrayed his in countless ways throughout the trial. Clearly, from the beginning he thought I was guilty, and his sympathies lay with the prosecution. For one thing, he condescended to Black witnesses, speaking to them as if they were not capable of understanding the issues. It was obvious that he was totally unaware of the development of Black consciousness in the past decade. Even his tone of voice was revealing. As the trial progressed, he constantly overruled my lawyer and sustained almost every objection of the prosecutor. Sometimes, when he did not like the way things were going, he looked over to the prosecutor's table as if inviting an objection, which he would then sustain. On interpretation, he was extremely rigid. Whenever a legal point could not be solved by legal mechanics, he would pass it off as unimportant, thereby leaving it for some higher court to deal with or for some political statement to be made through the legislature. Nothing was considered that was not in the book. He acknowledged that some laws were good and reluctantly followed those he disliked. Never for one moment did I consider him a fair arbitrator.

The most crucial aspect of the trial was the jury selection, and on that first trial day several hundred prospective jurors came to the courthouse. Charles Garry wanted a certain kind of juror, and he faced terrific odds in finding him. For one thing, everyone in the Oakland area had read or seen prejudicial accounts of the shooting. It was difficult to find anyone without an opinion about the case. Then, too, we wanted some Black people. This was a vital issue and, as we learned through our investigations, a formidable hurdle to overcome. Our inquiries revealed that the assistant district attorney and prosecutor in my trial, Lowell Jensen, had developed a system whereby Blacks would ostensibly be on jury panels called for duty but would always be eliminated before they were seated in an actual trial. Under Jensen's direction whenever a Black was removed from a prospective jury for cause, or through peremptory challenges, he was then returned to the jury panel and called in another trial. That way, it always appeared the Blacks were an active part of the system, even though it was unlikely a Black would ever serve on an actual jury. When my trial began, the routine changed; other district attorneys in the area did not remove Blacks from their jury panels. Therefore, while my trial was in session there were juries in other courts with as many as six Blacks on them.

The Party instructed Garry to use all his peremptory challenges on prospective jurors. In a capital case in the state of California each side is allowed twenty; that is, both defense and prosecution can reject twenty jurors without giving a reason. We gave Garry these instructions to demonstrate to the people that something is wrong with a trial system that defies the right of a defendant to be tried by a true cross-section of his community. We used all our peremptory challenges to emphasize this point. The prosecution did not exhaust all theirs, since it was not hard for them to find their kind of people. (Charles Garry found racism in almost every prospective juror he questioned.)

Selecting the jury took a long time—about two weeks. All in all, three panels of prospective jurors—about 180 people—were questioned before a jury and four alternates were chosen. Out of the nearly two hundred people available for my jury, there were sixteen Blacks, a few Orientals, and one or two Chicanos. The population of Oakland was then 38 per cent Black.

The final jury consisted of eleven whites and one Black. The Black man, David Harper, actually looked enough like me to pass as a relative, although we were strangers before the trial. At the time, he was an executive in a branch of the Bank of America, but he has since become president of a Black bank in Detroit. I wondered why the district attorney did not excuse him from serving. Perhaps he figured it would help his case in the appeals court to have at least one Black on the jury. Also, he had tried to get a safe one. I figured that the district attorney saw Harper as a "house nigger," a Black bank official who "had it made," so to speak. They probably thought Harper could be counted on because of his status and his ambition to go further in the white world.

Throughout the trial I studied Harper, trying to get the measure of the man. Would he go along with the madness of the system? With a jury it is always a guessing game. You know the judge and the prosecutor are your enemies and will do anything to keep you down. Every other paid employee in the courtroom, regardless of his color, is a slave to the system. But the jurors are something else. I watched every move Harper made, yet I could not detect where he was, or where he was going. I began to wonder if the fact that he had a good job in a bank gave him satisfaction. I asked myself whether he was so blinded by the crumbs the system offered him that he would go along with the racists on the jury and a corrupt state apparatus to secure his future—or what he hoped might be his future.

These questions went through my mind almost daily as the proceedings crept along. Sometimes, pondering Harper, I found myself paying no attention at all to the boring testimony of the prosecution witnesses, such as the ballistics experts. Not until I took the stand myself and began talking to the jury did I feel Harper knew his friends better than the district attorney had estimated. When I finally testified, I directed my words to Harper. He was my audience. An unspoken bond grew up between us that convinced me he not only understood but he also agreed with me. Only then did I see a glimmer of hope with the jury—he was it. However, I never placed much confidence in his ability to sway the others.

The prosecutor in my case was Lowell Jensen, who later became district attorney of Alameda County. Jensen is a witty and intelligent man and a worthy opponent as far as the law is concerned. He appears to have a photographic memory, and on the basis of legal knowledge alone he is a good lawyer. In my case, he meant to get a conviction of first-degree murder, no matter how far he had to stretch the law, and to that end, he ignored the possibility that there were a number of grounds for reversal and that in time a higher court would decide against the verdict of this trial. A conviction was all he cared about. He knew that if he won his case against me—a person hated by the Establishment—he would be rewarded with fame and rising fortune. What would a reversal matter? A ruling by a higher court would take from two to five years, and by that time he would have achieved what he wanted. My trial was nothing more than an ego trip for him.

Throughout the trial an unspoken "game" or challenge went on in the courtroom between Jensen, the judge, and myself, although a lot of people—especially the jury—knew nothing about it. The jury probably believed that the prosecutor and the judge were honorable men, with only their jobs and justice on their minds. But my lawyers and I understood the undercurrents and intangibles that were always present, difficult as they were to expose. And we knew that if the jury were aware of them also they would see the political nature of much that went on in the courtroom. For example, we surmised from the very start of the trial that Jensen had engineered the racist system by which Blacks would be on jury panels called for duty but eliminated before they could be seated for trial. And we knew that Jensen did not have justice on his mind but wanted victory at any cost to further his own personal ambitions. These were some of the things that made the whole trial scene like a game—a grim game with my life at stake—but a game nonetheless.

In his opening statement to the jury Jensen charged that I had murdered Officer John Frey with full intent, that I had shot Officer Herbert Heanes, and that I had kidnapped Dell Ross. He said that when the first policeman stopped me I had given him false identification, but when the second officer came up, I had correctly identified myself. Then the first officer, Frey, placed me under arrest. He claimed that when the police officer walked me back to his car, I produced a gun and began firing. According to Jensen, I shot Officer Frey with my own gun, which I pulled from inside my shirt, then took his gun and continued shooting. I was charged with shooting Officer Frey five times and Officer Heanes three times. Officer Heanes was supposed to have shot me once. After this, the prosecutor said, I escaped and forced Dell Ross to take me to another part of Oakland.

The most crucial challenge facing the prosecution was to establish motivation for my alleged actions. Jensen claimed that I had three motives for my alleged crimes. First, he said, I had had a prior conviction for a felony and was on probation. Because of this, I knew that having a concealed weapon on my person could lead to another felony conviction if the police officers found the gun on me. Second, they claimed that I had marijuana in the car and that bits of marijuana had been found in the pocket of my pants; this, too, could lead to another felony beef. And, third, they claimed that I had given false identification to the police officer, which was a violation of the law. For these reasons, the prosecutor claimed I was so desperate to escape another felony charge that I killed an officer, wounded another, and kidnapped a citizen. As I said before, the prosecutor was willing to go to any lengths to win his case.

The truth of the matter is that when Frey stopped me, he knew full well who I was, as did every other policeman on the Oakland force, and he tried to execute me in an urban variation of the old-style southern lynching. My attorneys had investigated Frey's background, and they found a long history of harassing and mistreating Black people and making racist statements about Blacks and to Blacks. Unfortunately for Frey, his habits boomeranged that time. I do not know what happened because I was unconscious, but things did not work out as he wanted or expected them to. I guess he thought that if he could bring me in dead, he would be given a promotion.

The marijuana charge was sheer fabrication. First of all, no member of the Black Panther Party uses drugs. It is absolutely forbidden. Anyone discovered violating this rule is expelled from the Party. Narcotics prohibition is part of the Black Panther principle of obeying the law to the letter. Both Charles Garry and I believed that the marijuana found in the car and in my trousers was planted there by the police. Having been stopped by members of the Oakland police force more than fifty times in the past year, why would I take the risk? Knowing that at any moment of the day or night I was liable to be thoroughly searched and my car inspected, I would never have been reckless enough to carry marijuana, even if I had wanted to use it—which I didn't. If the matchboxes really were in LaVerne's car that night, there is no way of knowing how they got there. Dozens of people used her car, many of whom she knew only slightly, since they were friends of friends. But it is far more likely that the police were behaving as usual, leaving out no possibility in their determination to railroad me to jail.

As for being a felon with a gun, I, of course, was not carrying a weapon but had been out celebrating the end of my probation that night. There was no reason for me to have a gun and no reason to avoid arrest on this count. Nor did I consider myself a felon. The original conviction of felony was a complicated one, anyway, going back to the Odell Lee case in 1964. Under California law, the sentence a defendant receives determines whether he is a "felon" or a "misdemeanant." If he is sentenced to a state prison, he is a felon; a misdemeanant usually goes to a county jail. When I was convicted of assaulting Odell Lee with a deadly weapon, I was sentenced to three years' probation, a condition being that I serve six months in the county jail. This meant I was a misdemeanant. However, in my murder trial the judge testified that I had been sentenced to the state prison and that then the sentence had been suspended. As a condition of my probation I spent six months in the county jail. Technically the state considered me a felon. In the end, this proved to be reversible error. Although I could have changed my legal status in the courts, I never petitioned because I did not consider myself a felon.

But the prosecution did, and planned its whole case around the point. Not only did they want to show I would commit murder to avoid arrest, but they also wanted to take advantage of the fact that a felon's testimony can be discredited and he can receive a severer sentence. Despite Charles Garry's objections and arguments, Judge Friedman ruled that I had been convicted of a felony in 1964, and this charge against me was added to the other three. This question of the Odell Lee conviction came up repeatedly during the trial, since the prosecution needed to establish a motive. Eventually, when I testified, I told the jury again that I had not considered myself a felon. It was actually a ridiculous basis for motivation, since I had dozens of witnesses who saw me out celebrating on the night of October 27—a fact which proved beyond doubt that I had no reason to resist arrest as a felon.

When my trial was just beginning, Eldridge Cleaver put out a leaflet that was widely distributed in the Black community. In it he charged that the police, with murder on their minds, had violated the territorial integrity of the Black community and that I had dealt with their transgression in a necessary way. The leaflet went on to say that Black people are justified in killing all policemen who do this. Behind Eldridge's message lay the inference that I had killed the police officer, even though I had not.

The leaflet could not have been used against me in the courts. Even so, my family was very upset over it, and they protested strongly to Eldridge. They felt he cared little about me and that he was, in effect, trying to gas me. I told them as gently as I could not to interfere with anything Eldridge or other Party members did during the trial because such actions could not be brought into the legal proceedings. As far as I was concerned, Eldridge was free to write and mobilize the community by any means necessary; I supported him in that. Issuing the leaflet was a political act using the trial to heighten the consciousness of the community. I was willing to go along with Party actions in the interest of educating the people, mobilizing the community, and taking the contradictions to a higher level. After that my family did not interfere with political activities.

The trial caused much grief and worry to my family. They wanted to save me, but I felt death was ahead, and my main concern was the community. Because my family continued to hope, I could not tell them this, however, and I was very moved by their faith and support. In fact, the only strain I felt during the trial was the pull between trying to comfort my family and carrying out the political activities I knew were necessary. It has all worked out for the best now, but at the time it was a tremendous weight on my family, and on me.

Another matter of concern was whether to reveal to my attorneys the name of Gene McKinney, my passenger on the night the incident went down. Gene had never been apprehended by the police, despite a diligent search. What is more, they did not even know his name. From the start, the police had cleared Gene, and Heanes had testified before the grand jury that my companion had not taken part in any violence. Right after I was captured, the police sent broadcasts all through California saying that they had apprehended the "guilty" party and they wanted the passenger to come in for questioning. They repeatedly said in these broadcasts that the passenger had nothing to do with the incident. I suspected that they wanted to use him against me, and at first I refused to give his name to my attorneys. I saw no point in involving Gene, even though I knew his testimony might help free me. Only when my lawyers had convinced me that legally the prosecution could not do anything to him did I agree to reveal Gene's identity. From my own knowledge of the law, I became aware that the courts were powerless to hurt him. However, Gene was skeptical. When my lawyers finally met him, they explained very carefully that he could not be hurt by testifying for the defense, and he did eventually testify despite his doubts. This showed supreme courage on his part, because the prosecutors were not above pulling some trick to involve him.

The prosecution took about three weeks to present its case and called about twenty witnesses to the stand. They included people like the nurse who had admitted me at Kaiser Hospital, the doctor who did the autopsy on Officer Frey, ballistics experts from the police department, various policemen who arrived at the scene of the shooting, and so on. But their three most important witnesses were Patrolman Heanes, Henry Grier, the bus driver who allegedly witnessed the shooting, and Dell Ross, who claimed that McKinney and I had kidnapped him. The first of these to testify was Herbert Heanes.

When Officer Heanes took the witness stand, it soon became apparent that he was a very disturbed man. He told of recurring dreams in which the Black Panthers were attacking him. Heanes is not very bright, and as time and again he had trouble keeping his story straight, the impression grew that he was completely confused. The prosecutor had obviously rehearsed him, but Heanes was so tense that he made mistakes; with each mistake he dropped his head as if to say, I'll try the script over again. He was no good at all at improvisation and reconciling contradictions in his testimony.

Heanes testified that after Frey ordered me out of my car, the two of us walked to Heanes's patrol car (parked behind LaVerne's Volkswagen) while he, Heanes, remained near the front door of Frey's patrol car, about thirty-five feet away from us. As Frey and I reached the rear of Heanes's car, Heanes testified that I "turned around and started shooting," and that Frey and I then started to "tussle" on the trunk of his car. At this point, Heanes said, he was shot in the right arm, whereupon he switched his gun to his left hand. Immediately after this, he noticed out of the corner of his eye that the passenger in my car (McKinney) had gotten out of the Volkswagen and was standing on the curb with his arms up in the air. Heanes turned his gun on him, but after the passenger assured him he was not armed, Heanes turned back to Frey and me. By this time, Heanes said, Frey and I had separated, although Frey was still hanging on to me, and he, Heanes, shot at my stomach as I faced him. He did not say that he saw his bullet hit me, only that he fired at my "midsection." After that, Heanes said he remembered only two things: first, sending out a 940B—the police emergency number—over the police radio; and second, seeing two men run into the darkness.

When Garry cross-examined Heanes after his testimony, many contradictions and unanswered questions emerged. Heanes repeatedly stated that he never saw a gun in my hand, yet he testified that I had turned around and started to shoot. He was never able to say who had shot him in the arm, although when he shot me in the stomach, he said I was facing him. He would not state that I had shot him, even though, as a police officer, he is supposedly trained to observe such facts as whether or not a suspect has a gun. He was confused in his descriptions of what McKinney was wearing; some of his testimony contradicted the description given later by Henry Grier, the bus driver.

Perhaps the greatest weakness of his testimony, which Garry skillfully brought to the jury's attention, was that Heanes had turned his back on McKinney, having only McKinney's word that he was unarmed. Since the Oakland police distrusted and hated all Black Panthers, and since McKinney, who was unknown to Heanes, and who was riding with the Black Panther Minister of Defense, could very well have been a Black Panther, why had he left himself so unprotected, particularly since he said he did not know where all the shots were coming from? As Garry suggested in his cross-examination of Heanes, it was probably because Heanes was more worried about what Frey would do. Among the police Frey was known to need watching in the Black community; he was even worse than the normal cop, which made him extremely dangerous.

It was clear from Heanes's testimony and the way he had been coached by the prosecutor that great pains had been taken to avoid any implication that Frey and Heanes had shot each other. Charles Garry's first question on cross-examination dealt with this: "Did you shoot and kill Officer Frey?" Heanes said no. Yet several facts pointed that way, and Heanes's evasions were not helpful to the prosecution. For instance, Heanes made a point of saying that he fired at me only when Frey and I had broken apart after our struggle on the car. A more damaging piece of evidence came from the ballistics section of the police department itself. The expert who testified concluded that the bullets that had hit both Frey and Heanes came from police revolvers. They were lead bullets—not copper-jacketed, as were the two nine-millimeter casings found on the ground at the scene of the shooting. This damaged the prosecution's case, because Jensen had maintained from the beginning that I had shot Heanes and Frey with my own .38 pistol, whose bullets would have matched the nine-millimeter casings found on the ground. Of course, this mythical gun was never found.

All in all, Heanes's testimony did little for the prosecution. He became even more muddled during my second trial, and by the time he appeared at the third trial, he found it impossible to deal with his own inconsistencies. It was then that he broke down on the stand and admitted seeing a third party at the scene of the shooting. But even at my first trial his testimony was too vague and inconsistent to be taken seriously.

The testimony of Henry Grier, a Black man, and the next major witness for the prosecution, was therefore all-important. He was the only person besides Heanes who claimed I had had a gun at the scene of the shooting. Grier was a bus driver for the Alameda–Contra Costa Transit system in Oakland. According to his testimony, he had been driving his bus along Seventh Street shortly after 5:00 A.M. on the morning of October 28, 1967, when he stopped his vehicle and under its bright lights witnessed the shooting of Frey and Heanes from a distance of about ten feet or less. Asked by Jensen to identify the gunman, Grier left the stand, walked over to where I sat with my attorneys, and put his hand on my shoulder.

When he testified for the first time, on the afternoon of August 7, 1968, a feeling of disgust for him overwhelmed me; he was obviously a bought man who had sold out from terror of the white power structure and perhaps because the district attorney had promised him a few handouts. My attorneys also had reason to suspect, after investigation, that he was in some kind of trouble with his job or the law, and only by cooperating with the district attorney's office could he get out of his predicament. Yet, as the first trial wore on, my feelings of disgust turned to pity. He was, after all, a brother. As a Black, I understood that he was coerced into selling his integrity for survival, and I knew he must have been disgusting to himself. After the first trial, I felt Grier would not be able to live with himself, but when he came back and did it twice again, in the second and third trials, I realized he had been totally destroyed as a person, too corrupt even to feel shame. He was a complete mystery to me.

It is an indication of Grier's importance to the prosecution that Charles Garry learned of his existence only on August 1, six days before he appeared on the witness stand. On August 1, jury selection had been completed, and under the rules of the court, the prosecution was required to give the defense the names and addresses of all the witnesses it intended to call during the trial. It was on this day that Garry first saw Grier's name and learned who he was. During the entire nine months of preparation for the trial, Jensen had seen to it that Grier was kept completely out of sight and never mentioned. He did not appear before the grand jury. In all the police reports, in all the official statements that were issued covering every detail of the incident, the name of the most important "witness" to the shooting was withheld. Jensen had carried out his Machiavellian tactics with supreme cunning. Only when it was no longer possible to hide Grier did Garry learn of his identity and that he claimed to have witnessed the incident.

At the time my lawyers received the prosecution list with Grier's name on it, they were also given another staggering piece of evidence: a transcript of a recorded conversation between Grier and Police Inspector Frank McConnell, which took place at the Oakland police station only ninety minutes after the shooting on October 28. The police had brought Grier to the station house for a statement almost immediately after the incident, and in it he described everything he had allegedly seen. He also identified me as the gunman from a photograph in the police files that Inspector McConnell showed him.

When my attorneys read Grier's statement, given to the police while everything was still fresh in his mind, we learned why the police and prosecution had hidden him away. If Charles Garry had had a chance to talk to him earlier, he would have convinced Grier in a very short time that his eyewitness account of the shooting would never stand up in court. First of all, Grier did not make a "statement" to the police. His interview at the police station was a classic case of verbal entrapment. The inspector led Grier, who was not only weak but also in many instances unsure of everything he had seen, and fed him the questions that would produce answers the police wanted. Whenever Grier hesitated or stopped while trying to remember what he had seen, Inspector McConnell put words in his mouth or suggested the way things had happened; then Grier would agree. But, serious as this was, some of Grier's most crucial statements were so damaging to the prosecution's case it seems incredible that Jensen was willing to gamble every-thing on him as a principal witness. The fact that Grier swore I had a gun in my hand must have affected Jensen's judgment concerning the rest of Grier's testimony.

First, in describing the gunman whom he later identified as me, Grier said he was no taller than five feet; "sort of a pee-wee type you might call him" were his exact words to Inspector McConnell. Since I am five feet ten and a half inches, Grier's impression of my height was wildly inaccurate. He also said I was wearing a black shirt, a light tan jacket, and that I was clean-shaven. The police had kept all the clothing I was wearing that night, and it was a matter of record that I wore a black jacket, a white shirt, and had two weeks' growth of beard (this was confirmed by a close-up photograph taken by the police when I was lying on the gurney at Kaiser Hospital). Then, too, many of the things Grier said in the transcript were at variance with Officer Heanes's depiction of what took place.

Grier told Inspector McConnell that he had first come upon the scene while driving his bus westbound on Seventh Street. As he approached Willow Avenue on Seventh, directly across from the con-struction site of a new post office, he said, he observed two parked police cars and near them two policemen and two civilians standing in the street. It was Grier's impression that the police were probably giving the two civilians a ticket or making a routine check, and so he thought little of it as he continued west to the end of his run. (This contradicted the testimony of Heanes, who said that the second pas-senger [McKinney] had remained in the Volkswagen until after he, Heanes, was shot.) Grier related how he went to the end of his route, turned around, and began his eastbound run back along Seventh Street, picking up three passengers on his way. When he got back to where the police cars were, he said, he arrived at the moment Frey and I were walking toward one of the police cars, with Officer Heanes walking behind us. (Heanes had testified that he stayed beside Frey's car as we walked toward the other police car and had not accompanied us.) At this point, Grier said, while Frey was walking beside me, I reached into my jacket, pulled out a gun, and fired at Heanes, who was walking behind me. Heanes fell to the ground. By this time, Grier told McConnell, he had stopped the bus about thirty or forty yards away from us. Then, he continued, Frey and I began wrestling, and he heard a second shot. He reached for the phone in his bus to call the central dispatcher of the transit system, and when he looked again, Frey had fallen on his back, and I was standing over him and firing three or four more shots at him while he lay on his back on the ground. The next thing he knew, said Grier, I had turned and fled west, and within minutes people and police were arriving at the scene from every direction. He told Inspector McConnell that he had not seen the second civilian after he first passed the four of us on his eastbound trip. During the shooting, the man was nowhere to be seen, according to Grier's testimony (Heanes had testified that McKinney was standing near the curb with his hands in the air).

As soon as Garry and my other attorneys read this transcript and received Grier's name and address on August 1, they tried to get in touch with him. He did not appear at work for the next six days. They called his home over and over again, but could never reach him; a recorded message said that the number was out of order. For six days a constant vigil was maintained outside his home. No one was there, and neither he nor any member of his family could be found. Grier had simply disappeared. None of my lawyers laid eyes on Henry Grier until he walked into the courtroom on August 7 to testify for the prosecution. On the afternoon his name had been given to the defense, Grier had been taken into protective custody by the district attorney's office and secretly installed in the Lake Merritt Hotel in downtown Oakland, completely unavailable for questioning by the defense. When Grier finally appeared, Garry had only a matter of hours to prepare his cross-examination on the basis of prosecution testimony. However, he had had six days to go over Grier's sworn statement to Inspector McConnell, enough time to discredit totally Grier's statements on the witness stand, because—unbelievably—Grier changed a lot of his earlier testimony under questioning by Jensen.

At this point the jury had not read the transcript of Grier's sworn statement to Inspector McConnell. And so, when Jensen put Grier on the stand on August 7, the jurors were hearing for the first time Grier's account of the shooting. Jensen handled his testimony very slickly, emphasizing particularly that part in which Grier said I pulled a gun from inside my shirt, shot at Heanes, and then shot and killed Frey, standing over him and firing three or four more shots into his body. When Grier walked over and identified me, the jury must have been convinced of my guilt, for Grier was a calm, assured witness.

But Jensen made a crucial mistake. He thought he could get away with the inconsistencies between Grier's statements made an hour and a half after the shooting and what Jensen coached him to say on the stand. He had Grier tell the jury that he was less than ten *feet* away from the participants in the shooting, whereas in his sworn statement to McConnell, Grier had said he was thirty or forty *yards* away. He told the jury in the courtroom that I had reached into my shirt for my gun, but in his original statement, he had said I reached into the pocket of my *jacket* or *coat* to get it. Grier testified during the trial that Frey fell forward, face down, while he had told McConnell that Frey fell on his back. On the stand Grier claimed that the bus lights were shining directly on the scene and he could see plainly, but he had told McConnell that he could not tell how old the gunman was because he had his head down and he "couldn't get a good look." He told Jensen on the stand that I had fled toward the post office construction site, but when McConnell had asked him if that was where I was headed when he had last seen me, Grier said no, that I was running northwest, toward a gas station.

It took only about three and a half hours of cross-examination for Charles Garry to demolish Grier's credibility. In his examination of him and in his final summation, Garry showed that there were at least fifteen crucial statements in which Grier's two sworn testimonies were in conflict. "For a while," Garry said to the jury near the end of the trial, "I thought Mr. Grier was making an honest mistake. I really thought that for a long time. But I've now come to the conclusion that this man was either deliberately lying or that he is a psychopath and that he can't be depended upon in relating any kind of facts. As far as Huey Newton is concerned, either choice is deadly."

In his cross-examination of Grier, Garry first demonstrated that there had been absolutely no reason for his having been taken into protective custody. Over the strenuous objections of Jensen, who constantly leaped up and called Garry's questions "incompetent, irrelevant, and immaterial," Garry got Grier to admit that not only had the district attorney's office never told him why he was being taken into custody, but also that Grier himself had always felt perfectly safe, had never been threatened, and had never felt a need for any protection. This was an effective beginning, because it showed the jury that the trial was being conducted by a ruthless prosecutor who had denied the defense lawyers their legal right to question a prospective witness.

Then Garry proceeded to develop his masterly strategy to expose Grier's fraudulence. He had him describe all over again in the same words the story he had told the jury for the prosecution. Garry wanted the jury to understand very clearly what was happening (the jury was still unaware of Grier's first statement to McConnell). When Grier had finished, Garry took off. He demonstrated in one instance after another all the discrepancies in Grier's two stories. This is how his cross-examination went at one point:

> GARRY: How was the civilian dressed?
> GRIER: Well, sir, he had on a dark jacket and a light shirt.
> GARRY: As a matter of fact, sir, didn't he—didn't that civilian have on a *dark* shirt and a *light* tan jacket?
> GRIER: No, sir.
> GARRY: I want you to think about this before you answer it. I am going to ask you again. Isn't it a fact that the person you have described as the civilian was a person who had a dark shirt on, a black shirt on, and a light tan jacket?
> (Silence) . . .
> GARRY: A light tan jacket?
> GRIER: No, sir. It was dark.
> JUDGE FRIEDMAN: What was the answer?
> GRIER: Dark.
> JUDGE FRIEDMAN: Dark what?
> GRIER: The outer garment was dark.
> GARRY: How tall was that civilian?
> GRIER: From up in the coach, sir, to look down at an angle like that, I wouldn't dare say, sir.
> GARRY: Isn't it a fact that that civilian was under five feet?
> GRIER: I do not know, sir.
> GARRY: Would you say that that civilian was heavy-set, thin, or otherwise?
> GRIER: I didn't pay that close attention, Counselor.
> GARRY: Mr. Grier, you know that you are under oath, do you not?

GRIER: I do, sir. I do.

JENSEN: Object to that as being argumentative, Your Honor.

GARRY: Mr. Grier, you made a statement to Inspector McConnell on the twenty-eighth day of October, 1967, at the hour of 6:30 A.M.?

GRIER: That's right, sir.

GARRY: And in that statement didn't you tell Inspector McConnell that the person that was involved was under five feet?

GRIER: I could have, sir.

GARRY: Did you or did you not say so?

GRIER: I don't recall making any specific statement, sir, as to that fact, sir.

At this point the court adjourned for the day. Next morning, Thursday, August 8, in the absence of the jury, Garry made two motions for a mistrial. The first was based on the evidence that the prosecution had hidden a witness from the defense. "We found out for the first time yesterday," said Garry to Judge Friedman, "that immediately after these documents were given to us and the list of the witnesses, that the prosecution immediately took this man out of circulation to a point where we did not know where he was, under the guise of so-called protective custody. He was put into the Hotel Merritt, and we didn't find this out until he was on the stand yesterday afternoon. Our motion is based upon the grounds that the prosecution has gone out of its way to circumvent the right and the obligation and the duty of the defense to prepare its case and to present it in a serious case as this one is. I feel hamstrung, I feel tied up. And I am asking the court for relief."

Jensen immediately responded that if Garry had wanted to talk to any witness he should have come to the district attorney's office the following day and talked to him there.

"I have a right to see the witnesses under my own circumstances and my own conditions.... I spent hours and hours of investigation time trying to locate this man, and all the time he had him under wraps," Garry replied. Then he went on to present his second motion for a mistrial:

> My second motion is based upon the atmosphere of the courthouse. I feel impelled to call to the court's attention that the entire courthouse, as you walk in through the front door, is permeated and surrounded by deputies of the Alameda County Sheriff's Department

and other police agencies, making it embarrassing and insulting, and has, in my opinion, a direct bearing and effect on the jury itself.

In this particular case, under these circumstances, I feel impelled to call to the court's attention that we don't feel we can get a fair trial with a jury walking through these same doors with bailiffs finding out who they are and what they are doing in the building, and this kind of atmosphere; and for that same reason I am going to renew a motion for mistrial.

JUDGE FRIEDMAN: Motion is denied. Bring the jury down.

With that, the jury returned, and Garry resumed his cross-examination of Henry Grier.

> GARRY: Mr. Grier, isn't it a fact that you first saw this officer and this civilian walking alongside of each other, as you have described it, when your bus was at least thirty to thirty-five yards from the scene?
> GRIER: I did not, sir.
> GARRY (reading from transcript): "...And then I noticed as I approached—I saw the officer walking—one guy towards the second patrol car and this guy was short, sort of a small-built fellow. He—just as I approached within thirty, thirty or forty yards of it I noticed the man begins going into his jacket—" You gave that answer to Inspector McConnell on that hour of the morning, did you not, sir?
> GRIER: I did, sir.
> GARRY: Mr. Grier, this man was under five feet, isn't that right? Would you answer that question either yes or no....
> GRIER: I don't know, Counselor.
> GARRY (reading from transcript):
>   "Q. And how tall would you say he was?
>   A. No more than five feet.
>   Q. Very short?
>   A. Very short."
> You gave that answer, did you not, at the time?
> GRIER: I did.
> GARRY: Mr. Grier, how much did this man weigh?
> GRIER: I don't know.
> GARRY: In your estimation?
> GRIER: I don't know, Counselor.
> GARRY (reading from transcript):
>   "Q. About how much would you say he weighed?
>   A. Oh, 125."
> Did you give that answer to that question?

GRIER: I could have, Counselor.
GARRY: Was this fellow, this man that you saw on that morning, was this fellow a husky fellow or a thin person, or a medium person, or what?
GRIER: Medium, I would say.
GARRY: As a matter of fact, the person you have described was a little pee-wee fellow, isn't that right?
GRIER: He was not, sir.
GARRY (reading from transcript):
 "Q. Was he heavy, husky?
 A. No.
 Q. Slender?
 A. Sort of pee-wee type fellow, you might call him."
Isn't that right, that is what you said?
GRIER: I could have, Counselor.
GARRY: That is what you did say, isn't it, sir?
GRIER: Possibly, yes. I could have said that, yes, sir.
GARRY: Not possibly; that is exactly what you did say, isn't it, sir?
GRIER: As I said before, Counselor, without any mistake, I could have.
GARRY: It was the truth, wasn't it, sir?
GRIER: It was, sir.

After this, and while Jensen registered his disapproval, Garry read to the jury the entire transcript of Grier's statement to Inspector McConnell. There could be no question in the jurors' minds then that something was suspicious, if not rotten, about the prosecution's star witness.

Garry's most dramatic refutation of Grier's testimony—and the one that went to the heart of the matter—came during his final summary for the defense. He walked over to the table in the courtroom where all the evidence for the trial was on display and picked up the black leather jacket I had been wearing on October 28. Then he picked up Heanes's .38 revolver and walked over to the jury box. Standing before the jurors, he quoted Grier's original statement that I had gone into my jacket or coat pocket and pulled out a gun. The gun that the prosecution claimed I had hidden, a .38 pistol, could not have been much smaller than Heanes's revolver, Garry said, as he put the gun into the jacket pocket. It immediately fell out. He put it into the other pocket, and it fell out again. He tried putting the gun in the pockets several times, and each time it fell out; the pocket was too small to hold it. He reminded the jury again of Grier's statement. "And if this isn't a diabolical lie," he said, "then I don't know what a lie is. That's the reason that he changed it from his coat to his shirt. Could it be doctored in any more fashionable way? Try it. This is a shallow pocket. It's about three and one half inches deep. That's why his testimony was changed. And it was changed with the condonation and the knowledge of the prosecution in this case. To get a conviction."

On Monday morning, August 12, Dell Ross, accompanied by his own lawyer, arrived at court to testify for the prosecution. At this point Jensen needed him desperately. The first two major witnesses—Heanes and Grier—had not been as strong as he had hoped. Ross was his last chance. Dell Ross had testified before the grand jury in November, 1967, that right after the shooting I had jumped into his car with another man and forced him at gunpoint to flee the scene. He was the second person to claim I had had a gun in my hand. The kidnapping charge was important, too, since it demonstrated that I knew I had committed a crime and was using desperado tactics to escape. Ross had told the grand jury that I had jumped into the back seat of his car, and my companion had gotten into the front. At first, he said, he had refused to drive us to the corner of Thirty-second and Chestnut as we requested, but when I pulled a gun on him, he complied. He testified that I had said to him, "I just shot two dudes," and "I'd have kept shooting if my gun hadn't jammed." When a picture of me was shown to him, Ross identified me as the man with the gun.

When Jensen put him on the stand on August 12, he had no reason to suspect that Ross would not repeat all his grand jury testimony. Ross answered his first few questions about where he lived, whether he had owned a car in October, 1967, what make it was, et cetera, et cetera. But when Jensen asked him where he had been at five o'clock on the morning of October 28, Ross would not tell him. "I refuse to answer on the grounds it would tend to incriminate me," he said. Jensen could not believe his ears. He asked the court reporter to read the answer back to him, as if to reassure himself of what he had just heard. Ross was a *prosecution* witness. Moreover, he was a *victim*, not a defendant, and victims do not take the Fifth Amendment. When Ross persisted in refusing to answer, Jensen became furious. From his point of view, Ross's insistence on not answering could damage his case seriously and result in bad publicity. It would look as if something fishy was going on (which, of course, it was) and put the district attorney's office in an unfavorable light. He appealed to Judge Friedman, asking that the witness be obligated to respond to his questions, pointing out that he had already testified fully on the case before the grand jury nine months before. At this point, the judge ordered the jury to retire from the courtroom. Ross's lawyer argued that Ross was making a personal claim for his own protection under the Fifth Amendment. He pointed out that questions put to Ross during the trial might well go beyond the factual answers he had given to the grand jury and lead to further questions that could incriminate him. Ross's lawyer suggested that Ross perhaps knew more about what had happened on the morning of October 28 than he had told the grand jury.

Here was a dilemma for both prosecutor and judge. Judge Friedman responded by cutting short the proceedings for that day. The next day he granted Ross immunity and told him he could not be prosecuted for anything that arose out of his testimony, except perjury or contempt for failing to answer questions directed at him. Now, Ross had to answer Jensen's questions and could no longer invoke the Fifth Amendment. But when the prosecutor began all over again and asked the same question Ross had refused to answer the previous day—where he had been at 5:00 A.M. on October 28, 1967—Ross again refused to answer on the grounds that it would incriminate him. The judge became totally exasperated and told him that he must now answer the questions since he had immunity. Otherwise, he would go to jail for contempt. Ross just sat there stolidly, refusing to go on. Just as Judge Friedman was preparing to sentence him for contempt, Jensen suddenly realized what he could do with this intransigent witness in order to save the day for the prosecution.

"Mr. Ross," he asked him, "do you *remember* what happened on the morning of October 28, 1967?" Ross stalled. Judge Friedman was quick to interject, "If you don't remember what happened that morning," he said, "why, you should say you don't remember. The court does not desire to force you into anything. Is it perhaps that you don't remember what happened that morning?" Ross agreed that he couldn't remember.

It was incredible to see the way the judge aided Jensen. What they planned to do was clear. The judge chose to point out that a witness cannot be punished for having a faulty memory, and so the prosecution was going to help Ross remember by reading back to him all his grand jury testimony, which ordinarily is never allowed as evidence in a trial. Charles Garry protested strongly, but Judge Friedman was adamant. Jensen read all Ross's testimony back to him in front of the jury, and it went into the official record of the trial.

Never was Judge Friedman's bias in favor of Jensen more blatantly obvious than in his dealings with Dell Ross as a witness. It was typical of the arbitrary way the trial was conducted. When their man would not testify because of self-incrimination, they gave him immunity so that anything he said could not be used against him. Then the judge actually coaxed Ross into saying he could not remember what he had said before the grand jury so that the prosecution had an excuse to read his testimony into the transcript. On the other hand, when our man, Gene McKinney, refused to testify twelve days later, because of self-incrimination, they did not offer him immunity or coax him in any way; they just threw him into jail. The police had already exonerated McKinney of any involvement in the incident, but they still would not offer him immunity to protect himself. This was the only time that the contradiction between justice and what the judge and prosecution were doing came out in open court. Their people got immunity when they knew their testimony would incriminate them. Our people, who had been exonerated but who did not trust the system anyway, got tossed into jail. The whole trial was nothing but a big charade to get me railroaded into the gas chamber.

But all their chicanery to get Dell Ross's testimony came to nothing in the end, because Charles Garry had called the last trump. Two weeks before the trial, he had interviewed Ross in his office and taped the conversation, during the course of which Ross admitted that he had lied to the grand jury. He had gone along with the authorities, he said, because they had warrants out on him for parking violations, and he was afraid of them. Ross told Garry in this interview that I did not have a gun that night, that I was barely conscious and had said nothing at all to him. Of course, when Garry got up to cross-examine him during the trial, Ross could not remember this interview, either, so Garry played the whole tape in court, over Jensen's vehement objections.

As a result, the kidnapping charge against me was dropped for lack of evidence—and I was now being tried on three counts instead of four. Ross's appearance as a witness for the prosecution had been a complete failure. Yet he was brought back for my second and third trials, and both times he repudiated his position during the first trial. Despite this, I felt no anger toward him. Like Grier, he was a crushed and broken man, pathetically terrified of the power of the state. I felt more angry at the prosecution for using him as a dupe of the state than against Ross, who could not defend himself.

Ross was the last important witness that Jensen produced, and after he appeared the prosecution rested its case. In any trial the burden of proof lies with the prosecution to establish beyond reasonable doubt the evidence of guilt. Jensen had not achieved this. Many of his accusations were made through implication and innuendo, not facts. Despite his single-minded determination to place me at the scene with a gun in my hand, a lot of his evidence had backfired in ways he had not anticipated. In addition to weaknesses in the testimony of both Grier and Heanes—and the fact that their two stories did not jibe at crucial points—there were a number of serious flaws and omissions in the prosecutor's case.

Jensen never dealt satisfactorily with the shooting—for instance, the location of the two nine-millimeter casings that were found at the scene by police officers. Jensen had suggested throughout the trial that these casings, which did not match police guns, belonged to the .38 revolver I allegedly carried that night. The casings were found lying twenty to twenty-five feet apart, one between the two police vehicles and one near the rear left fender of Heanes's car, right where Frey was shot. Since both Heanes's and Grier's testimony coincided in stating that Frey and I had walked to the back of Heanes's car and that no shooting had occurred until we reached this point, how could the second casing have gotten twenty-five feet away? I could not have been in two places at once. This was an insurmountable puzzle in the prosecution argument. The only possible solution seems to be that a third person was firing at the scene, and the prosecution had totally excluded this possibility since it wanted only one assailant—me.

Then, too, my lawyers found the police tapes from that morning very mystifying. They carefully went over the transcript of all the police conversations that were recorded between the police cars at the scene and Radio Dispatch in the police administration building. The tapes began with a request from Officer Frey just after he had stopped me shortly before 5:00 A.M. The request was for information about me and the car I was driving. They continued through all the communications that took place after other police cars arrived at the scene following the shooting. In analyzing the messages that passed between Radio Dispatch and the patrol car radios, my lawyers found indications that the police dispatcher in the administration building was sending out information to other police in the Oakland area that was not being radioed in by the police at the scene. This suggested that either the tapes were tampered with or that witnesses were phoning in accounts of the shooting and giving descriptions that the police at the scene did not have.

For instance, the dispatcher assumed that I was connected with the crime since Frey had asked information about me before he was shot, and so he sent out a bulletin about 5:15 A.M. describing me as the "suspect" and stating that I was wearing a tan jacket. Half an hour later, he inexplicably sent out another bulletin that said I was wearing "dark clothing." There had been no incoming police radio message on the tape to tell him this, and no indication of how he got this information. How did he learn that I was wearing dark clothing? Henry Grier, too, had mentioned in his interview with Inspector McConnell a "peewee" type wearing a tan jacket. Was there a third person answering this description at the scene? Throughout the trial Jensen never allowed this possibility to be suggested to the jury, even though the police had interviewed witnesses who had heard the shots and arrived at the scene seconds after the shooting. My lawyers even suspect that a number of people in the area were close and had witnessed the incident. One woman, a Black prostitute, told the police that she had seen three men running away in the direction of the gas station at the corner of Seventh Street and Willow Avenue. Another witness, a young man, told the police that he had seen two cars speeding away north on Seventh Street. Jensen never called these people to testify because he wanted to create the impression that I was the only person who could possibly have killed Frey. Yet the accounts of others who were there (and later Heanes's own admission at my third trial that there had been a third person present) contradicted his theory.

Another piece of evidence that Jensen found hard to dismiss was the lawbook I was carrying when Frey ordered me to the back of Heanes's car. Charles Garry pointed out that I could not very well have carried a gun and a lawbook in my right hand at the same time. But even more crucial was my reason for carrying it. Reading to the police from lawbooks was the only defense I had in case of unlawful arrest. I had done it countless times in the past, and there are hundreds of people in the Black community who have seen me do it and can testify that it was my common practice. I carried it again on the morning of October 28 to read the law to Officer Frey. It was an action that Jensen could not distort for his own ends.

Perhaps Jensen's most grievous and callous omission during the entire trial was his failure to point out that a vital word in the transcript of Grier's conversation with Inspector McConnell had been changed. It was only by accident that Charles Garry discovered that this word had been incorrectly transcribed by a typist in the district attorney's office from the tape that Inspector McConnell had made with Grier. And yet this one word was so important that it called into doubt Grier's identification of me from the picture McConnell showed him at police headquarters. To make matters worse, Garry discovered this error only after the trial proper was over and the jury had been out deliberating the verdict for a day.

On September 5, the jury requested to see the transcript, and Judge Friedman called Garry and Jensen into his chambers to ask them for a copy. There was no court copy (the trial clerk had forgotten to acquire one as evidence), and Charles Garry had lent his only copy to someone else. So Jensen went to get his and came back with the original working copy of the transcription. As Garry quickly looked through it, he paused in disbelief over a section of Grier's testimony. There, over the crucial word, was a handwritten correction, completely reversing the meaning of the sentence. This section read:

Q. About how old?
A. I couldn't say because I had only my lights on. I couldn't—I DID get a clear picture, clear view of his face, but—because he had his

head kind of down facing the headlights of the coach and I could-
n't get a good look—.

Over the word "did" someone had written in the correct word:
"didn't." But throughout the trial, Jensen, knowing that this issue was
crucial, had neglected to inform Garry, the jury, and the court that there
was a question in the transcript of how clearly Grier had been able to
see. Indeed, Jensen's contention was that Grier *had* gotten a good look
and was therefore in a position to identify that person as me. As long
as there was the slightest doubt in his mind about whether the word
was "did" or "didn't" he had a moral obligation to inform the court and
the defense counsel, and it was an absolute matter of conscience that
he listen again to the tape to see what the word actually was. He never
bothered.

In this important matter and in all the other dubious issues—the
position of the bullet casings, the police tapes, the hiding of Grier, the
keeping of important witnesses off the stand, the changing of Grier's
original testimony—Lowell Jensen proved less than honorable. It is
the prosecutor's job to convict a *guilty* man—not an *innocent* one. And
in my case Jensen had many reasons to believe I was innocent. He chose
to ignore them all.

When the prosecution rested its case, Charles Garry, on the morning of August 19, moved for another mistrial. He based his motion
on the fact that it was impossible for me to receive a fair trial in Oakland because of the atmosphere of hatred, violence, and controversy.
As proof of this, he read to the court samples of hate mail that he and
I had been receiving. One of the letters was from four retired marines
who said they had known Frey. The letter stated that neither Garry
nor I would be alive ten days after the trial was over, no matter what
the verdict. Another letter was signed "KKK" and read:

> Nigger Lover:
> I guess you feel that the murdering coon's gonna get off because
> the jury and witnesses have all been intimidated to the extent that
> no one dares convict. I hope he will be gunned down in the streets
> by some friends of the poor policeman he killed. The Black Panthers
> parade all over the place and I don't see why the KKK and Ameri-
> can Nazi Parties couldn't do the same. It is supposed to be a free coun-

try for everybody. It is too bad we ever stopped lynching. At least the dam niggers knew their place in those days and didn't cause any trouble. I remember reading about one time they strung up some coons and pulled out pieces of their flesh with corkscrews. That must have been a lot of fun. I wish I had been there to take part in the good work. I hope this race war that we are having starts right away. We outnumber the blacks ten to one, so we know who will win. And a lot of damn nigger lovers will be laying right there beside them. I wish Hitler had won and then we could have kicked off the shinnies and started in on the coons.

KKK

Garry's request for a mistrial was denied by Judge Friedman, who refused to acknowledge that I was receiving anything but a fair trial. He felt the letters were negligible and unimportant.

After this, Garry opened the defense and began on the morning of August 19 to show the jury where the truth lay. He introduced a group of witnesses who were essential to those political aspects of the case that we had been so determined to explore from the beginning. These were people from the Black community—ordinary, honest working people—who could testify with sincerity and conviction about how their lives were frequently made difficult by the occupying army of racist police. These people described being stopped, questioned, bullied, pushed around, and insulted for no reason other than the sadistic whim of some southern cracker who hated Blacks. These were the people brutalized by intruders in their own community. All had one thing in common: encounters with Officer John Frey.

Daniel King, sixteen, related on the stand how he had met Frey around four o'clock one morning in West Oakland, where he was visiting his sister. They had gone out to get something to eat on Seventh Street, and there, incredibly enough, had encountered a white man with no pants on. He was with Frey. Frey told King he was violating curfew, and the white man accused him of knowing the girl who had taken his pants. When King denied this, both Frey and the white man called him "nigger," "pimp," and other "dirty words." Frey had held King while the white man hit him. Then he put him in a paddy wagon and took him to Juvenile Hall where he spent the rest of the night. Frey did not even bother to call King's parents.

Luther Smith, Sr., who worked with a youth organization in Oakland, told of a number of run-ins with Frey. He testified that Frey was "awful mean" and had used racial epithets when talking to him. Frey had called Smith's brother a "little Black nigger" and his son's wife a "Black bitch."

Belford Dunning, an employee of the Prudential Life Insurance Company, described an encounter with Frey the day before he died. When Frey pushed Dunning around while he was being given a ticket by another policeman for a minor violation on his car, Dunning had said to him, "What's the matter with you? You act like you're the Gestapo or something." Frey's hand went to his revolver. "I *am* the Gestapo," he said.

A young white schoolteacher, Bruce Byson, who had taught Frey in high school, invited him to come back and speak to the class about his work as a policeman. While he was talking to the high school students, Byson testified, Frey referred to people in the Black community as "niggers" and spoke disparagingly of them as criminals and lawbreakers.

Garry wanted the jury to understand what Black people are subjected to by cops like Frey, hung up on power. He also wanted them to realize that Frey's bloodthirstiness was responsible for his own death. Belford Dunning, the insurance man, had said to him the day before he died, "Man, if you don't lick this, you are not going to last very long around here." As a matter of fact, Frey's superiors had already decided to move him out of the Black community into another area, where he would be less of a lethal threat to innocent human beings. But they were too late, and Frey himself fulfilled Dunning's prophecy. Garry stressed this aspect of Frey's behavior (and by implication, most other policemen) over and over again during his defense. Frey was not only a bully to helpless people; he was also determined to exterminate anyone whom he considered a threat to his own dubious masculinity. "You know," Garry said to the jury during his summation,

> since the day I got into this case, one thing has bothered me. Why in tarnation was Officer Frey so headstrong in stopping Huey Newton's automobile? I wake up at night trying to find an answer to that, and I can't find an answer. This bothers me. It is just not part of legal due process. It is not part of any understanding of justice. It is not

part of any understanding of the proper administration of the law. Frankly, it is not the type of police action that I have personally witnessed, but then again, I am not a Black man. I am not a Black Panther. I am part of accepted society. I don't think any officer would stop me unless I was actually, openly, overtly violating the law.

What was Huey Newton doing when he was driving down Seventh Street, between 4:50 and five o'clock in the morning, that warranted this officer to call in and ask for PIN [Police Intelligence Network] information, saying, "I got a Black Panther car. See if there is something on it."

In my opening statement I told you that there was a plan, a concerted plan by the Oakland Police Department, together with other police departments in Alameda County, to get Huey Newton, to get the Black Panther Party. Huey Newton above all…

Another thing that bothers me, and bothers me very, very much about the evidence, and it should bother you when you start analyzing it: If it is true that Officer Frey intended to arrest Huey Newton and, in fact, said, "I now place you under arrest," which we contend is not so, but let's assume for the sake of argument that he did, I don't understand why he didn't put handcuffs on him, since the Panthers are supposed to be such desperadoes.

I further don't understand, if he was placing him under arrest, why he passed his own automobile. I don't understand why Officer Frey took Mr. Newton to the third automobile, to the back end of it. Why? Was he going to beat him up? You know he could very well do it. He was a heavier man, weighing 200 pounds. He went to the gym regularly, according to Officer Heanes. Huey is a 165-pounder and Huey had a lawbook in his hand.

Perhaps the most significant comment that can be made about the testimony of these defense witnesses from the Black community is that Jensen offered no rebuttal. His silence was eloquent. I guess no one could be found to speak well of Frey. What can you say about a policeman who owned three guns, carried extra ammunition on his cartridge belt, and was the only member of the Oakland force who did not use the regular bullets issued by the department but spent his own money to buy a special high-velocity type?

On August 24, Charles Garry called Gene McKinney to the witness stand. When McKinney entered the courtroom that afternoon with his lawyer, Harold Perry, a feeling of excitement and expectation could be felt among the spectators. Here was one of the most important witnesses to the shooting of Heanes and Frey. Up until then, there had been considerable speculation about whether even the defense lawyers knew the name of my companion that morning. Throughout the trial reporters and newsmen had been asking Charles Garry whether the mysterious witness would testify.

When McKinney took the stand, Garry rose and asked him first his name and then whether he had been a passenger in the Volkswagen with me at the corner of Seventh and Willow on the morning of October 28, 1967. "Yes, I was," McKinney answered. His response electrified the courtroom. But those two questions were the only ones he ever answered. When Garry asked, "Now, Mr. McKinney, at the time and place on that morning, at approximately five o'clock in the morning, did you by chance or otherwise shoot at Officer John Frey?" McKinney said, "I refuse to answer on the grounds it may tend to incriminate me." Jensen was outraged. He jumped to his feet and demanded that Judge Friedman direct the witness to answer. "Inasmuch as he has already started to testify," said Jensen, "saying he was there at the scene, he has obviously waived [his right to silence]. Let's hear him tell what he knows. He said he was there, and I ask that that question now be read to him and the court direct him to answer."

Then followed a discussion between the prosecutor, Perry, and the judge about McKinney's constitutional rights, with Perry claiming McKinney need only be cross-examined on the two questions he had chosen to respond to—his name and where he was on October 28. Beyond that, Perry claimed, he was entirely within his rights to claim the Fifth Amendment. When Jensen insisted on cross-examining him, McKinney refused to answer. Here Garry was trying to raise the question of "reasonable doubt"—doubt about whether there could have been only one possible person who did the shooting—me, as the prosecution claimed.

But Garry and Harold Perry were also using another brilliant strategy, and Jensen understood immediately what was involved. The prosecution believed that McKinney was inviting Judge Friedman to grant him immunity in his testimony—the same immunity he had given to Dell Ross—whereby nothing he said could be used against him. Then, with this protection, he could say that *he* had killed Frey and shot at Heanes, and that he had escaped with me. Because no evidence had been submitted during the trial to prove otherwise, he could not have been convicted of perjury. Thus, having absolved me of the crime and having freed himself of any danger of prosecution, since his testimony could not be used against him, both of us could have walked out of the courtroom—at liberty.

But Jensen and Friedman, believing this to be the strategy, were having none of it. After questioning McKinney carefully to make sure he realized he was liable for contempt, Judge Friedman ordered him immediately sent to jail for refusing to testify. He later sentenced him to six months, but the California Superior Court reversed the decision, stating that McKinney had acted within his constitutional rights. After spending a few weeks in the county jail, McKinney was released on bail. As I said, he is a courageous man.

Finally, on the morning of August 22, I took the witness stand. A number of people had doubted I would testify because they thought I would not be able to handle a merciless cross-examination by Jensen. But actually I looked forward to it. For six weeks I had sat beside Charles Garry in the courtroom and listened to Jensen claim that I had murdered Frey in cold blood. I had watched him try to sell the jury on the fact that I loved violence, that I had a history of provoking policemen, and that there was reason to believe I did not tell the truth. I wanted to set the record straight and prove to the jury that I was innocent. I also was determined to let him know what it meant to be a Black man in America and why it had been necessary to form an organization like the Black Panther Party. After that, I hoped they would understand why Frey had illegally stopped my car on the morning of October 28.

Garry opened up by asking me the two all-important questions: whether I had killed Officer John Frey and whether I had shot and wounded Officer Herbert Heanes. I gave the only possible answers— the truth. No, I had not. After that, we went through the necessary background leading up to the incident, which in this case began the day I was born. I told the court about my family, about growing up in Oakland, where there was no place to play except in the rubble and garbage-strewn streets and vacant lots, because Black kids have no swimming pools, no parks, no playgrounds. I told them about degrading experiences in the public school system, experiences that countless thousands of other Black children have endured and continued to endure in an oppressive and indifferent world. I told them how the Black community is occupied by police who need no excuse to harass and bully its inhabitants. I told them that when I graduated from Oakland Technical High School I was unable to read or write and that most of my classmates were in the same boat, because no one in the school system cared whether we learned to read or write. Then I told how, under the influence of my brother Melvin, I had taught myself to read by going again and again through Plato's *Republic*. I tried to explain what a deep impression Plato's allegory of the cave had made on me and how the prisoners in that cave were a symbol of the Black man's predicament in this country. It was a seminal experience in my life, I explained, for it had started me thinking and reading and trying to find a way to liberate Black people. Then I told of meeting Bobby Seale at Oakland City College and how the Black Panther Party grew out of our talks.

Garry led me through an exposition of what the Black Panther Party stood for and an explication of its ten-point program. I recited the ten points in the courtroom and explained them. Blacks, I said, are a colonized people used only for the benefit and profit of the power structure whenever it suits their purposes. After the Civil War, Blacks were kicked off plantations and had nowhere to go. For nearly one hundred years they were either unemployed or used for the most menial tasks, because industry preferred to use the labor of more acceptable immigrants—the Irish, the Italians, and the Jews. However, when World War II started, Blacks were again employed—in factories and by industry—because, with the white male population off fighting, there was a labor shortage. But when that war ended, Blacks were once again kicked off "the plantation" and left stranded with no place to go in an industrial society. Growing up in the late forties, I was aware of it in Oakland, because major defense plants had been built there during the war, and a large Black population was condemned to unemployment after the war. I quoted the second point in our program as a way of changing all this: "We want full employment for our people. We believe that the Federal Government is responsible and obligated to give every man employment or a guaranteed income. We believe that if the white American businessman will not give full employment, then the means of production should be taken from the businessmen and placed in the community so that the people of the community can organize and employ all of its people and give a high standard of living."

Sometimes, while I was explaining Black history and the aims of the Black Panther Party to the court, I forgot that I was on trial for my life. The subjects were so real and important to me that I would get lost in what I was saying. There were moments when I even enjoyed myself, especially when I had a chance to score points against Judge Friedman and Jensen.

On one occasion I saw an opportunity to show my contempt for the judge, and I took it. I was describing how some immigrant groups had been subjected to oppression and discrimination when they first arrived in this country, but that after they began to make economic gains some of them had joined their oppressors, even when the oppressors continued to discriminate against the immigrants' own people. I used as an example Jews who join the Elks Club, even though they know that this organization is racist and anti-Semitic. Judge Friedman had been the first Jew admitted to the Elks Club in Oakland, a fact that had been given a great deal of publicity. The Elks wanted it believed that they were no longer anti-Semitic, but everybody knew better.

Another time, talking about contemporary racism in American society, I deliberately used the Mormon church as one of the most blatant proponents of ethnic discrimination. Knowing that Jensen was a Mormon, I looked at him when I said this, instead of at the jury. He gave me a smirk, and I kept right on looking at him. He could say nothing in front of the jury lest they learn the truth about him.

Jensen often became impatient with the way Garry was conducting his examination of me and frequently interrupted, but even he sometimes seemed interested in what I was saying. Throughout, however, those meaningful glances passed between Jensen and Judge Friedman, the judge asking for an objection and Jensen giving it to him. Friedman could hardly hide his disapproval of everything I was saying and kept telling me to stick to the present and the incident itself. Then Garry would remind him that everything I said was relevant to the defense. Somehow, we managed to get in all the most important political aspects of the case, and that was what mattered most. Only when that was accomplished did I turn to my version of what had happened that morning. I described it exactly as it took place up until Frey shot me. After that, of course, I had passed out, so I could describe only those things I remembered and my hazy impressions of them.

I had spent nearly the entire day on the stand when Garry turned me over to the enemy. For the first time in eight weeks Jensen and I were face to face.

My sister Leola had told me of an incident that occurred at the beginning of the trial when she was standing on the courthouse steps watching one of the many demonstrations. Jensen, not knowing who she was, was standing near her, watching with an associate. She heard Jensen tell his friend that he meant to make me lose my temper before the jury. Then, he said, all the demonstrations on my behalf would be meaningless. So, when he approached me that afternoon, I knew what to expect: he wanted me to explode rather than engage in a good debating session. I felt that the whole exchange would be nothing more than another debate, only this time the stakes were high. I had spent too much time on corners, in bars, and in the classroom debating very complex subjects to get upset with Jensen's probing. He was a worthy opponent, but I knew that once he began to push me, he was going to be surprised at my responses. He had a false impression of me and expected me to respond in a way I was incapable of doing. Throughout almost two days of cross-examination, we struggled to see whose approach would prevail, mine or his, and I felt that during almost all of this time I controlled the situation. In responding to Jensen, just as I had responded to Garry, I did not pull any punches about criticizing the system or its agents. Though my life was at stake, I wanted to show my contempt. I sought to use their own apparatus to defy them, which was consistent with the revolutionary practices I have attempted to live by.

Jensen's entire cross-examination, nearly every incident he brought up, was intended to demonstrate that I loved violence and guns and that I was a personal threat and a menace to police officers merely trying to do their duty. He began by asking about our early patrols in the Oakland community, emphasizing for the benefit of the jury, in insidious ways, the fact that we had carried shotguns. He tried to imply that I would have preferred to carry a concealed pistol on these patrols but that the terms of my probation did not allow this. He reinforced this suggestion by having me read a poem, "Guns, Baby, Guns," I had once written for *The Black Panther* newspaper, which was filled with symbols and metaphors that have a particular meaning for Black people but are utterly lost on most whites. In the poem I had mentioned a P-38 revolver, and Jensen tried to suggest that this was the type of gun I had shot Frey with and that my poem suggested I liked this gun and would use it if the occasion demanded.

"What is a P-38?" he asked.

"It's an automatic pistol," I answered.

"Does it fire nine-millimeter Luger cartridges?" was his next question.

I explained to Jensen that I don't know much about hand guns. I always preferred a shotgun and would never touch hand guns while I was on probation. I explained to him that in this matter, as in all others, Black Panthers obey the law.

At that, he asked me if I remembered an incident in Richmond in 1967 when I *had not* obeyed the law, when, as he put it, I "got into a combat with Richmond police"? He was referring to the time the police had lain in wait for us until 5:00 A.M. outside a house where we were partying. I had taken an arrest that time in order to avoid combat after one young police officer had stepped on all the brothers' feet and another got me in a choke hold against a police car. I carefully explained the details to Jensen and the jury and told how an all-white conservative jury at my trial in Richmond had believed the police version of what had taken place, as they always do, and sentenced me to sixty days on the county farm. I made sure the jury learned about the policeman's remark after viciously beating the brother: "I have to go now because I promised to take my wife and kids to church at nine."

Then Jensen brought up the time the Black Panthers had responded to the little boy who ran into headquarters asking for help. The police had burst into his house when his father was away and were tearing up the place on some phony pretext of looking for a shotgun. We asked the police to leave because they had no search warrant, and in their rage they had arrested me for wearing a dagger in a holster, accusing me of "displaying a weapon in a rude and threatening fashion."

While describing this incident, I really got the best of Jensen. He had been on my right when he first asked the question, and the jury on my left. He wanted me to speak toward him, but I turned my back and began giving details of the incident to the jury, which took a while. Since he had asked the question about the incident, he could not interrupt my answer without looking stupid, so I seized the time and took the play away from him.

The jury seemed fascinated with my description of the affair and was with me all the way. Jensen obviously got so disgusted with what was happening that he left his position near the clerk's desk and sat down looking very dejected—as I was later told. At any rate, I described the incident fully, leaned back, and turned to my right for Jensen's next question; he was no longer there. I was surprised at not seeing him where he had last been standing, so I said, "Where is he?" Then I saw him seated at the table, and I smiled at him and said, "Oh, there you are. I thought you had gone home." The courtroom broke up at this, and the judge admonished me.

Much of Jensen's cross-examination had continual reference to official reports and documents, which he kept consulting while I was on the stand. Reading a report that is filed in some record system and stamped with an official seal of approval can be very impressive: the printed page somehow suggests that whatever is described represents the truth, that it faithfully describes what took place. And so, when Jensen brought up official police testimony of what had happened to me in the past—in arrests, in courts, in various trials—he thought he was offering the jury proof of my violent and crime-filled past. But, far from distressing or embarrassing me, every one of his challenges presented a chance to tell the jury what had really taken place and to describe them in the larger context of what life is like for Black people in this country. In this way, I was able to demonstrate how the police had harassed the Black Panthers and looked for every opportunity they could to arrest us and destroy our organization.

To give Jensen credit, he did not miss very much. But I countered every piece of "official" evidence with an explanation that went beyond words on a page. And I think the jury came to understand that no official document ever contains the whole truth. Events are dictated by a number of mitigating circumstances and a whole system of values and customs that can never be conveyed in print.

Jensen made another mistake by examining some of my speeches and writings and reading into them exhortations to violence. On this tack he quickly got out of his depth; he did not understand the way language is used among Blacks and often took literally what was meant symbolically. Every time he brought up something I had written or said that he thought sounded dangerous, I patiently explained what it meant in terms of organizing the Black community. In this way, I was able to describe to the jury the goals the Party had for Black people. I had hoped to do this—to take the initiative from Jensen and develop certain political points in the courtroom. It was surprising how often I succeeded.

Finally, Jensen got around to the morning of October 28. He came meticulously prepared, armed with photographs and maps, to present his version of what had happened. Leading me carefully through the whole incident, he had me describe my every move and gesture. At one point I was even asked to demonstrate with him how Frey had "smeared" me. He also chose to bring up an encounter that Bobby Seale and I had had with two policemen in 1966, because he believed the event related to the shooting of Officer Frey. As Jensen described this incident, I had gotten into a fight with a policeman and had tried to take his gun away from him. If Jensen had been able to prove this, he could have used it as a foreshadowing of what had happened in 1967 and as evidence that I had done the same thing with Frey. I do not know where he got his information, but I pointed out to the court that it was on record that one of the policemen who was hassling us in 1966 had admitted in court that he was drunk when he met Bobby and me. Jensen said, "Mr. Newton, isn't it a fact that you entered a plea of guilty to battery upon that police officer, the man in uniform?" I answered, "I accepted the deal that the district attorney's department offered."

> "I see. And you pled guilty to a battery on a policeman?"
> "I think it was simple assault."
> (Sarcastically) "Is that right? Mr. Newton, did you see anyone shoot John Frey?"
> "No."
> "Did you see anyone shoot Officer Heanes?"
> "No. I did not."
> "You have no explanation at all of how John Frey was killed?"
> "None whatsoever."
> "I have no further questions."

With that, Jensen's cross-examination was completed. It had not gone according to his plan. I had never lost my cool. It was Jensen, in fact, who lost his.

Garry was masterful in his closing arguments. A defense lawyer has to be good at that point, because the prosecution gives the closing argument first, and then has the last word after the defense has spoken. Garry reviewed the evidence, showing the holes and the discrepancies in the prosecution testimony. He had brought a number of large posters into court with Grier's conflicting testimony lined up side by side, and with a pointer he painstakingly indicated all the contradictions in Grier's two sworn statements. The whole thrust of Garry's summing up was to illustrate how much of a "reasonable doubt" there was in the evidence presented by the prosecution.

But Garry did more than this. In a moving and heartfelt closing speech he addressed himself to the conscience of the jury and to their understanding of social conditions that had led to the death of Officer Frey:

> The Black community today, the Black ghetto, is fighting for the right of survival. The white community is sitting smug and saying, Let's have more police! Let's have more guns! Let's arm ourselves against the Blacks!
>
> That is not the answer. If you think that is the answer, we are all destroyed. If you think that Mayor Daley has the answer, we are all destroyed. If you think that this nation with all of its power and all of its strength can eliminate violence on the street with more violence, they have another thought coming.
>
> My client and his party are not for destruction; they want to build. They want a better America for Black people. They want the police out of their neighborhoods. They want them off their streets. Every one of you here possibly knows a policeman in your neighborhood. I know several men in police departments. I think they are wonderful people. I live in Daly City; I have a beautiful relationship with them. Those police live in my neighborhood, within three or four blocks. I know where one of them lives. I can call on him if I need him. But no police officer lives in the ghetto. Why don't they live in the ghetto? Because a man that is making eight or nine or ten thousand dollars isn't going to live in the kind of hovel that the ghetto is.
>
> Has anybody thought of uplifting the ghetto? So that it doesn't exist in the manner that it has? These are the things that Huey Newton and the Black Panthers and other people are trying to do....

White America, listen! White America, listen! The answer is not to put Huey Newton in the gas chamber. It is not the answer to put Huey Newton and his organization into jail. The answer is to wipe out the ghetto, the conditions of the ghetto, so that Black brothers and sisters can live with dignity, so that they can walk down the street with dignity.

The fire and eloquence of Charles Garry's final argument are difficult to describe; he was pleading for the principles and beliefs he feels most deeply about and to which he has dedicated his entire life. When he stood and spoke out for justice and truth and tolerance, he was not simply defending a man whose life was in jeopardy; he was speaking for all the downtrodden and oppressed in the world, and he was asking the jury to think about them also. Few people in the courtroom that day were unaffected by what he said.

In contrast, Jensen devoted most of his closing arguments to the particulars of the trial. He asked the jury to find me guilty of murdering John Frey and defended in detail the testimony of Grier and Heanes. Yet at a point in Jensen's summation in which he discussed the meaning of law and the process of justice the words could very well have been spoken by Garry. It was what my lawyers and I had been fighting for. But I feel sure Jensen had no idea of the irony in his remarks:

We put together in the courtroom the notion that every right that goes to every citizen is implemented in our courts. I think that is so. And I think you should reflect on this: the notion that society accords a right to an individual has something that goes along with it, and that is that there is no such thing as a right without a duty that goes along with it. That is, if the law says a man has a right, the law also says that every other person must honor that right. He has a duty to honor that right.

What is more fundamental, ladies and gentlemen, than the right to life? What is more fundamental than the right to a peaceful occupation and life?

What we do in a courtroom is to seek out and declare a truth. We must, as I say, declare those truths in a courtroom. If we cannot declare those truths in a courtroom we are lost.

And in a courtroom, just as there must be a duty to implement a right, a courtroom must exist on the basis of the declaration of truth.

With Jensen's final declaration that I was a murderer, the arguments were finished. The struggle between defense and prosecution was over, and the judge began to instruct the jury about what they must do to reach a verdict. "The function of the jury," said Judge Friedman, "is to determine the issues of fact that are presented by the allegations of the indictment filed in this court and the defendant's plea of not guilty. This duty you should perform uninfluenced by pity for a defendant or by passion or prejudice against him. You must not suffer yourselves to be biased against a defendant because of the fact that he had been arrested for these offenses, or because an indictment has been filed against him, or because he has been brought before this court to stand trial. None of these facts is evidence of his guilt, and you are not permitted to infer or speculate from any or all of them that he is more likely to be guilty than innocent."

As the jury filed out, led by David Harper, I felt everything was over for me. Some jurors had been impressed with my testimony and believed in me. I had watched them throughout the trial and felt they were sympathetic to the defense, but I had no hope of their steadfastness under the pressure of jury deliberations. Often, in such circumstances, people will appear to lean one way but change their minds when conflicting opinions bear down on them. So I went back to my cell prepared for a decision that would send me to the gas chamber. My work had prepared me well; organizing defense groups in the community had continually made me aware that I could be killed at any time, and I knew that when serious actions begin to go down against you, you must be ready. If you wait to prepare for death when the gas chamber is facing you, it is too late. It is the difference between having your raft ready when high tide comes or trying to make it after the waves are there. When death is staring you in the face, the heavy things take over.

The jury deliberated for four days—from September 5 until September 8—and despite the fact that my lawyers were with me constantly, the time passed very slowly. Nonetheless, I was in good spirits. My thoughts kept me occupied. I re-examined everything that I had done before and during the trial and found nothing to regret, nothing I had to square myself with. Our activities as Black Panthers had been worth all the trouble and pain we had seen, and there was no reason to feel we were losing everything. If I had had a chance to start again, nothing would have been any different.

I contemplated the gas chamber. Only two thoughts concerned me: how the last minute would be and how it would affect my family. First of all, I resolved to face it with dignity right to the end. Second, I worried about my family having to live through yet another ordeal. The whole experience had been terrible for them. Yet I knew that if necessary I would do it again, even though it meant more suffering for them. I felt great love for them and valued their support. If I had caused them anguish, I was sustained by the knowledge that one day the people would have the victory, and that this would bring some measure of satisfaction to those I loved.

Many people wondered what the Black Panthers would do when the verdict came down. The brothers had repeatedly said that the sky was the limit if the oppressor did not free me. At the time that was said, we meant that an unfavorable decision would be taken to the highest judicial level. But the statement was intentionally ambiguous and open to interpretation in order to put the whole Oakland power structure up tight. That plan certainly worked. An open interpretation not only attracted considerable publicity but also left us free to make specific decisions about action after the verdict was in, rather than before.

It was in the early evening of September 5, the first day of the jury's deliberations, that we were notified that the jury was returning to the courtroom. At first we thought they had reached a verdict, but no, they wanted to have Grier's statement to McConnell read to them again, and they also asked if they could see my bullet wound. When everyone was assembled, I went over to the jury box, lifted up my sweater to show the scar in my abdomen, and then turned around to show the exit wound. (Later, we found out that a disagreement had arisen among the jury members over the location of the wound. If Heanes's testimony were true [he testified that he was in a kneeling position and I was in a standing position], the wound near my navel would be lower than the exit wound in my back. But if Frey had stood and shot me while I was in a kneeling position, the navel wound would be higher than the rear exit wound. I had testified that Frey had shot me as I fell to my knees. My demonstration supported my testimony.)

It was also during the jury's first day of deliberations that Garry found the mistake in Grier's testimony left uncorrected by Jensen. The jury had asked to see the transcript again, but when Garry discovered the error, he refused to allow the uncorrected copy to be sent in. Judge Friedman commented that he did not think the error made much difference. But Garry knew better. It was a vital correction as far as the defense was concerned, a mistake so serious that it could mean a new trial. Garry insisted that he and Jensen listen to the original tape, find out whether the word really was "didn't"—and send the correction in to the jury. Jensen at first claimed that his office did not have the proper machine to play the original tape. That evening one of my lawyers listened to a dub of the original on his own machine and swore the word was "didn't." Jensen did not listen to the tape until the next morning. It was a tense period for all of us, since the jury could have come in with a verdict at any moment. On Friday, September 5, my attorneys played the original tape in the press room for reporters and representatives of the media. Most of them thought the word was "didn't," and the news on television, radio, and in the press that day carried stories about this new discovery. Meanwhile, my attorneys went to an audio engineer who worked for a radio station in Oakland. He agreed to transfer the crucial part of Grier's testimony to another tape and then blow it up on his own hi-fi equipment so that they could hear the correct word distinctly, and once and for all. When this was done, the word Grier actually had said—"didn't"—came through loud and clear. Meanwhile, the defense was working frantically against time, preparing a motion to reopen the case and trying to get the proper equipment into court to play the blown-up tape for Judge Friedman and Jensen. It was a real hassle, but in the end, over the vigorous objections of Jensen, who claimed it was too late and that Garry should have done this during the trial, the judge did listen to the blown-up tape and had to recognize that the word was "didn't." A corrected statement was sent in to the jury late Saturday afternoon, but Friedman would not allow any mention of the original error to accompany the transcript. We never learned whether the jury even noticed it, let alone understood how important and significant a correction it was.

Finally, on the fourth day of deliberations, September 8, around ten o'clock in the evening, the jury reached a verdict. I came back into the courtroom with my lawyers to hear it read by the clerk:

Verdict of the jury. We, the jury in the above entitled cause, find the above named defendant Huey P. Newton guilty of a felony, to wit, voluntary manslaughter, a violation of Section 192, Subdivision 1 of the Penal Code of the State of California, a lesser and included offense within the offense charged in the first count of the Indictment. David B. Harper, Foreman.

The next verdict, with the title of the Court and cause the same: We, the jury in the above entitled cause, find the above named defendant Huey P. Newton not guilty of a felony, to wit, assault with a deadly weapon upon a police officer, a violation of Section 245B of the Penal Code of the State of California as charged in the second count of the Indictment. David B. Harper, Foreman.

The following verdict, with the title of the Court and cause the same: We, the jury in the above entitled cause, find that the charge of previous conviction as set forth in the Indictment is true. David B. Harper, Foreman.

Manslaughter, not murder. *That* was a surprise. But Garry and I were unhappy with such an equivocal decision. It meant the jury believed I had killed Officer Frey, but only after severe provocation, and in a state of passion. It was absurd, however, that they did not think I had also shot Officer Heanes. Did the jury think someone else had shot him, and if so, who, and how did the two shootings connect? The verdict was a compromise that showed no justice at all, for there was clearly a reasonable doubt about my guilt in the minds of some jurors, although they failed to bring about my exoneration. All these questions began to surface when I realized that although I would have to go to jail, I had escaped the gas chamber. Some people thought the verdict was better than a hung jury and a mistrial; the state could not try me again for first-degree murder. But I disagreed with them.

The verdict caused a lot of dissatisfaction in the Black community. Some people were particularly angry at David Harper, the jury foreman, who, to them, had sold out in typical Uncle Tom fashion. I did not think so. To counteract this opinion, I sent out a message to the community shortly after I had a chance to analyze the verdict. This, in part, was my statement:

The question has been asked: What do I think of the verdict of the jury? I think the verdict reflected the racism that exists here in

America, and that all Black people are subjected to. Some specific things I would like to say about certain people on the jury: first, Brother Harper and other members of the jury who believed in my innocence owed an obligation to me and the Black community to adhere to their convictions that I was not guilty. I am sure that they, the people on the jury who agreed with Brother Harper (a strong man and also jury foreman), were in the minority. I believe that Brother Harper was interested in doing the best thing for my welfare. I think that the verdict was a compromise verdict; a compromise between a first-degree murder and an acquittal or not guilty. Why did Brother Harper compromise? He compromised because he truly believed that it was in my best interest. Mr. Harper made his decision based on the assumption that if a hung jury resulted, I would be tried in the next trial by an all-white jury and possibly convicted of first-degree murder. I believe that he based his action or his decision upon the fact that he saw how racist the majority of the jury was acting, and their whole attitude toward the case. I believe that there were few people joining Brother Harper and his just conclusion that I was innocent, and that I am innocent, but he did compromise. Because Harper failed to persuade the jury, or he felt that he could not persuade them or show them the truth or the fact that I was innocent, he thought that he would then give the lowest possible sentence. He might have considered that I had been in jail for the last ten months and that I might be in jail for another ten months awaiting a new trial and then stand the possibility of having the first-degree murder conviction stand, simply because of the racism that exists here in America. These are all my speculations, and I will tell you why I speculate on these things later on while I have this conversation with you.

Brother Harper, like many people, believes that on a manslaughter charge, you would spend maybe two years or three years at the most in the state penitentiary, and further, that due to the fact that I have already been in jail for one year, that while waiting trial another year as a result of a hung jury, I would already serve that time and even more. So, therefore, because he couldn't get an acquittal, he then chose to compromise and get the lowest sentence. The only problem with that, though, is that in a political case, the defendant is subject to do the maximum length of time. The sentence on a manslaughter charge with a prior felony conviction is from two to fifteen years. But I don't believe that Brother Harper had any idea of what he was doing, so, therefore, I want to ask the Black community sincerely and Brother Harper's son to forgive not only him, but also the other people who believed in my innocence, and who were compromising because they did not know what they were doing. I believe that they thought they were doing the best thing in my interest, and the best thing in the interest of the Black community, under the racist circumstances wherein which they had to operate ....

Even though he was unknowingly operating against it, he felt that he was acting in the capacity of one who loves the community. Therefore, I am asking the community that in the event that he teaches at Oakland City College next semester, that he be given all respect due to a Black man because he did not know what he was compromising to.

I am very sure...that we will get a new trial not because of the kindness that the appellate courts will show us, but because of the political pressure that we have applied to the establishment, and we will do this by organizing the community so that they can display their will. The will of the Black people must be done, and I would like to compliment the people on the revolutionary fervor that they have shown thus far. They have been very beautiful, and they have exceeded my expectations. Let us go on outdoing ourselves; a revolutionary man always transcends himself or otherwise he is not a revolutionary man, so we always do what we ask of ourselves or more than what we know we can do.... At this time I would like to admonish my revolutionary brothers and sisters to use restraint and that we would not show violent eruption at this time for the reason that the establishment would like to see violence occur in the community in order to have an excuse to send in 2,000 or 8,000 troops. The mayor has already stated that he would be very happy if something were to happen in the community while the establishment is in a favorable situation. They would like to wipe the community out .... It is up to the VAN-GUARD PARTY to protect the community and teach the community to protect itself, and therefore at this time we should admonish the community to use restraint and not to open ourselves for destruction.

I cautioned restraint to the people because I knew the police were eager for a chance to kill Black people indiscriminately. They had been waiting a long time for this day, and an angry eruption by the community would have given them the excuse they needed. The community responded to my request and stayed cool. Any spontaneous and unorganized outburst would have caused great suffering. With everything quiet the night after the decision came down, the police felt cheated; they wanted some action, and that meant killing Blacks.

Unable to find any provocation, two drunken colleagues of Frey created one. They drove in their police cars to our office on Grove Street and fired a shattering volley of bullets into the front window. Then they went to the corner, turned around, and came back, shooting into the office again. By this time, some citizens had called police headquarters, and the two policemen were apprehended.

Fortunately for us, the office was purposely empty, and no one in the streets or the buildings nearby was hit by the bullets. But if Black Panthers had been in the office, the police probably would have claimed that we had fired on them first, and then tried to wipe us out. This time, however, they could not hide their treachery behind their usual lie—"justifiable homicide." The true nature of their crime—an unprovoked and unjustified attack on our office—had been exposed before the community. The two policemen were eventually dismissed from the force, but they were never brought to trial for breaking the law.

But the incident should also help make it clear to doubters that I was in fact innocent. Just as Frey's two colleagues felt free to go in search of Black people to kill, so, too, did Frey in the early morning hours of October 28, 1967. There are many who do not believe that a police officer, without provocation or danger, would draw his service revolver and fire upon a citizen. But that morning Frey had murder on his mind.

Charles Garry summed it all up when he told the jury that the Black community is in constant danger from the violence of the police:

> I wonder how many people are going to die before we recognize the brotherhood of man. I wonder how many more people are going to die before the police departments of our nation, the mayors of our nation, the leaders of our nation recognize that you can't have a society that is 66 per cent white racists ignoring the role of the Black man, the brown man, the red man, and the yellow man....
> Officer Frey bothers me. His death bothers me, and the things that caused his death bother me. I can see this young man going through high school, varsity football, basketball, and all the other things that young men do, in good physical condition. Joining the police department and without proper orientation, without proper attitudes and without proper psychological training and all the other training which is necessary to being a policeman. Being thrown into the ghetto. In a year's time he becomes a rank and outright racist to such a point

that when he comes to class to talk about his success as a police officer, the schoolteacher has to cringe and grimace to let him know that
the use of the word "nigger" was not appropriate. I just wonder how
many more Officer Freys there are. His death bothers me, but Huey
Newton is not responsible for his death."

Part Two

The Greatest Threat

FOLLOWING THE OPENING months of Huey's trial in the summer of 1968, FBI director J. Edgar Hoover issued his infamous pronouncement that the Black Panther Party was "the greatest threat" to the domestic security of the United States. Hoover's fear bore no relation to the nation's safety, of course, reflecting instead his own repressive concerns over the Party's radicalizing influence on the political consciousness of the New Left and on African Americans in general.

Between Huey's arrest in 1967 and his acquittal in 1970, the Black Panthers became the vanguard movement of the post–civil rights era. In response, a diverse coalition of activists—from the white Peace and Freedom Party to the Puerto Rican Young Lords to the Gay Liberation Front to San Francisco Chinatown's Red Guard—rallied behind the Party in answer to Huey's call for national solidarity against social injustice. The FBI's most violent attacks on the Panthers were accordingly launched over this formative four-year period, with 79 percent of all counterintelligence actions against African-American political groups targeting the destruction of the Black Panther Party.

This segment of the book offers a window into Huey's political and intellectual maturation during this volatile time. Beginning with defining texts such as "In Defense of Self-Defense" and "The Correct Handling of a Revolution," we see how his preoccupation with African Americans and armed self-defense evolves to more inclusive discussions on topics beyond the black liberation struggle strictly speaking. Essays like "On the Peace Movement" and "The Women's and Gay Liberation Movements" attest to Huey's growing awareness of the necessity for "uniting against a common enemy," as he later puts it. Although the Black Panthers remained fundamentally an African-American liberation movement, the Party's vision had grown to embrace all who struggled in social protest.

fear and doubt: May 15, 1967

The lower socio-economic Black male is a man of confusion. He faces a hostile environment and is not sure that it is not his own sins that have attracted the hostilities of society. All his life he has been taught (explicitly and implicitly) that he is an inferior approximation of humanity. As a man, he finds himself void of those things that bring respect and a feeling of worthiness. He looks around for something to blame for his situation, but because he is not sophisticated regarding the socio-economic milieu and because of negativistic parental and institutional teachings, he ultimately blames himself.

When he was a child his parents told him that they were not affluent because "we didn't have the opportunity to become educated," or "we did not take advantage of the educational opportunities that were offered to us." They tell their children that things will be different for them if they are educated and skilled but there is absolutely nothing other than this occasional warning (and often not even this) to stimulate education. Black people are great worshipers of education, even the lower socio-economic Black person, but at the same time they are afraid of exposing themselves to it. They are afraid because they are vulnerable to having their fears verified; perhaps they will find that they can't compete with White students. The Black person tells himself that he could have done much more if he had really wanted to. The fact is, of course, that the assumed educational opportunities were never available to the lower socio-economic Black person due to the unique position assigned him in life.

It is a two-headed monster that haunts this man. First, his attitude is that he lacks the innate ability to cope with the socio-economic problems confronting him, and second, he tells himself that he has the abil-

131

ity, but he simply has not felt strongly enough to try to acquire the skills needed to manipulate his environment. In a desperate effort to assume self-respect he rationalizes that he is lethargic; in this way, he denies a possible lack of innate ability. If he openly attempts to discover his abilities he and others may see him for what he is—or is not—and this is the real fear. He then withdraws into the world of the invisible, but not without a struggle. He may attempt to make himself visible by processing his hair, acquiring a "boss mop," or driving a long car even though he cannot afford it. He may father several "illegitimate" children by several different women in order to display his masculinity. But in the end, he realizes that his efforts have no real effect.

Society responds to him as a thing, a beast, a nonentity, something to be ignored or stepped on. He is asked to respect laws that do not respect him. He is asked to digest a code of ethics that acts upon him, but not for him. He is confused and in a constant state of rage, of shame, of doubt. This psychological state permeates all his interpersonal relationships. It determines his view of the social system. His psychological development has been prematurely arrested. This doubt begins at a very early age and continues throughout his life. The parents pass it on to the child and the social system reinforces the fear, the shame, and the doubt. In the third or fourth grade he may find that he shares the classroom with White students, but when the class is engaged in reading exercises, all the Black students find themselves in a group at a table reserved for slow readers. This may be quite an innocent effort on the part of the school system. The teacher may not realize that the Black students feared (in fact, feel certain) that Black means dumb, and White means smart. The children do not realize that the head start White children get at home is what accounts for the situation. It is generally accepted that the child is the father of the man; this holds true for the lower socio-economic Black people.

With whom, with what, can he, a man, identify? As a child he had no permanent male figure with whom to identify; as a man, he sees nothing in society with which he can identify as an extension of himself. His life is built on mistrust, shame, doubt, guilt, inferiority, role confusion, isolation and despair. He feels that he is something less than a man, and it is evident in his conversation: "The White man is 'THE MAN,' he got everything, and he knows everything, and a nigger ain't nothing." In a society where a man is valued according to occupation and material possessions, he is without possessions. He is unskilled and more often than not, either marginally employed or unemployed. Often his wife (who is able to secure a job as a maid, cleaning for White people) is the breadwinner. He is, therefore, viewed as quite worthless by his wife and children. He is ineffectual both in and out of the home. He cannot provide for, or protect his family. He is invisible, a nonentity. Society will not acknowledge him as a man. He is a consumer and not a producer. He is dependent upon the White man ("THE MAN") to feed his family, to give him a job, educate his children, serve as the model that he tries to emulate. He is dependent and he hates "THE MAN" and he hates himself. Who is he? Is he a very old adolescent or is he the slave he used to be?

"What did he do to be so Black and blue?"

from "In Defense of Self-Defense" I: June 20, 1967

en were not created in order to obey laws. Laws are created to obey men. They are established by men and should serve men. The laws and rules which officials inflict upon poor people prevent them from functioning harmoniously in society. There is no disagreement about this function of law in any circle—the disagreement arises from the question of which men laws are to serve. Such lawmakers ignore the fact that it is the duty of the poor and unrepresented to construct rules and laws that serve their interests better. Rewriting unjust laws is a basic human right and fundamental obligation.

Before 1776 America was a British colony. The British government had certain laws and rules that the colonized Americans rejected as not being in their best interests. In spite of the British conviction that Americans had no right to establish their own laws to promote the general welfare of the people living here in America, the colonized immigrant felt he had no choice but to raise the gun to defend his welfare. Simultaneously he made certain laws to ensure his protection from external and internal aggressions, from other governments, and his own agencies. One such form of protection was the Declaration of Independence, which states: ". . . whenever any government becomes destructive to these ends, it is the right of the people to alter or to abolish it, and to institute a new government, laying its foundations on such principles and organizing its powers in such forms as to them shall seem most likely to effect their safety and happiness."

Now these same colonized White people, these bondsmen, paupers, and thieves, deny the colonized Black man not only the right to abol-

134

ish this oppressive system, but to even speak of abolishing it. Having carried this madness and cruelty to the four corners of the earth, there is now universal rebellion against their continued rule and power. But as long as the wheels of the imperialistic war machine are turning, there is no country that can defeat this monster of the West. It is our belief that the Black people in America are the only people who can free the world, loosen the yoke of colonialism, and destroy the war machine. Black people who are within the machine can cause it to malfunction. They can, because of their intimacy with the mechanism, destroy the engine that is enslaving the world. America will not be able to fight every Black country in the world and fight a civil war at the same time. It is militarily impossible to do both of these things at once.

The slavery of Blacks in this country provides the oil for the machinery of war that America uses to enslave the peoples of the world. Without this oil the machinery cannot function. We are the driving shaft; we are in such a strategic position in this machinery that, once we become dislocated, the functioning of the remainder of the machinery breaks down.

Penned up in the ghettos of America, surrounded by his factories and all the physical components of his economic system, we have been made into "the wretched of the earth," relegated to the position of spectators while the White racists run their international con game on the suffering peoples. We have been brainwashed to believe that we are powerless and that there is nothing we can do for ourselves to bring about a speedy liberation for our people. We have been taught that we must please our oppressors, that we are only ten percent of the population, and therefore must confine our tactics to categories calculated not to disturb the sleep of our tormentors.

The power structure inflicts pain and brutality upon the peoples and then provides controlled outlets for the pain in ways least likely to upset them, or interfere with the process of exploitation. The people must repudiate the established channels as tricks and deceitful snares of the exploiting oppressors. The people must oppose everything the oppressor supports, and support everything that he opposes. If Black people go about their struggle for liberation in the way that the oppressor dictates and sponsors, then we will have degenerated to the level of groveling flunkies for the oppressor himself. When the oppressor makes a vicious attack against freedom-fighters because of the way that such freedom-fighters choose to go about their liberation, then we know we are moving in the direction of our liberation. The racist dog oppressors have no rights which oppressed Black people are bound to respect. As long as the racist dogs pollute the earth with the evil of their actions, they do not deserve any respect at all, and the "rules" of their game, written in the people's blood, are beneath contempt.

The oppressor must be harassed until his doom. He must have no peace by day or by night. The slaves have always outnumbered the slavemasters. The power of the oppressor rests upon the submission of the people. When Black people really unite and rise up in all their splendid millions, they will have the strength to smash injustice. We do not understand the power in our numbers. We are millions and millions of Black people scattered across the continent and throughout the Western Hemisphere. There are more Black people in America than the total population of many countries now enjoying full membership in the United Nations. They have power and their power is based primarily on the fact that they are organized and united with each other. They are recognized by the powers of the world.

We, with all our numbers, are recognized by no one. In fact, we do not even recognize our own selves. We are unaware of the potential power latent in our numbers. In 1967, in the midst of a hostile racist nation whose hidden racism is rising to the surface at a phenomenal speed, we are still so blind to our critical fight for our very survival that we are continuing to function in petty, futile ways. Divided, confused, fighting among ourselves, we are still in the elementary stage of throwing rocks, sticks, empty wine bottles and beer cans at racist police who lie in wait for a chance to murder unarmed Black people. The racist police have worked out a system for suppressing these spontaneous rebellions that flare up from the anger, frustration, and desperation of the masses of Black people. We can no longer afford the dubious luxury of the terrible casualties wantonly inflicted upon us by the police during these rebellions.

Black people must now move, from the grass roots up through the perfumed circles of the Black bourgeoisie, to seize by any means necessary a proportionate share of the power vested and collected in the structure of America. We must organize and unite to combat by long resistance the brutal force used against us daily. The power structure depends upon the use of force within retaliation. This is why they have made it a felony to teach guerrilla warfare. This is why they want the people unarmed.

The racist dog oppressors fear the armed people; they fear most of all Black people armed with weapons and the ideology of the Black Panther Party for Self-Defense. An unarmed people are slaves or are subject to slavery at any given moment. If a government is not afraid of the people it will arm the people against foreign aggression. Black people are held captive in the midst of their oppressors. There is a world of difference between thirty million unarmed submissive Black people and thirty million Black people armed with freedom, guns, and the strategic methods of liberation.

When a mechanic wants to fix a broken-down car engine, he must have the necessary tools to do the job. When the people move for liberation they must have the basic tool of liberation: the gun. Only with the power of the gun can the Black masses halt the terror and brutality directed against them by the armed racist power structure; and in one sense only by the power of the gun can the whole world be transformed into the earthly paradise dreamed of by the people from time immemorial. One successful practitioner of the art and science of national liberation and self-defense, Brother Mao Tse-tung, put it this way: "We are advocates of the abolition of war, we do not want war; but war can only be abolished through war, and in order to get rid of the gun it is necessary to take up the gun."

The blood, sweat, tears, and suffering of Black people are the foundations of the wealth and power of the United States of America. We were forced to build America, and if forced to, we will tear it down. The immediate result of this destruction will be suffering and bloodshed. But the end result will be perpetual peace for all mankind.

from "In Defense of Self-Defense" II: July 3, 1967

Historically the power structure has demanded that Black leaders cater to their desires and to the ends of the imperialistic racism of the oppressor. The power structure has endorsed those Black leaders who have reduced themselves to nothing more than apologizing parrots. They have divided the so-called Black leaders within the political arena. The oppressors sponsor radio programs, give space in their racist newspapers, and show them the luxury enjoyed only by the oppressor. The Black leaders serve the oppressor by purposely keeping the people submissive, passive, and non-violent, turning a deaf ear to the cries of the suffering and downtrodden, the unemployed and welfare recipients who hunger for liberation by any means necessary.

Historically there have been a few Black men who have rejected the handouts of the oppressor and who have refused to spread the oppressor's treacherous principles of deceit, gradual indoctrination, and brainwashing, and who have refused to indulge in the criminal activity of teaching submission, fear, and love for an enemy who hates the very color Black and is determined to commit genocide on an international scale.

There has always existed in the Black colony of Afro-America a fundamental difference over which tactics, from the broad spectrum of alternatives, Black people should employ in their struggle for national liberation.

One side contends that Black people are in the peculiar position where, in order to gain acceptance into the "mainstream" of American life, they must employ no tactic that will anger the oppressor Whites. This view holds that Black people constitute a hopeless minority and that salvation for Black people lies in developing brotherly relations. There are certain tactics that are taboo. Violence against the oppressor must be avoided at all costs because the oppressor will retaliate with superior violence. So Black people may protest, but not protect. They can complain, but not cut and shoot. In short, Black people must at all costs remain non-violent.

On the other side we find that the point of departure is the principle that the oppressor has no rights that the oppressed is bound to respect. Kill the slavemaster, destroy him utterly, move against him with implacable fortitude. Break his oppressive power by any means necessary. Men who have stood before the Black masses and recommended this response to the oppression have been held in fear by the oppressor. The Blacks in the colony who were wed to the non-violent alternative could not relate to the advocates of implacable opposition to the oppressor. Because the oppressor always prefers to deal with the less radical, i.e., less dangerous, spokesmen for his subjects. He would prefer that his subjects had no spokesmen at all, or better yet, he wishes to speak for them himself. Unable to do this practically, he does the next best thing and endorses spokesmen who will allow him to speak through them to the masses. Paramount among his imperatives is to see to it that implacable spokesmen are never allowed to communicate their message to the masses. Their oppressor will resort to any means necessary to silence them.

The oppressor, the "endorsed spokesmen," and the implacables form the three points of a triangle of death. The oppressor looks upon the endorsed spokesmen as a tool to use against the implacables to keep the masses passive within the acceptable limits of the tactics he is capable of containing. The endorsed spokesmen look upon the oppressor as a guardian angel who can always be depended upon to protect him from the wrath of the implacables, while he looks upon the implacables as dangerous and irresponsible madmen who, by angering the oppressor, will certainly provoke a blood bath in which they themselves might get washed away. The implacables view both the oppressors and the endorsed leaders as his deadly enemies. If anything, he has a more profound hatred for the endorsed leaders than he has for the oppressor himself, because the implacables know that they can deal with the oppressor only after they have driven the endorsed spokesmen off the scene.

Historically the endorsed spokesmen have always held the upper hand over the implacables. In Afro-American history there are shining brief moments when the implacables have outmaneuvered the oppressor and the endorsed spokesmen and gained the attention of the Black masses. The Black masses, recognizing the implacables in the depths of their despair, respond magnetically to the implacables and bestow a devotion and loyalty to them that frightens the oppressor and endorsed spokesmen into a panic-stricken frenzy, often causing them to leap into a rash act of murder, imprisonment, or exile to silence the implacables and to get their show back on the road.

The masses of Black people have always been deeply entrenched and involved in the basic necessities of life. They have not had time to abstract their situation. Abstractions come only with leisure, the people have not had the luxury of leisure. Therefore, the people have been very aware of the true definition of politics. Politics is merely the desire of individuals and groups to satisfy their basic needs first: food, shelter, and clothing, and security for themselves and their loved ones. The Black leaders endorsed by the power structure have attempted to sell the people the simpleminded theory that politics is holding a political office; being able to move into a $40,000 home; being able to sit near White people in a restaurant (while in fact the Black masses have not been able to pay the rent of a $40.00 rat-infested hovel).

The Black leaders have led the community to believe that brutality and force could be ended by subjecting the people to this very force of self-sacrificing demonstrations. The Black people realize brutality and force can only be inflicted if there is submission. The community has not responded in the past or in the present to the absurd, erroneous and deceitful tactics of so-called legitimate Black leaders. The community realizes that force and brutality can only be eliminated by counterforce through self-defense. Leaders who have recommended these tactics have never had the support and following of the downtrodden Black masses who comprise the bulk of the community. The grass roots, the downtrodden of the Black community, though rejecting the hand-picked "handkerchief heads" endorsed by the power structure have not had the academic or administrative knowledge to form a long resistance to the brutality.

Marcus Garvey and Malcolm X were the two Black men of the twentieth century who posed an implacable challenge to both the oppressor and the endorsed spokesmen.

In our time, Malcolm stood on the threshold with the oppressor and the endorsed spokesmen in a bag that they could not get out of. Malcolm, implacable to the ultimate degree, held out to the Black masses the historical, stupendous victory of Black collective salvation and liberation from the chains of the oppressor and the treacherous embrace of the endorsed spokesmen. Only with the gun were the Black masses denied this victory. But they learned from Malcolm that with the gun they can recapture their dreams and make them a reality.

The heirs of Malcolm now stand millions strong on their corner of the triangle, facing the racist dog oppressor and the soulless endorsed spokesmen. The heirs of Malcolm have picked up the gun and taking first things first are moving to expose the endorsed spokesmen so the Black masses can see them for what they are and have always been. The choice offered by the heirs of Malcolm to the endorsed spokesmen is to repudiate the oppressor and to crawl back to their own people and earn a speedy reprieve or face a merciless, speedy, and most timely execution for treason and being "too wrong for too long."

the correct handling of a revolution: July 20, 1967

T he Black masses are handling the resistance incorrectly. When the brothers in East Oakland, having learned their resistance fighting from Watts, amassed the people in the streets, threw bricks and Molotov cocktails to destroy property and create disruption, they were herded into a small area by the gestapo police and immediately contained by the brutal violence of the oppressor's storm troops. Although this manner of resistance is sporadic, short-lived, and costly, it has been transmitted across the country to all the ghettos of the Black nation.

The identity of the first man who threw a Molotov cocktail is not known by the masses, yet they respect and imitate his action. In the same way, the actions of the party will be imitated by the people—if the people respect these activities.

The primary job of the party is to provide leadership for the people. It must teach by words and action the correct strategic methods of prolonged resistance. When the people learn that it is no longer advantageous for them to resist by going into the streets in large numbers, and when they see the advantage in the activities of the guerrilla warfare method, they will quickly follow this example.

But first, they must respect the party which is transmitting this message. When the vanguard group destroys the machinery of the oppressor by dealing with him in small groups of three and four, and then escapes the might of the oppressor, the masses will be impressed and more likely to adhere to this correct strategy. When the masses hear that a gestapo policeman has been executed while sipping coffee at a counter, and the revolutionary executioners fled without being traced, the masses will see the validity of this kind of resistance. It is not necessary to organize thirty million Black people in primary groups of two's and three's, but it is important for the party to show the people how to stage a revolution.

There are three ways one can learn: through study, observation, and experience. Since the Black community is composed basically of activists, observation of or participation in activity are the principle ways the community learns. To learn by studying is good, but to learn by experience is better. Because the Black community is not a reading community it is very important that the vanguard group be essentially activists. Without this knowledge of the Black community a Black revolution in racist America is impossible.

The main function of the party is to awaken the people and teach them the strategic method of resisting a power structure which is prepared not only to combat with massive brutality the people's resistance but to annihilate totally the Black population. If it is learned by the power structure that Black people have "X" number of guns in their possession, that information will not stimulate the power structure to prepare itself with guns; it is already prepared.

The end result of this revolutionary education will be positive for Black people in their resistance, and negative for the power structure in its oppression because the party always exemplifies revolutionary defiance. If the party does not make the people aware of the tools and methods of liberation, there will be no means by which the people can mobilize.

The relationship between the vanguard party and the masses is a secondary relationship. The relationship among the members of the vanguard party is a primary relationship. If the party machinery is to be effective it is important that the members of the party group maintain a face-to-face relationship with each other. It is impossible to put together functional party machinery or programs without this direct relationship. To minimize the danger of Uncle Tom informers and opportunists the members of the vanguard group should be tested revolutionaries.

The main purpose of the vanguard group should be to raise the consciousness of the masses through educational programs and other activities. The sleeping masses must be bombarded with the correct approach to struggle and the party must use all means available to get this information across to the masses. In order to do so the masses must know that the party exists. A vanguard party is never underground in the beginning of its existence; that would limit its effectiveness and educational goals. How can you teach people if the people do not know and respect you? The party must exist aboveground as long as the dog power structure will allow, and, hopefully, when the party is forced to go underground, the party's message will already have been put across to the people. The vanguard party's activities on the surface will necessarily be short-lived. Thus the party must make a tremendous impact upon the people before it is driven into secrecy. By that time the people will know the party exists and will seek further information about its activities when it is driven underground.

Many would-be revolutionaries work under the fallacious notion that the vanguard party should be a secret organization which the power structure knows nothing about, and that the masses know nothing about except for occasional letters that come to their homes by night. Underground parties cannot distribute leaflets announcing an underground meeting. Such contradictions and inconsistencies are not recognized by these so-called revolutionaries. They are, in fact, afraid of the very danger that they are asking the people to confront. These so-called revolutionaries want the people to say what they themselves are afraid to say, to do what they themselves are afraid to do. That kind of revolutionary is a coward and a hypocrite. A true revolutionary realizes that if he is sincere death is imminent. The things he is saying and doing are extremely dangerous. Without this realization it is pointless to proceed as a revolutionary.

If these imposters would investigate the history of revolution they would see that the vanguard group always starts out aboveground and is driven underground by the aggressor. The Cuban Revolution is an example: when Fidel Castro started to resist the butcher Batista and the American running dogs, he began by speaking publicly on the University of Havana campus. He was later driven to the hills. His impact upon the dispossessed people of Cuba was tremendous and his teachings were received with much respect. When he went into hiding, the Cuban people searched him out, going to the hills to find him and his band of twelve.

Castro handled the revolutionary struggle correctly, and if the Chinese Revolution is investigated it will be seen that the Communist Party operated quite openly in order to muster support from the masses. There are many more examples of successful revolutionary struggle from which one can learn the correct approach: the revolution in Kenya, the Algerian Revolution discussed in Fanon's *The Wretched of the Earth*, the Russian Revolution, the works of Chairman Mao Tse-tung, and a host of others.

Millions and millions of oppressed people may not know members of the vanguard party personally but they will learn of its activities and its proper strategy for liberation through an indirect acquaintance provided by the mass media. But it is not enough to rely on the media of the power structure; it is of prime importance that the vanguard party develop its own communications organ, such as a newspaper, and at the same time provide strategic revolutionary art, and destruction of the oppressor's machinery. For example in Watts the economy and property of the oppressor was destroyed to such an extent that no matter how the oppressor tried in his press to whitewash the activities of the Black brothers, the real nature and cause of the activity was communicated to every Black community. And no matter how the oppressor tried in his own media to distort and confuse the message of Brother Stokely Carmichael, Black people all over the country understood it perfectly and welcomed it.

The Black Panther Party for Self-Defense teaches that, in the final analysis, the guns, hand grenades, bazookas, and other equipment necessary for defense must be supplied by the power structure. As exemplified by the Vietcong, these weapons must be taken from the oppressor. Therefore, the greater the military preparation on the part of the oppressor, the greater the availability of weapons for the Black community. It is believed by some hypocrites that when the people are taught by the vanguard group to prepare for resistance, this only brings "the man" down on them with increasing violence and brutality; but the fact is that when the man becomes more oppressive he only heightens revolutionary fervor. So if things get worse for oppressed people they will feel the need for revolution and resistance. The people make revolution; the oppressors, by their brutal actions, cause resistance by the people. The vanguard party only teaches the correct methods of resistance.

The complaint of the hypocrites that the Black Panther Party for Self-Defense is exposing the people to deeper suffering is an incorrect observation. By their rebellions in the Black communities across the country the people have proved that they will not tolerate any more oppression by the racist dog police. They are looking now for guidance to extend and strengthen their resistance struggle. The vanguard party must exemplify the characteristics that make them worthy of leadership.

a functional definition of politics: January 17, 1969

Politics is war without bloodshed. War is politics with bloodshed. When the peaceful means of politics are exhausted and the people do not get what they want, politics is continued. Usually this ends up in physical conflict, which is called war and is also political.

Black people are not free because we lack political power. Historically, Black Reconstruction failed after the Civil War because Blacks had neither political nor military power. The masses of Black people at the time, nevertheless, were very clear on the definition of political power. It is evident in the songs of the time; on the Day of Jubilee we'd have forty acres and two mules. This was promised Black people by the Freedman's Bureau, and, as far as the Black masses were concerned, this was freedom.

For the "Talented Tenth" of Blacks living during the latter nineteenth century, freedom was operative in more explicitly political arenas such as electoral politics. Although many of these Blacks were often better educated than most whites in the south, having received schooling in France, Canada, and England, early Black elected officials lacked the influence necessary to empower Blacks at large. And it was for this reason, among others, that Reconstruction failed.

When one operates in the political arena, it is assumed that he has access to or at least represents power. There are essentially three forms of political power in this respect: economic, land (feudal power), and military. If Black people had received 40 acres and 2 mules, we would have developed a political force and chosen a representative to speak on our behalf of our interests as a people. Instead, Blacks received noth-

147

ing from the government, thereby contributing to the continuation of our oppressed status. It was absurd to have a Black representative in the political arena where no real political influence existed for Black people.

Whites, however, had and have a base of power from which they exert political consequence. This is evident in the fact that when the farmers are not given adequate prices for their crops, the economy receives a political consequence. Farmers let their crops rot in the field. To be political, you must have a political consequence when you do not receive your desires—otherwise you are non-political.

When Black people send a representative, he is somewhat absurd because he has very little political influence. He does not represent land power, because we do not own any land. He does not represent economic or industrial power, because Black people do not own the means of production. The only way he can become political is to represent what is commonly called a military power, which the Black Panther Party for Self-Defense calls Self-Defense Power. Black people develop Self-Defense Power by arming themselves from house to house, block to block, community to community, throughout the nation. Then we will choose a political representative, and he will state the desires of the black masses. If the desires are not met, the power structure will receive a political consequence. We will make it economically non-profitable for those in power to go on with their oppressive ways. Now, we will negotiate as equals. There will be a balance between the people who are economically powerful and the people who are potentially economically destructive.

The white racist oppresses Black people for reasons not only related to racism but also for purposes having to do with the fact that it is economically profitable to do so. Black people must develop the political power that will make it unprofitable for racists to continue oppressing us. If the white racist imperialists in America continue to wage war against all people of color throughout the world, while also waging a civil war against Blacks here in America, it will be economically impossible for him to survive. This racist United States operates with the motive of profit; he lifts the gun and escalates war for profit. We will make him lower his guns because they will no longer serve his profit motive.

Every man is born; therefore he has a right to live and a right to share in the wealth of his nation. If he is denied the right to work, he is denied the right to live. If he can't work, he deserves a high standard of living, regardless of his education or skill. Those who control our economic system are obligated to furnish each man with a livelihood. If they cannot or will not do this, they do not deserve the position of administrators. The means of production should be taken away and placed in the hands of the people, who can organize a system that will provide everyone with a source of livelihood. Motivated by a sincere interest in our general welfare and not the interest of private property, the people will choose capable administrators to control the means of production and the land that is rightfully theirs. Until the people are in possession of these controls, there will be no peace. Black people must control the destiny of their community.

Black people desire to determine their own destiny. As a result, they are constantly inflicted with brutality from the occupying army, embodied by the police department. There is a great similarity between the occupying army in Southeast Asia and the occupation of our communities by the racist police. The armies were sent not to protect the people of South Vietnam but to brutalize and oppress them in the self-interests of imperial powers.

There should be no division or conflict of interest between the people and the police. Once there is a division, the police become the enemy of the people. The police should serve the interest of the people, and be one and the same. When this principle breaks down, the police become an occupying army. When one race has oppressed another and policemen are recruited from the oppressor race to patrol the communities of the oppressed people, an intolerable contradiction exists.

The racist dog policemen must withdraw immediately from our communities, cease their wanton murder and brutality and torture of Black people, or face the wrath of the armed people.

on the Peace Movement: August 15, 1969

The Peace Movement is extremely important, more important than I thought it was two years ago. The reason I place so much more emphasis on the Peace Movement is that I now see that if peace were to come about, it would revolutionize the basic economic composition of the country.

We all know now this is a garrison state, a warfare state. And not by accident. When capitalism reaches a point where it can no longer expand, it looks for other avenues, other deposits, other places to expand the capitalists interest. At this time super-capitalists (General Motors, Chrysler, General Dynamics, and all the super companies—I understand there's about seventy-six that control the whole economy of this country) and their companies are the main contractors for the Pentagon. In other words, super-capitalists are now putting their over-expanded capitalistic surplus into military equipment. This military equipment is then placed in foreign countries such as Vietnam and the Dominican Republic. With the wedding of industry and the Pentagon, there is a new avenue to invest in. Military equipment is an expendable avenue, because the purpose of the equipment is to explode. Therefore, you must keep building new explosives. A perpetual process.

We know that the U.S. has a secret pact with Thailand. These pacts are all part of a super-plan to keep the economy going. What would happen then, if peace were to come about? There would not be that final depository for expendable goods, and the surplus could then be returned to the country. The military plants, related defense plants, and industrial plants would be brought to a grinding halt.

This is why some union representatives support the war effort. The AFL-CIO supported the invasion of the Dominican Republic. It forced out Juan Bosch for the simple reason that, as long as the war continues, they know they can exploit the people through taxation and human lives. We sent soldiers, you see, brothers, because they're expendable too; people are expendable.

One of the favored arguments of the capitalists is that America is not an imperialistic country because the traditional ways and means of imperialism is to go into a developing country, rape it of its raw materials, refine them either in the colony or the mother country, and sell them back at a high price to the colonized people. And the argument is that "America is not doing that. We don't need any equipment or raw materials out of Vietnam." And this is very true. This contradiction puzzled me for a while. But now I understand that something new has happened; with the wedding of science and industry, the industrial plants in America have solved the basic problem of raw materials through synthetics and the knowledge of using raw materials that are already here in a variety of ways, therefore keeping the plants going. The favored argument of the capitalist is "We must be there to stop communism or wars of subversion." What is overlooked is the fact that the super-capitalists know we don't need to rape the country. I think Cuba was the turning point away from the traditional colonized country.

Another argument is that we need the strategic military positions. But we know that the U.S. does not need strategic military positions because they already have enough equipment to defend this country from any point in the world if attacked. So they could only be there to use this developing country as depository for expendable goods.

In traditional imperialism, people from the mother country usually go to the colony, set up government, and the leaders of the military, but this is not so in America. People from the mother country have not gone to the colonized country of Vietnam and jockeyed for position, but the profit has all been turned back to America. The defense contractors jockey for position now in the mother country for defense contracts. Then they set up a puppet government or a military regime to supply these developing countries with military equipment. They really do not want to be in Vietnam or any of the developing countries because they feel (and they have all done this) that they have bought off the militaries in these various developing countries so that they will only be an arm of the Pentagon. The military regime in Greece is a good example. They have full control of the military officers, paying them high salaries so they feel that they will not have to send American troops and disturb the mother country.

But what happens when one battalion of military is defeated? Then you send in reinforcements for the defeated puppet army in that developing country. The whole government becomes subject to the army. And the army becomes suspicious of the civil government in these developing countries because they are told by the Pentagon through indoctrination and money that the civil government is a communist threat to the nation. Military coups follow, and this is what happens over and over with the support of the U.S.

We have actually an imperialistic variation of imperialism. The jockeying for positions of power is inside of the mother country now, so, in fact, the American people have become colonized.

At one time I thought that only Blacks were colonized. But I think we have to change our rhetoric to an extent because the whole American people have been colonized, if you view exploitation as a colonized effect. Seventy-six companies have exploited everyone. American people are a colonized people even more so than the people in developing countries where the military operates.

This is why the Peace Movement is so important. If the Peace Movement is successful, then the revolution will be successful. If the Peace Movement fails, then the revolution in the mother country fails. In other words, the people would be pushed so uptight once war were to stop that the whole economy would go down the drain. Only a planned economy could combat the chaos that an absence of incentive causes. Now war is the incentive for the military contractors.

This is why it is very important that we have communications with the Peace Movement. Not only should we communicate with it, we should actually get out and support it fully in various ways including literature and demonstrations.

We have to realize our position, and we have to know ourselves and know our enemies. A thousand wars and a thousand victories. And until we know who the enemy is and what the situation is we will only be marking time. Even the Peace Movement doesn't compromise our defense principles. We still defend ourselves against attack and against aggression. But overall, we are advocating the end to all wars. But, yet, we support the self-defense of the Vietnamese people and all the people who are struggling.

prison, where is thy victory?: January 3, 1970

When a person studies mathematics he learns that there are many mathematical laws that determine the approach he must take to solving the problems presented to him. In the study of geometry one of the first laws a person learns is that "the whole is not greater than the sum of its parts." This means simply that one cannot have a geometrical figure such as a circle or a square that contains more than it does when broken down into smaller parts. Therefore, if all the smaller parts add up to a certain amount, the entire figure cannot add up to a larger amount. The prison cannot have a victory over the prisoner because those in charge take the same kind of approach and assume if they have the whole body in a cell that they have contained all that makes up the person. But a prisoner is not a geometrical figure, and an approach that is successful in mathematics is wholly unsuccessful when dealing with human beings.

In the case of the human we are not dealing only with the single individual, we are also dealing with the ideas and beliefs that have motivated him and that sustain him, even when his body is confined. In the case of humanity the whole is much greater than its parts because the whole includes the body, which is measurable and confineable and also the ideas, which cannot be measured and cannot be confined.

The ideas that can and will sustain our movement for total freedom and dignity of the people cannot be imprisoned, for they are to be found in the people, all the people, wherever they are. As long as the people live by the ideas of freedom and dignity, there will be no prison that can hold our movement down. Ideas move from one person to another by the association of brothers and sisters who recognize that a most

154

evil system of capitalism has set us against each other, although our real enemy is the exploiter who profits from our poverty. When we realize such an idea, then we come to love and appreciate our brothers and sisters who we may have seen as enemies, and those exploiters who we may have seen as friends are revealed for what they truly are to all oppressed people. The people are the idea. The respect and dignity of the people as they move toward their freedom are the sustaining forces that reach into and out of the prison. The walls, the bars, the guns, and the guards can never encircle or hold down the idea of the people. And the people must always carry forward the idea, which is their dignity and their beauty.

The prison operates with the concept that since it has a person's body it has his entire being, because the whole cannot be greater than the sum of its parts. They put the body in a cell and seem to get some sense of relief and security from that fact. The idea of prison victory, then, is that when the person in jail begins to act, think, and believe the way they want him to, they have won the battle and the person is then "rehabilitated." But this cannot be the case because those who operate the prisons have failed to examine their own beliefs thoroughly, and they fail to understand the types of people they attempt to control. Therefore, even when the prison thinks it has won the victory, there is no victory.

There are two types of prisoners. The largest number are those who accept the legitimacy of the assumptions upon which the society is based. They wish to acquire the same goals as everybody else: money, power, and conspicuous consumption. In order to do so, however, they adopt techniques and methods that the society has defined as illegitimate. When this is discovered such people are put in jail. They may be called "illegitimate capitalists" since their aim is to acquire everything this capitalistic society defines as legitimate. The second type of prisoner is the one who rejects the legitimacy of the assumptions upon which the society is based. He argues that the people at the bottom of the society are exploited for the profit and advantage of those at the top. Thus, the oppressed exist and will always be used to maintain the privileged status of the exploiters. There is no sacredness, there is no dignity, in either exploiting or being exploited. Although this system may make the society function at a high level of technological efficiency,

156 | *The Huey P. Newton Reader*

it is an illegitimate system, since it rests upon the suffering of humans who are as worthy and as dignified as those who do not suffer. Thus, the second type of prisoner says that the society is corrupt and illegitimate and must be overthrown. This second type of prisoner is the "political prisoner." They do not accept the legitimacy of the society and cannot participate in its corrupting exploitation, whether they are in the prison or on the block.

The prison cannot gain a victory over either type of prisoner no matter how hard it tries. The "illegitimate capitalist" recognizes that if he plays the game the prison wants him to play, he will have his time reduced and be released to continue his activities. Therefore, he is willing to go through the prison programs and say the things the prison authorities want to hear. The prison assumes he is "rehabilitated" and ready for the society. The prisoner has really played the prison's game so that he can be released to resume pursuit of his capitalistic goals. There is no victory, for the prisoner from the "git-go" accepted the idea of the society. He pretends to accept the idea of the prison as a part of the game he has always played.

The prison cannot gain a victory over the political prisoner because he has nothing to be rehabilitated from or to. He refuses to accept the legitimacy of the system and refuses to participate. To participate is to admit that the society is legitimate because of its exploitation of the oppressed. This is the idea that the political prisoner does not accept, this is the idea for which he has been imprisoned, and this is the reason why he cannot cooperate with the system. The political prisoner will, in fact, serve his time just as will the "illegitimate capitalist." Yet the idea that motivated and sustained the political prisoner rests in the people. All the prison has is a body.

The dignity and beauty of man rests in the human spirit, which makes him more than simply a physical being. This spirit must never be suppressed for exploitation by others. As long as the people recognize the beauty of their human spirits and move against suppression and exploitation, they will be carrying out one of the most beautiful ideas of all time. Because the human whole is much greater than the sum of its parts. The ideas will always be among the people. The prison cannot be victorious because walls, bars, and guards cannot conquer or hold down an idea.

the women's liberation and gay liberation movements: August 15, 1970

During the past few years strong movements have developed among women and among homosexuals seeking their liberation. There has been some uncertainty about how to relate to these movements.

Whatever your personal opinions and your insecurities about homosexuality and the various liberation movements among homosexuals and women (and I speak of the homosexuals and women as oppressed groups), we should try to unite with them in a revolutionary fashion. I say "whatever your insecurities are" because as we very well know, sometimes our first instinct is to want to hit a homosexual in the mouth, and want a woman to be quiet. We want to hit a homosexual in the mouth because we are afraid we might be homosexual; and we want to hit the woman or shut her up because we are afraid that she might castrate us, or take the nuts that we might not have to start with.

We must gain security in ourselves and therefore have respect and feelings for all oppressed people. We must not use the racist attitude that the White racists use against our people because they are Black and poor. Many times the poorest White person is the most racist because he is afraid that he might lose something, or discover something that he does not have. So you're some kind of threat to him. This kind of psychology is in operation when we view oppressed people and we are angry with them because of their particular kind of behavior, or their particular kind of deviation from the established norm.

Remember, we have not established a revolutionary value system; we are only in the process of establishing it. I do not remember our ever constituting any value that said that a revolutionary must say offensive things towards homosexuals, or that a revolutionary should make sure that women do not speak out about their own particular kind of oppression. As a matter of fact, it is just the opposite: we say that we recognize the women's right to be free. We have not said much about the homosexual at all, but we must relate to the homosexual movement because it is a real thing. And I know through reading, and through my life experience and observations, that homosexuals are not given freedom and liberty by anyone in the society. They might be the most oppressed people in the society.

And what made them homosexual? Perhaps it's a phenomenon that I don't understand entirely. Some people say that it is the decadence of capitalism. I don't know if that is the case; I rather doubt it. But whatever the case is, we know that homosexuality is a fact that exists, and we must understand it in its purest form: that is, a person should have the freedom to use his body in whatever way he wants.

That is not endorsing things in homosexuality that we wouldn't view as revolutionary. But there is nothing to say that a homosexual cannot also be a revolutionary. And maybe I'm now injecting some of my prejudice by saying that "even a homosexual can be a revolutionary." Quite the contrary, maybe a homosexual could be the most revolutionary.

When we have revolutionary conferences, rallies, and demonstrations, there should be full participation of the gay liberation movement and the women's liberation movement. Some groups might be more revolutionary than others. We should not use the actions of a few to say that they are all reactionary or counterrevolutionary because they are not.

We should deal with the factions just as we deal with any other group or party that claims to be revolutionary. We should try to judge, somehow, whether they are operating in a sincere revolutionary fashion and from a really oppressed situation. (And we will grant that if they are women they are probably oppressed.) If they do things that are unrevolutionary or counterrevolutionary, then criticize that action. If we feel that the group in spirit means to be revolutionary in practice, but they make mistakes in interpretation of the revolutionary philosophy, or they do not understand the dialectics of the social forces in operation, we

should criticize that and not criticize them because they are women trying to be free. And the same is true for homosexuals. We should never
say a whole movement is dishonest when in fact they are trying to be
honest. They are just making honest mistakes. Friends are allowed to
make mistakes. The enemy is not allowed to make mistakes because
his whole existence is a mistake, and we suffer from it. But the women's
liberation front and gay liberation front are our friends, they are potential allies, *and we need as many allies as possible.*

We should be willing to discuss the insecurities that many people
have about homosexuality. When I say "insecurities," I mean the fear
that they are some kind of threat to our manhood. I can understand
this fear. Because of the long conditioning process that builds insecurity in the American male, homosexuality might produce certain hang-
ups in us. I have hang-ups myself about male homosexuality. But on
the other hand, I have no hang-up about female homosexuality. And
that is a phenomenon in itself. I think it is probably because male
homosexuality is a threat to me and female homosexuality is not.

We should be careful about using those terms that might turn our
friends off. The terms "faggot" and "punk" should be deleted from our
vocabulary, and especially we should not attach names normally
designed for homosexuals to men who are enemies of the people, such
as Nixon or Mitchell. Homosexuals are not enemies of the people.

We should try to form a working coalition with the gay liberation
and women's liberation groups. We must always handle social forces
in the most appropriate manner.

speech delivered at Boston College: November 18, 1970

Power to the people, brothers and sisters. I would like to thank you for my presence here tonight because you are responsible for it. I would be in a maximum-security penitentiary if it were not for the power of the people.

I would like to petition you to do the same for Bobby Seale, our Chairman, for Ericka Huggins, for Angela Davis, for the New York 21 and the Soledad Brothers. For all political prisoners and prisoners of war. On the 28th and 29th of November we will have a People's Revolutionary Constitutional convention in Washington, D.C. We cannot have that convention if the people do not come. After all, the people are the makers of world history and responsible for everything. How can we have a convention if we have no people? Some believe a people's convention is possible without the people being there. As I recall, that was the case in 1777.

Tonight, I would like to outline for you the Black Panther Party's program and explain how we arrived at our ideological position and why we feel it necessary to institute a Ten-Point Program. A Ten-Point Program is not revolutionary in itself, nor is it reformist. *It is a survival program.* We, the people, are threatened with genocide because racism and fascism are rampant in this country and throughout the world. And the ruling circle in North America is responsible. We intend to change all of that, and in order to change it, there must be a total transformation. But until we can achieve that total transformation, we must exist. In order to exist, we must survive; therefore, we need a survival kit: the Ten-Point Program. It is necessary for our children to grow up healthy with functional and creative minds. They cannot do this if they do not get the correct nutrition. That is why we have a breakfast program for children. We also have community health programs. We have a busing program. We call it "The Bus for Relatives and Parents of Prisoners." We realize that the fascist regime that operates the prisons throughout America would like to do their treachery in the dark. But if we get the relatives, parents, and friends to the prisons they can expose the treachery of the fascists. This too is a survival program.

We must not regard our survival programs as an answer to the whole problem of oppression. We don't even claim it to be a revolutionary program. Revolutions are made of sterner stuff. We do say that if the people are not here revolution cannot be achieved, for the people and only the people make revolutions.

The theme of our Revolutionary People's Constitutional Convention is "Survival Through Service to the People." At our convention we will present our total survival program. It is a program that works very much like the first-aid kit that is used when a plane falls and you find yourself in the middle of the sea on a rubber raft. You need a few things to last until you can get to the shore, until you can get to that oasis where you can be happy and healthy. If you do not have the things necessary to get you to that shore, then you will probably not exist. At this time the ruling circle threatens us to the extent that we are afraid that we might not exist to see the next day or see the revolution. The Black Panther Party will not accept the total destruction of the people. As a matter of fact, we have drawn a line of demarcation and we will no longer tolerate fascism, aggression, brutality, and murder of any kind. We will not sit around and allow ourselves to be murdered. Each person has an obligation to preserve himself. If he does not preserve himself then I accuse him of suicide: reactionary suicide because reactionary conditions will have caused his death. If we do nothing we are accepting the situation and allowing ourselves to die. We will not accept that. If the alternatives are very narrow we still will not sit around, we will not die the death of the Jews in Germany. We would rather die the death of the Jews in Warsaw!

Where there is courage, where there is self-respect and dignity, there is a possibility that we can change the conditions and win. This is called *revolutionary enthusiasm* and it is the kind of struggle that is needed in order to guarantee a victory. If we must die, then we will die the death of a revolutionary suicide that says, "If I am put down, if I am driven out, I refuse to be swept out with a broom. I would much rather be driven out with a stick because if I am swept out with the broom it will humiliate me and I will lose my self-respect. But if I am driven out with the stick, then, at least, I can claim the dignity of a man and die the death of a man rather than the death of a dog." Of course, our real desire is to live, but we will not be cowed, we will not be intimidated.

I would like to explain to you the method that the Black Panther Party used to arrive at our ideological position, and more than that, I would like to give to you a framework or a process of thinking that might help us solve the problems and the contradictions that exist today. Before we approach the problem we must get a clear picture of what is really going on; a clear image divorced from the attitudes and emotions that we usually project into a situation. We must be as objective as possible without accepting dogma, letting the facts speak for themselves. But we will not remain totally objective; we will become subjective in the application of the knowledge received from the external world. We will use the scientific method to acquire this knowledge, but we will openly acknowledge our ultimate subjectivity. Once we apply knowledge in order to *will* a certain outcome our objectivity ends and our subjectivity begins. We call this integrating theory with practice, and this is what the Black Panther Party is all about.

In order to understand a group of forces operating at the same time, science developed what is called the scientific method. One of the characteristics or properties of this method is disinterest. Not *un*interest, but disinterest: no special interest in the outcome. In other words, the scientist does not promote an outcome, he just collects the facts. Nevertheless, in acquiring his facts he must begin with a basic premise. Most basic premises stem from a set of assumptions because it is very difficult to test a first premise without these assumptions. After an agreement is reached on certain assumptions, an intelligent argument can follow, for then logic and consistency are all that is required to reach a valid conclusion.

Tonight I ask you to assume that an external world exists. An external world that exists independently of us. The second assumption I would like for you to make is that things are in a constant state of change, transformation, or flux. With agreement on these two assumptions we can go on with our discussion.

The scientific method relies heavily on empiricism. But the problem with empiricism is that it tells you very little about the future; it tells you only about the past, about information which you have already discovered through observation and experience. It always refers to past experience.

Long after the rules of empirical knowledge had been ascertained, a man by the name of Karl Marx integrated these rules with a theory developed by Immanuel Kant called rationale. Kant called his process of reasoning pure reason because it did not depend on the external world. Instead it only depended on consistency in manipulating symbols in order to come up with a conclusion based upon reason. For example, in this sentence "If the sky is above my head when I turn my head upwards, I will see the sky" there is nothing wrong with the conclusion. As a matter of fact, it is accurate. But I haven't said anything about the existence of the sky. I said "if." With rationale we are not dependent upon the external world. With empiricism we can tell very little about the future. So what will we do? What Marx did. In order to understand what was happening in the world Marx found it necessary to integrate rationale with empiricism. He called his concept dialectical materialism. If, like Marx, we integrate these two concepts or these two ways of thinking, not only are we in touch with the world outside us but we can also explain the constant state of transformation. Therefore, we can also make some predictions about the outcome of certain social phenomena that is not only in constant change but also in conflict.

Marx, as a social scientist, criticized other social scientists for attempting to explain phenomena, or one phenomenon, by taking it out of its environment, isolating it, putting it into a category, and not acknowledging the fact that once it was taken out of its environment the phenomenon was transformed. For example, if in a discipline such as sociology we study the activity of groups—how they hold together and why they fall apart—without understanding everything else related to that group, we may arrive at a false conclusion about the nature of the group. What Marx attempted to do was to develop a way of thinking that would explain phenomena realistically.

In the physical world, when forces collide they are transformed. When atoms collide, in physics, they divide into electrons, protons, and neutrons, if I remember correctly. What happened to the atom? It was transformed. In the social world a similar thing happens. We can apply the same principle. When two cultures collide a process or condition occurs which the sociologists call acculturation: the modification of cultures as a result of their contact with each other. Marx called the collision of social forces or classes a contradiction. In the physical world, when forces collide we sometimes call it just that—a collision. For example, when two cars meet head on, trying to occupy the same space at the same time, both are transformed. Sometimes other things happen. Had those two cars been turned back to back and sped off in opposite directions they would not be a contradiction; they would be contrary, covering different spaces at different times. Sometimes when people meet they argue and misunderstand each other because they think they are having a contradiction when they are only being contrary. For example, I can say the wall is ten feet tall and you can say the wall is red, and we can argue all day thinking we are having a contradiction when actually we are only being contrary. When people argue, when one offers a thesis and the other offers an anti-thesis, we say there is a contradiction and hope that if we argue long enough, provided that we agree on one premise, we can have some kind of synthesis. Tonight I hope I can have some form of agreement or synthesis with those who have criticized the Black Panther Party.

I think that the mistake is that some people have taken the apparent as the actual fact in spite of their claims of scholarly research and following the discipline of dialectical materialism. They fail to search deeper, as the scientist is required to do, to get beyond the apparent and come up with the more significant. Let me explain how this relates to the Black Panther Party. The Black Panther Party is a Marxist-Leninist party because we follow the dialectical method and we also integrate theory with practice. We are not mechanical Marxists and we are not historical materialists. Some people think they are Marxists when actually they are following the thoughts of Hegel. Some people think they are Marxist-Leninists but they refuse to be creative, and are, therefore, tied to the past. They are tied to a rhetoric that does not apply to the present set of conditions. They are tied to a set of thoughts that approaches dogma—what we call flunkyism.

Marx attempted to set up a framework which could be applied to a number of conditions. And in applying this framework we cannot be afraid of the outcome because things change and we must be willing to acknowledge that change because we are objective. If we are using the method of dialectical materialism we don't expect to find anything the same even one minute later because "one minute later" is history. If things are in a constant state of change, we cannot expect them to be the same. Words used to describe old phenomena may be useless to describe the new. And if we use the old words to describe new events we run the risk of confusing people and misleading them into thinking that things are static.

In 1917 an event occurred in the Soviet Union that was called a revolution. Two classes had a contradiction and the whole country was transformed. In this country, 1970, the Black Panther Party issued a document. Our Minister of Information, Eldridge Cleaver, who now is in Algeria, wrote a pamphlet called "On the Ideology of the Black Panther Party." In that work Eldridge Cleaver stated that neither the proletarians nor the industrial workers carry the potentialities for revolution in this country at this time. He claimed that the left wing of the proletarians, the lumpen proletarians, have that revolutionary potential, and in fact, acting as the vanguard, they would carry the people of the world to the final climax of the transformation of society. It has been stated by some people, by some parties, by some organizations, by the Progressive Labor Party, that revolution is impossible. How can the lumpen proletarians carry out a successful socialist transformation when they are only a minority? And in fact how can they do it when history shows that only the proletarians have carried out a successful social revolution? I agree that it is necessary for the people who carry out a social revolution to represent the popular majority's interests. It is necessary for this group to represent the broad masses of the people. We analyzed what happened in the Soviet Union in 1917. I also agree that the lumpen proletarians are the minority in this country. No disagreement. Have I contradicted myself? It only goes to show that what's apparent might not actually be a fact. What appears to be a contradiction may be only a paradox. Let's examine this apparent contradiction.

The Soviet Union, in 1917, was basically an agricultural society with a very large peasantry. A set of social conditions existing there at that time was responsible for the development of a small industrial base. The people who worked in this industrial base were called proletarians. Lenin, using Marx's theory, saw the trends. He was not a historical materialist, but a dialectical materialist, and therefore very interested in the ever-changing status of things. He saw that while the proletarians were a minority in 1917, they had the potential to carry out a revolution because their class was increasing and the peasantry was declining. That was one of the conditions. The proletarians were destined to be a popular force. They also had access to the properties necessary for carrying out a socialist revolution.

In this country the Black Panther Party, taking careful note of the dialectical method, taking careful note of the social trends and the ever-changing nature of things, sees that while the lumpen proletarians are the minority and the proletarians are the majority, technology is developing at such a rapid rate that automation will progress to cybernation, and cybernation probably to technocracy. As I came into town I saw MIT over the way. If the ruling circle remains in power it seems to me that capitalists will continue to develop their technological machinery because they are not interested in the people. Therefore, I expect from them the logic that they have always followed: to make as much money as possible, and pay the people as little as possible—until the people demand more, and finally demand their heads. If revolution does not occur almost immediately, and I say almost immediately because technology is making leaps (it made a leap all the way to the moon), and if the ruling circle remains in power the proletarian working class will definitely be on the decline because they will be unemployables and therefore swell the ranks of the lumpens, who are the present unemployables. Every worker is in jeopardy because of the ruling circle, which is why we say that the lumpen proletarians have the potential for revolution, will probably carry out the revolution, and in the near future will be the popular majority. Of course, I would not like to see more of my people unemployed or become unemployables, but being objective, because we're dialectical materialists, we must acknowledge the facts.

Marx outlined a rough process of the development of society. He said that society goes from a slave class to a feudalistic class structure to a capitalistic class structure to a socialistic class structure and finally to communism. Or in other words, from capitalist state to socialist state to nonstate: communism. I think we can all agree that the slave class in the world has virtually been transformed into the wage slave. In other words, the slave class in the world no longer exists as a significant force, and if we agree to that we can agree that classes can be transformed literally out of existence. If this is so, if the slave class can disappear and become something else—or not disappear but just be trans-formed—and take on other characteristics, then it is also true that the proletarians or the industrial working class can possibly be transformed out of existence. Of course the people themselves would not disappear; they would only take on other attributes. The attribute that I am interested in is the fact that soon the ruling circle will not need the workers, and if the ruling circle is in control of the means of produc-tion the working class will become unemployables or lumpens. That is logical; that is dialectical. I think it would be wrong to say that only the slave class could disappear.

Marx was a very intelligent man. He was not a dogmatist. Once he said, "One thing I'm not, I'm not a Marxist." In those words, he was trying to tell the Progressive Labor Party and others not to accept the past as the present or the future, but to understand it and be able to predict what might happen in the future and therefore act in an intel-ligent way to bring about the revolution that we all want.

After taking those things into consideration we see that as time changes and the world is transformed we need some new definitions, for if we keep using the old terms people might think the old situa-tion still exists. I would be amazed if the same conditions that existed in 1917 were still existing today.

You know Marx and Lenin were pretty lazy dudes when it came to working for somebody. They looked at toil, working for your neces-sities, as something of a curse. And Lenin's whole theory, after he put Marx's analysis into practice, was geared to get rid of the proletari-ans. In other words, when the proletarian class or the working class seized the means of production, they would plan their society in such a way as to be free from toil. As a matter of fact, Lenin saw a time in which man could stand in one place, push buttons and move mountains. It sounds to me as though he saw a proletarian working class transformed and in possession of a free block of time, to indulge in productive creativity, to think about developing their universe, so that they could have the happiness, the freedom, and the pleasure that all men seek and value.

Today's capitalist has developed machinery to such a point that he can hire a group of specialized people called technocrats. In the near future he will certainly do more of this, and the technocrat will be too specialized to be identified as a proletarian. In fact that group of technocrats will be so vital we will have to do something to explain the presence of other people; we will have to come up with another definition and reason for existing.

But we must not confine our discussion to theory; we must have practical application of our theory to come up with anything worthwhile. In spite of the criticism that we have received from certain people, the Party has a practical application of its theories. Many of our activities provide the working class and the unemployed with a reason and a means for existing in the future. The people will not disappear—not with our survival programs they will not. They will still be around. The Black Panther Party says it is perfectly correct to organize the proletarians because after they are kicked out of the factory and are called unemployable or lumpen, they still want to live, and in order to live they have to eat. It is in the proletarian's own best interest to seize the machinery that he has made in order to produce in abundance, so he and his brethren can live. We will not wait until the proletarian becomes the lumpen proletarian to educate him. Today we must lift the consciousness of the people. The wind is rising and the rivers flowing, times are getting hard and we can't go home again. We can't go back to our mother's womb, nor can we go back to 1917.

The United States, or what I like to call North America, was transformed at the hands of the ruling circle from a nation to an empire. This caused a total change in the world, because no part of an interrelated thing can change and leave everything else the same. So when the United States, or North America, became an empire it changed the whole composition of the world. There were other nations in the world. But "empire" means that the ruling circle who lives in the empire (the imperialists) control other nations. Now some time ago there existed a phenomenon we called—well, I call—primitive empire. An example of that would be the Roman Empire because the Romans controlled all of what was thought to be the known world. In fact they did not know all of the world, therefore some nations still existed independent of it. Now, probably all of the world is known. The United States as an empire necessarily controls the whole world either directly or indirectly.

If we understand dialectics we know that every determination brings about a limitation and every limitation brings about a determination. In other words, while one force may give rise to one thing it might crush other things, including itself. We might call this concept "the negation of the negation." So, while in 1917 the ruling circle created an industrial base and used the system of capitalism they were also creating the necessary conditions for socialism. They were doing this because in a socialist society it is necessary to have some centralization of the wealth, some equal distribution of the wealth, and some harmony among the people.

Now, I will give you roughly some characteristics that any people who call themselves a nation should have. These are economic independence, cultural determination, control of the political institutions, territorial integrity, and safety.

In 1966 we called our Party a Black Nationalist Party. We called ourselves Black Nationalists because we thought that nationhood was the answer. Shortly after that we decided that what was really needed was revolutionary nationalism, that is, nationalism plus socialism. After analyzing conditions a little more, we found that it was impractical and even contradictory. Therefore, we went to a higher level of consciousness. We saw that in order to be free we had to crush the ruling circle and therefore we had to unite with the peoples of the world. So we called ourselves Internationalists. We sought solidarity with the peoples of the world. We sought solidarity with what we thought were the nations of the world. But then what happened? We found that because everything is in a constant state of transformation, because of the development of technology, because of the development of the mass media, because of the fire power of the imperialist, and because of the fact that the United States is no longer a nation but an empire, nations could not exist, for they did not have the criteria for nationhood. Their self-determination, economic determination, and cultural determination has been transformed by the imperialists and the ruling circle. They were no longer nations. We found that in order to be Internationalists we had to be also Nationalists, or at least acknowledge nationhood. Internationalism, if I understand the word, means the interrelationship among a group of nations. But since no nation exists, and since the United States is in fact an empire, it is impossible for us to be Internationalists. These transformations and phenomena require us to call ourselves "intercommunalists" *because nations have been transformed into communities of the world.* The Black Panther Party now disclaims internationalism and supports intercommunalism.

Marx and Lenin felt, with the information they had, that when the non-state finally came to be a reality, it would be caused or ushered in by the people and by communism. A strange thing happened. The ruling reactionary circle, through the consequence of being imperialists, transformed the world into what we call "Reactionary Intercommunalism." They laid siege upon all the communities of the world, dominating the institutions to such an extent that the people were not served by the institutions in their own land. The Black Panther Party would like to reverse that trend and lead the people of the world into the age of "Revolutionary Intercommunalism." This would be the time when the people seize the means of production and distribute the wealth and the technology in an egalitarian way to the many communities of the world.

We see very little difference in what happens to a community here in North America and what happens to a community in Vietnam. We see very little difference in what happens, even culturally, to a Chinese community in San Francisco and a Chinese community in Hong Kong. We see very little difference in what happens to a Black community in Harlem and a Black community in South Africa, a Black community in Angola and one in Mozambique. We see very little difference.

So, what has actually happened, is that the non-state has already been accomplished, but it is reactionary. A community by way of definition is a comprehensive collection of institutions that serve the people who live there. It differs from a nation because a community evolves around a greater structure that we usually call the state, and the state has certain control over the community if the administration represents the people or if the administration happens to be the people's commissar. It is not so at this time, so there's still something to be done. I mentioned earlier the "negation of the negation," I mentioned earlier the necessity for the redistribution of wealth. We think that it is very important to know that as things are in the world today socialism in the United States will never exist. Why? It will not exist because it cannot exist. It cannot at this time exist anyplace in the world. Socialism would require a socialist state, and if a state does not exist how could socialism exist? So how do we define certain progressive countries such as the People's Republic of China? How do we describe certain progressive countries, or communities as we call them, as the Democratic People's Republic of Korea? How do we define certain communities such as North Vietnam and the provisional government in the South? How do we explain these communities if in fact they too cannot claim nationhood? We say this: we say they represent the people's liberated territory. They represent a community liberated. But that community is not sufficient, it is not satisfied, just as the National Liberation Front is not satisfied with the liberated territory in the South. It is only the groundwork and preparation for the liberation of the world—seizing the wealth from the ruling circle, equal distribution and proportional representation in an intercommunal framework. This is what the Black Panther Party would like to achieve with the help of the power of the people, because without the people nothing can be achieved.

I stated that in the United States socialism would never exist. In order for a revolution to occur in the United States you would have to have a redistribution of wealth not on a national or an international level, but on an intercommunal level. Because how can we say that we have accomplished revolution if we redistribute the wealth just to the people here in North America when the ruling circle itself is guilty of *trespass de bonis asportatis*. That is, they have taken away the goods of the people of the world, transported them to America and used them as their very own.

In 1917, when the revolution occurred, there could be a redistribution of wealth on a national level because nations existed. Now, if you talk in terms of planning an economy on a *world-wide* level, on an intercommunal level, you are saying something important: that the people have been ripped off very much like one country being ripped off. Simple reparation is not enough because the people have not only been robbed of their raw materials, but of the wealth accrued from the investment of those materials—an investment which has created the technological machine. The people of the world will have to have control—not a limited share of control for "X" amount of time, but total control forever.

In order to plan a real intercommunal economy we will have to acknowledge how the world is hooked up. We will also have to acknowledge that nations have not existed for some time. Some people will argue that nations still exist because of the cultural differences. By way of definition, just for practical argument, culture is a collection of learned patterns of behavior. Here in the United States Black people, Africans, were raped from the mother country, and consequently we have literally lost most of our African values. Perhaps we still hold on to some surviving Africanisms, but by and large you can see the transformation which was achieved by time and the highly technological society whose tremendous mass media functions as an indoctrination center. The ruling circle has launched satellites in order to project a beam across the earth and indoctrinate the world, and while there might be some cultural differences, these differences are not qualitative but quantitative. In other words, if technology and the ruling circle go on as they are now the people of the world will be conditioned to adopt Western values. (I think Japan is a good example.) The differences between people are getting very small, but again that is in the interest of the ruling circle. I do not believe that history can be backtracked. If the world is really that interconnected then we have to acknowledge that and say that in order for the people to be free, they will have to control the institutions of their community, and have some form of representation in the technological center that they have produced. The United States, in order to correct its robbery of the world, will have to first return much of which it has stolen. I don't see how we can talk about socialism when the problem is world distribution. I think this is what Marx meant when he talked about the non-state.

I was at Alex Haley's house some time ago and he talked to me about his search for his past. He found it in Africa but when he returned there shortly afterward, he was in a state of panic. His village hadn't changed very much, but when he went there he saw an old man walking down the road, holding something that he cherished to his ear. It was a small transistor radio that was zeroed in on the British broadcasting network. What I'm trying to say is that mass media plus the development of transportation make it impossible for us to think of ourselves in terms of separate entities, as nations. Do you realize that it only took me approximately five hours to get from San Francisco to here? It only takes ten hours to get from here to Vietnam. The ruling circle no longer even acknowledges wars; they call them "police actions." They call the riots of the Vietnamese people "domestic disturbance." What I am saying is that the ruling circle must realize and accept the consequences of what they have done. They know that there is only one world, but they are determined to follow the logic of their exploitation.

A short time ago in Detroit, the community was under siege, and now sixteen members of the Party are in prison. The local police laid siege on that community and that house, and they used the same weapons they use in Vietnam (as a matter of fact, two tanks rolled up). The same thing happens in Vietnam because the "police" are there also. The "police" are everywhere and they all wear the same uniform and use the same tools, and have the same purpose: the protection of the ruling circle here in North America. It is true that the world is one community, but we are not satisfied with the concentration of its power. We want the power for the people.

I said earlier (but I strayed away) that the theory of the "negation of the negation" is valid. Some scholars have been wondering why in Asia, Africa, and Latin America the resistance always seeks the goal of a collective society. They seem not to institute the economy of the capitalist. They seem to jump all the way from feudalism to a collective society, and some people can't understand why. Why won't they follow historical Marxism, or historical materialism? Why won't they go from feudalism to the development of a capitalistic base and finally to socialism? They don't do it because they can't do it. They don't do it for the same reason that the Black community in Harlem cannot develop capitalism, that the Black community in Oakland or San Francisco cannot develop capitalism, because the imperialists have already preempted the field. They have already centralized the wealth. Therefore, in order to deal with them all we can do is liberate our community and then move on them as a collective force.

We've had long arguments with people about our convictions. Before we became conscious we used to call ourselves a dispersed collection of colonies here in North America. And people argued with me all day and all night, asking, "How can you possibly be a colony? In order to be a colony you have to have a nation, and you're not a nation, you're a community. You're a dispersed collection of communities." Because the Black Panther Party is not embarrassed to change or admit error, tonight I would like to accept the criticism and say that those critics were absolutely right. We are a collection of communities just as the Korean people, the Vietnamese people, and the Chinese people are a collection of communities—a dispersed collection of communities because we have no superstructure of our own. The superstructure we have is the superstructure of Wall Street, which all of our labor produced. This is a distorted form of collectivity. Everything's been collected but it's used exclusively in the interest of the ruling circle. This is why the Black Panther Party denounces Black capitalism and says that all we can do is liberate our community, not only in Vietnam but here, not only in Cambodia and the People's Republics of China and Korea but the communities of the world. We must unite as one community and then transform the world into a place where people will be happy, wars will end, the state itself will no longer exist, and we will have communism. But we cannot do this right away. When transformation takes place, when structural change takes place, the result is usually cultural lag. After the people possess the means of production we will probably not move directly into communism but linger with Revolutionary Intercommunalism until such time as we can wash away bourgeois thought, until such time as we can wash away racism and reactionary thinking, until such time as people are not attached to their nation as a peasant is attached to the soil, until such time as that people can gain their sanity and develop a culture that is "essentially human," that will serve the people instead of some god. Because we cannot avoid contact with each other we will have to develop a value system that will help us function together in harmony.

Part Three

The Second Wave

HUEY'S RELEASE from prison in July 1970 marked a period of renewal for the Party. Under the counsel of attorney Charles Garry and with the sweeping support of the people, Huey beat the odds and was personally reunited with the Party for the first time since 1967. Diminishing the atmosphere of jubilation, however, was the fact that other Black Panther leaders remained imprisoned: Chairman Bobby Seale and Ericka Huggins were held on an FBI-inspired murder charge; Black Panther field marshal George Jackson was incarcerated in San Quentin Penitentiary; and Eldridge Cleaver was living abroad in political exile. If the conspicuous absence of Huey's most trusted comrades was not in itself an alienating situation, then the many unfamiliar faces that cheered his freedom left him feeling estranged from his own supporters.

Recall that the Party's ranks swelled as a result of the "Free Huey" movement, and that the majority of Black Panthers were therefore acquainted with their leader only from his words and pictures in the newspaper. Although a small cadre had worked with Huey from the Party's inception (and some of us had even grown up with him), most rank-and-file members had never met Huey, much less knew him intimately. Consequently, his first months back on the streets were a period of familiarization with the very organization he had launched just four years earlier.

Whereas Huey's arrest had brought the first wave of political fervor to the Black Panther Party, his release engendered a number of equally historic changes from 1971 to 1972. Firstly, he traveled to Africa and Asia, where meetings with Mozambique president Samora Moises Machel and Chinese premier Chou En-lai among others helped inspire Huey's formulation of his groundbreaking philosophy of Intercommunalism. As outlined here in a 1971 excerpt from *In Search of Common Ground,* this farsighted and prophetic philosophy became the Party's official ideology regarding world affairs.

Another shift took place in March 1971 when Eldridge resigned from the Panthers. While much scholarly attention has been lavished on this so-called split, his defection, as Huey points out in "On the Defection of Eldridge Cleaver from the Black Panther Party and the Defection of the Black Panther Party from the Black Community," in reality had only a minor impact on our operations. More critically, however, Eldridge's departure signaled the need for the Party to rebuild its connection to people in the community. Huey's "Black Capitalism Re-analyzed" and "On the Relevance of the Church" thus illustrate a renewed commitment to speaking to and meeting the needs of the community on issues outside of the rhetoric of armed revolt.

intercommunalism: February 1971

We, the Black Panther Party, believe that everything is in a constant state of change, so we employ a framework of thinking that can put us in touch with the process of change. That is, we believe that the conclusions at which we arrive will always change, but the fundamentals of the method by which we arrive at our conclusions will remain constant. Our ideology, therefore, is the most important part of our thinking.

There are many different ideologies or schools of thought, and all of them start with an a priori set of assumptions. Mankind is still limited in its knowledge and finds it hard at this historical stage to talk about the very beginning of things and the very end of things without starting from premises that cannot yet be proved.

This is true of both general schools of thought—the idealist and the materialist. The idealists base their thinking on certain presumptions about things of which they have very little knowledge; the materialists like to believe that they are very much in contact with reality, or the real material world, disregarding the fact that they only assume there *is* a material world.

The Black Panther Party has chosen materialist assumptions on which to ground its ideology. This is a purely arbitrary choice. Idealism might be the real happening; we might not be here at all. We don't really know whether we are in Connecticut or in San Francisco, whether we are dreaming and in a dream state, or whether we are awake and in a dream state. Perhaps we are just somewhere in a void; we simply can't be sure. But because the members of the Black Panther Party are materialists, we believe that some day scientists will be able to deliver the information that will give us not only the evidence but the

181

proof that there is a material world and that its genesis was material —motion and matter—not spiritual.

Until that time, however, and for the purposes of this discussion, I merely ask that we agree on the stipulation that a material world exists and develops externally and independently of us all. With this stipulation, we have the foundation for an intelligent dialogue. We *assume* that there is a material world and that it exists and develops independently of us; and we assume that the human organism, through its sensory system, has the ability to observe and analyze that material world.

The dialectical materialist believes that everything in existence has fundamental internal contradictions. For example, the African gods south of the Sahara always had at least two heads, one for evil and one for good. Now people create God in their own image, what they think He—for God is always a "He" in patriarchal societies—is like or should be. So the African said, in effect: I am both good and evil; good and evil are the two parts of the thing that is me. This is an example of an internal contradiction.

Western societies, though, split up good and evil, placing God up in heaven and the Devil down in hell. Good and evil fight for control over people in Western religions, but they are two entirely different entities. This is an example of an external contradiction.

This struggle between mutually exclusive opposing tendencies within everything that exists explains the observable fact that all things have motion and are in a constant state of transformation. Things transform themselves because while one tendency or force is more dominating than another, change is nonetheless a constant, and at some point the balance will alter and there will be a new qualitative development. New properties will come into existence, qualities that did not altogether exist before. Such qualities cannot be analyzed without understanding the forces struggling within the object in the first place, yet the limitations and determinations of these new qualities are not defined by the forces that created them.

Class conflict develops by the same principles that govern all other phenomena in the material world. In contemporary society, a class that owns property dominates a class that does not own property. There is a class of workers and a class of owners, and because there exists a basic contradiction in the interests of those two classes, they are constantly struggling with one another. Now, because things do not stay the same we can be sure of one thing: the owner will not stay the owner, and the people who are dominated will not stay dominated. We don't know exactly how this will happen, but after we analyze all the other elements of the situation, we can make a few predictions. We can be sure that if we increase the intensity of the struggle, we will reach a point where the equilibrium of forces will change and there will be a qualitative leap into a new situation with a new social equilibrium. I say "leap," because we know from our experience of the physical world that when transformations of this kind occur they do so with great force.

These principles of dialectical development do not represent an iron law that can be applied mechanically to the social process. There are exceptions to those laws of development and transformation, which is why, as dialectical materialists, we emphasize that we must analyze each set of conditions separately and make concrete analyses of concrete conditions in each instance. One cannot always predict the outcome, but one can for the most part gain enough insight to manage the process.

The dialectical method is essentially an ideology, yet we believe that it is superior to other ideologies because it puts us more in contact with what we believe to be the real world; it increases our ability to deal with that world and shape its development and change.

You could easily say, "Well, this method may be successfully applied in one particular instance, but how do you know that it is an infallible guide in all cases?" The answer is that we don't know. We don't say "all cases" or "infallible guide" because we try not to speak in such absolute and inclusive terms. We only say that we have to analyze each instance, that we have found this method the best available in the course of our analyses, and that we think the method will continue to prove itself in the future.

We sometimes have a problem because people do not understand the ideology that Marx and Engels began to develop. People say, "You claim to be Marxists, but did you know that Marx was a racist?" We say, "Well, he probably was a racist: he made a statement once about the marriage of a white woman and a black man, and he called the black man a gorilla or something like that." The Marxists claim he was only kidding and that the statement shows Marx's closeness to the man, but of course that is nonsense. So it does seem that Marx was a racist.

If you are a *Marxist*, then Marx's racism affects your own judgment because a Marxist is someone who worships Marx and the thought of Marx. Remember, though, that Marx himself said, "I am not a Marxist." Such Marxists cherish the conclusions which Marx arrived at through his method, but they throw away the method itself—leaving themselves in a totally static posture. That is why most Marxists really are historical materialists: they look to the past to get answers for the future, and that does not work.

If you are a *dialectical materialist*, however, Marx's racism does not matter. You do not believe in the conclusions of one person but in the validity of a mode of thought; and we in the Party, as dialectical materialists, recognize Karl Marx as one of the great contributors to that mode of thought. Whether or not Marx was a racist is irrelevant and immaterial to whether or not the system of thinking he helped develop delivers truths about processes in the material world. And this is true in all disciplines. In every discipline you find people who have distorted visions and are at a low state of consciousness who nonetheless have flashes of insight and produce ideas worth considering. For instance, John B. Watson once stated that his favorite pastime was hunting and hanging niggers, yet he made great forward strides in the analysis and investigation of conditioned responses.

Now that I have said a word about the ideology of the Party, I am going to describe the history of the Party and how we have changed our understanding of the world.

When we started in October 1966, we were what one would call black nationalists. We realized the contradictions in society, the pressure on black people in particular, and we saw that most people in the past had solved some of their problems by forming into nations. We therefore argued that it was rational and logical for us to believe that our sufferings as a people would end when we established a nation of our own, composed of our own people.

After a while we saw that something was wrong with this resolution of the problem. In the past, nationhood was a fairly easy thing to accomplish. If we look around now, though, we see that the world—

the land space, the livable parts as we know them—is pretty well set-tled. So we realized that to create a new nation we would have to become a dominant faction in this one, and yet the fact that we did not have power was the contradiction that drove us to seek nation-hood in the first place. It is an endless circle, you see: to achieve nation-hood, we needed to become a dominant force; but to become a dominant force, we needed to be a nation.

So we made a further analysis and found that in order for us to be a dominant force we would at least have to be great in number. We developed from just plain nationalists or separatist nationalists into rev-olutionary nationalists. We said that we joined with all of the other people in the world struggling for decolonialization and nationhood, and called ourselves a "dispersed colony" because we did not have the geographical concentration that other so-called colonies had. But we did have black communities throughout the country—San Francisco, Los Angeles, New Haven—and there are many similarities between these communities and the traditional kind of colony. We also thought that if we allied with those other colonies we would have a greater num-ber, a greater chance, a greater force; and that is what we needed, of course, because only force kept us a colonized people.

We saw that it was not only beneficial for us to be revolutionary nationalists but to express our solidarity with those friends who suf-fered many of the same kind of pressures we suffered. Therefore we changed our self-definitions. We said that we are not only revolutionary nationalists—that is, nationalists who want revolutionary changes in everything, including the economic system the oppressor inflicts upon us—but we are also individuals deeply concerned with the other peo-ple of the world and their desires for revolution. In order to show this solidarity we decided to call ourselves internationalists.

Originally, as I said, we assumed that people could solve a number of their problems by becoming nations, but this conclusion showed our lack of understanding of the world's dialectical development. Our mis-take was to assume that the conditions under which people had become nations in the past still existed. To be a nation, one must satisfy cer-tain essential conditions, and if these things do not exist or cannot be created, then it is not possible to be a nation.

In the past, nation-states were usually inhabited by people of a certain ethnic and religious background. They were divided from other people either by a partition of water or a great unoccupied land space. This natural partition gave the nation's dominant class, and the people generally, a certain amount of control over the kinds of political, economic, and social institutions they established. It gave them a certain amount of control over their destiny and their territory. They were secure at least to the extent that they would not be attacked or violated by another nation ten thousand miles away, simply because the means to transport troops that far did not exist. This situation, however, could not last. Technology developed until there was a definite qualitative transformation in the relationships within and between nations.

We know that you cannot change a part of the whole without changing the whole, and vice versa. As technology developed and there was an increase in military capabilities and means of travel and communication, nations began to control other territories, distant from their own. Usually they controlled these other lands by sending administrators and settlers, who would extract labor from the people or resources from the earth—or both. This is the phenomenon we know as colonialism.

The settlers' control over the seized land and people grew to such an extent that it wasn't even necessary for the settler to be present to maintain the system. He went back home. The people were so integrated with the aggressor that their land didn't look like a colony any longer. But because their land didn't look like a free state either, some theorists started to call these lands "neocolonies." Arguments about the precise definition of these entities developed. Are they colonies or not? If they aren't, what are they? The theorists knew that something had happened, but they did not know what it was.

Using the dialectical materialist method, we in the Black Panther Party saw that the United States was no longer a nation. It was something else; it was more than a nation. It had not only expanded its territorial boundaries, but it had expanded all of its controls as well. We called it an empire. Now at one time the world had an empire in which the conditions of rule were different—the Roman Empire. The difference between the Roman and the American empires is that other nations were able to exist external to and independent of the Roman

Empire because their means of exploration, conquest, and control were all relatively limited.

But when we say "empire" today, we mean precisely what we say. An empire is a nation-state that has transformed itself into a power controlling *all* the world's lands and people.

We believe that there are no more colonies or neocolonies. If a people is colonized, it must be possible for them to decolonize and become what they formerly were. But what happens when the raw materials are extracted and labor is exploited within a territory dispersed over the entire globe? When the riches of the whole earth are depleted and used to feed a gigantic industrial machine in the imperialists' home? Then the people and the economy are so integrated into the imperialist empire that it's impossible to "decolonize," to return to the former conditions of existence.

If colonies cannot "decolonize" and return to their original existence as nations, then nations no longer exist. Nor, we believe, will they ever exist again. And since there must be nations for revolutionary nationalism or internationalism to make sense, we decided that we would have to call ourselves something new.

We say that the world today is a dispersed collection of communities. A community is different from a nation. A community is a small unit with a comprehensive collection of institutions that exist to serve a small group of people. And we say further that the struggle in the world today is between the small circle that administers and profits from the empire of the United States, and the peoples of the world who want to determine their own destinies.

We call this situation intercommunalism. We are now in the age of reactionary intercommunalism, in which a ruling circle, a small group of people, control all other people by using their technology.

At the same time, we say that this technology can solve most of the material contradictions people face, that the material conditions exist that would allow the people of the world to develop a culture that is essentially human and would nurture those things that would allow the people to resolve contradictions in a way that would not cause the mutual slaughter of all of us. The development of such a culture would be revolutionary intercommunalism.

Some communities have begun doing this. They have liberated their territories and have established provisional governments. We recognize them, and say that these governments represent the people of China, North Korea, the people in the liberated zones of South Vietnam, and the people in North Vietnam.

We believe their examples should be followed so that the order of the day would not be reactionary intercommunalism (empire) but revolutionary intercommunalism. The people of the world, that is, must seize power from the small ruling circle and expropriate the expropriators, pull them down from their pinnacle and make them equals, and distribute the fruits of our labor that have been denied us in some equitable way. We know that the machinery to accomplish these tasks exists and we want access to it.

Imperialism has laid the foundation for world communism, and imperialism itself has grown to the point of reactionary intercommunalism because the world is now integrated into one community. The communications revolution, combined with the expansive domination of the American empire, has created the "global village." The peoples of all cultures are under siege by the same forces and they all have access to the same technologies.

There are only differences in degree between what's happening to the blacks here and what's happening to all of the people in the world, including Africans. Their needs are the same and their energy is the same. And the contradictions they suffer will only be resolved when the people establish a revolutionary intercommunalism where they share all the wealth that they produce and live in one world.

The stage of history is set for such a transformation: the technological and administrative base of socialism exists. When the people seize the means of production and all social institutions, then there will be a qualitative leap and a change in the organization of society. It will take time to resolve the contradictions of racism and all kinds of chauvinism; but because the people will control their own social institutions, they will be free to re-create themselves and to establish communism, a stage of human development in which human values will shape the structures of society. At this time the world will be ready for a still higher level of which we can now know nothing.

•••

Question: I'm wondering: Now that you have established an ideology with which to view the kinds of imperialism going on in the United States, what do you do once the revolution has taken place? What happens once you have taken over the structures made by capitalism and have assumed responsibility for them? Aren't you going to encounter the same struggles between the dominant forms of government and the inferior?

Newton: It's not going to be the same because nothing remains the same. All things are in a constant state of transformation, and therefore you will have other contradictions inherent in that new phenomenon. We can be very sure that there will be contradictions after revolutionary intercommunalism is the order of the day, and we can even be sure that there will be contradictions after communism, which is an even higher stage than revolutionary intercommunalism. There will always be contradictions or else everything would stop. So it's not a question of "when the revolution comes": the revolution is always going on. It's not a question of "when the revolution is going to be": the revolution is going on every day, every minute, because the new is always struggling against the old for dominance.

We also say that every determination is a limitation, and every limitation is a determination. This is the struggle of the old and new again, where a thing seems to negate itself. For instance, imperialism negates itself after laying the foundation for communism, and communism will eventually negate itself because of its internal contradictions, and then we'll move to an even higher state. I like to think that we will finally move to a stage called "godliness," where man will know the secrets of the beginning and the end and will have full control of the universe —and when I say the universe, I mean all motion and matter. This is only speculation, of course, because science has not delivered us the answer yet; but we believe that it will in the future.

So of course there will be contradictions in the future. But some contradictions are antagonistic and some contradictions are not antagonistic. Usually when we speak of antagonistic contradictions, we are talking about contradictions that develop from conflicts of economic interest, and we assume that in the future, when the people have power, these antagonistic contradictions will occur less and less.

Could you speak to the question of how you are going to expropriate the expropriators when they are the ones with the army and the ones with the police force?

Well, all things carry a negative sign as well as a positive sign. That's why we say every determination has a limitation and every limitation has a determination. For example, your organism carries internal contradictions from the moment you are born and begin to deteriorate. First you are an infant, then a small child, then an adolescent, and so on until you are old. We keep developing and burning ourselves out at the same time; we are negating ourselves. And this is just how imperialism is negating itself now. It's moved into a phase we call reactionary intercommunalism and has thus laid the foundation for revolutionary intercommunalism, because as the enemy disperses its troops and controls more and more space, it becomes weaker and weaker, you see. And as they become weaker and weaker, the people become stronger and stronger.

You spoke of technological differences between the various countries of the world. How are you going to integrate all these countries into intercommunalism if these differences exist?

They are already integrated by the mere fact that the ruling circle has control of all of them. Inside the geographical region of North America, for example, you have Wall Street, you have the big plants in Detroit turning out automobiles, and you have Mississippi, where there are no automobile factories. Does that mean that Mississippi is not a part of the complete whole? No, it only means that the expropriators have chosen to put automobile plants in Detroit rather than in Mississippi. Instead of producing automobiles, they grow food in Mississippi that makes stronger the hands of people in Detroit or Wall Street. So the answer to your question is that systems are inclusive: just because you don't have a factory in every single community does not mean that the community is distinct and independent and autonomous, you see.

Well, then, do you see each of the dispersed communities having certain kinds of things to work out among themselves before they can take part in intercommunalism?

They are part of intercommunalism, reactionary intercommunalism. What the people have to do is become conscious of this condition. The primary concern of the Black Panther Party is to lift the level of consciousness of the people through theory and practice to the point where they will see exactly what is controlling them and what is oppressing them, and therefore see exactly what has to be done—or at least what the first step is. One of the greatest contributions of Freud was to make people aware that they are controlled much of their lives by their unconscious. He attempted to strip away the veil from the unconscious and make it conscious: that's the first step in feeling free, the first step in exerting control. It seems to be natural for people not to like being controlled. Marx made a similar contribution to human freedom, only he pointed out the external things that control people. In order for people to liberate themselves from external controls, they have to know about these controls. Consciousness of the expropriator is necessary for expropriating the expropriator, for throwing off external controls.

In the ultimate intercommune do you see separate, geographically defined communities that have had a specific history and a unique set of experiences? Would each community retain some kind of separate identity?

No, I think that whether we like it or not, dialectics would make it necessary to have a universal identity. If we do not have universal identity, then we will have cultural, racial, and religious chauvinism, the kind of ethnocentrism we have now. So we say that even if in the future there will be some small differences in behavior patterns, different environments would all be a secondary thing. And we struggle for a future in which we will realize that we are all Homo sapiens and have more in common than not. We will be closer together than we are now.

I would like to return to something we were talking about a minute or two ago. It seems to me that the mass media have, in a sense, psy-

chologized many of the people in our country, our own geographical area, so that they come to desire the controls that are imposed upon them by the capitalist system. So how are we going to fight this revolution if a great number of people, in this country at least, are in fact psychologically part of the ruling class?

Part of or controlled by?

Well, part of in the psychological sense, because they are not really in power. It's a psychological way of talking about the middle class. Do you have any feelings on that?

First, we have to understand that everything has a material basis, and that our personalities would not exist, what others call our spirit or our mind would not exist, if we were not material organisms. So to understand why some of the victims of the ruling class might identify with the ruling circle, we must look at their material lives; and if we do, we will realize that the same people who identify with the ruling circle are also very unhappy. Their feelings can be compared to those of a child: a child desires to mature so that he can control himself, but he believes he needs the protection of his father to do so. He has conflicting drives. Psychologists would call this conflict neurotic if the child were unable to resolve it.

In a sense, then, that is what we are all about. First, people have to be conscious of the ways they are controlled, then we have to understand the scientific laws involved, and once that is accomplished, we can begin to do what we want—to manipulate phenomena.

But if the opposing forces at this point include a very large number of people, including most of the middle classes, then where will the revolutionary thrust come from?

I see what you are getting at. That thrust will come from the growing number of what we call "unemployables" in this society. We call blacks and third world people in particular, and poor people in general, "unemployables" because they do not have the skills needed to work

Huey P. Newton, founding member of the
Black Panther Party, Oakland, California,
circa 1967. STEPHEN SHAMES/COURTESY OF
THE DR. HUEY P. NEWTON FOUNDATION

Huey P. Newton blowing bubbles with children at a Black Panther Party Liberation School, circa 1969.
PHOTOGRAPHER UNKNOWN/COURTESY OF THE DR. HUEY P. NEWTON FOUNDATION

Party volunteers regularly checked on and escorted elders to appointments, circa 1972. PHOTOGRAPHER UNKNOWN/COURTESY OF THE DR. HUEY P. NEWTON FOUNDATION

Bobby Seale (extreme right) and other Black Panther Party members registering voters and preparing for their community food distribution, Oakland, California, 1973. PHOTOGRAPHER UNKNOWN/COURTESY OF THE DR. HUEY P. NEWTON FOUNDATION

Children participating
in the Black Panther Party food
distribution program, 1972.
STEPHEN SHAMES/COURTESY OF THE
DR. HUEY P. NEWTON FOUNDATION

The Black Panther Party
sponsored free sickle-cell
anemia testing. San Pablo
Park, Oakland, California,
March 31, 1972.
HANK LEBO/COURTESY OF
THE DR. HUEY P. NEWTON
FOUNDATION

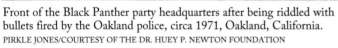

Front of the Black Panther party headquarters after being riddled with
bullets fired by the Oakland police, circa 1971, Oakland, California.
PIRKLE JONES/COURTESY OF THE DR. HUEY P. NEWTON FOUNDATION

The community gives a farewell salute to George Jackson, Revolutionary, Oakland, California, 1971.
STEPHEN SHAMES/COURTESY OF THE DR. HUEY P. NEWTON FOUNDATION

Huey P. Newton being greeted by Chinese Premier Chou En-lai, Beijing, 1971.

Iuey P. Newton and members of the Black Panther Party being greeted by PLO Chairman Yasser Arafat, 971. PLO UNIFIED INFORMATION/COURTESY OF THE DR. HUEY P. NEWTON FOUNDATION

ack Panther Party press conference after Party members' visit to China, 1972.
OTOGRAPHER UNKNOWN/COURTESY OF THE DR. HUEY P. NEWTON FOUNDATION

The Black Panther Youth, Oakland, California, 1972. STEPHEN SHAMES/COURTESY OF
THE DR. HUEY P. NEWTON FOUNDATION

in a highly developed technological society. You remember my saying that every society, like every age, contains its opposite: feudalism produced capitalism, which wiped out feudalism, and capitalism produced socialism, which will wipe out capitalism. Now the same is true of reactionary intercommunalism. Technological development creates a large middle class, and the number of workers increases also. The workers are paid a good deal and get many comforts. But the ruling class is still only interested in itself. They might make certain compromises and give a little—as a matter of fact, the ruling circle has even developed something of a social structure or welfare state to keep the opposition down—but as technology develops, the need for workers decreases.

It has been estimated that ten years from now only a small percentage of the present work force will be necessary to run the industries. Then what will happen to your worker who is now making four dollars an hour? The working class will be narrowed down, the class of unemployables will grow because it will take more and more skills to operate those machines and fewer people. And as these people become unemployables, they will become more and more alienated; even socialist compromises will not be enough. You will then find an integration between, say, the black unemployable and the white racist hard hat who is not regularly employed and mad at the blacks who he thinks threaten his job. We hope that he will join forces with those people who are already unemployable, but whether he does or not, his material existence will have changed. The proletarian will become the lumpen proletarian. It is this future change—the increase of the lumpen proletariat and the decrease of the proletariat—which makes us say that the lumpen proletariat is the majority and carries the revolutionary banner.

I'd like to ask you a question about the Party. You said that you see the Black Panther Party as primarily a force to educate people, raise their consciousness, end their oppression, and so on. Do you see the Party as educating black people specifically or as educating everybody?

We say that black people are the vanguard of the revolution in this country, and, since no one will be free until the people of America are free, that black people are the vanguard of world revolution. We don't say this in a boasting way. We inherit this legacy primarily because we are the last, you see, and as the saying goes, "The last will be the first."

We believe that black Americans are the first real internationalists; not just the Black Panther Party but black Americans. We are internationalists because we have been internationally dispersed by slavery, and we can easily identify with other people in other cultures. Because of slavery, we never really felt attached to the nation in the same way that the peasant was attached to the soil in Russia. We are always a long way from home.

And, finally, the historical condition of black Americans has led us to be progressive. We've always talked equality, you see, instead of believing that other people must equal us. What we want is not dominance but for the yoke to be released. We want to live with other people. We don't want to say that we are better: in fact, if we suffer a fault, it is that we tend to feel we are worse than other people because we have been brainwashed to think that way. So these subjective factors, based on the material existence of black people in America, contribute to our vanguard position.

Now as far as the Party is concerned, it has been exclusively black so far. We are thinking about how to deal with the racist situation in America and the reaction black people in America have to racism. We have to get to the black people first because they were carrying the banner first, and we try to do everything possible to get them to relate to us.

You were saying something a while ago about the problem of simplifying your ideology for the masses. Could you say a little more about it?

Yes, that's our big burden. So far I haven't been able to do it well enough to keep from being booed off the stage, but we are learning. I think one way to show how dialectics works is to use practical example after practical example. The reason I am sometimes afraid to do that is that people will take each example and think, "Well, if this is true in one case, then it must be true in all other cases." If they do that, then they become historical materialists like most Marxist scholars and most Marxist parties. These scholars and parties don't really deal in dialectics at all, or else they would know that at this time the revolutionary banner will not be carried by the proletarian class but by the lumpen proletariat.

Talking about contradictions, one of the most obvious contradictions within the black community is the difference in outlook between the black bourgeoisie and the black lower class. How do you raise the level of consciousness in the community to the point where the black bourgeoisie sees its own interests as being the same as those of the lower class?

Well, we are again dealing with attitudes and values that have to be changed. The whole concept of the bourgeoisie—black bourgeoisie—is something of an illusion. It's a fantasy bourgeoisie, and this is true of most of the white bourgeoisie too. There are very few controllers even in the white middle class. They can barely keep their heads above water, they are paying all the bills, living hand-to-mouth, and they have the extra expense of refusing to live like black people, you see. So they are not really controlling anything; they are controlled.

In the same way, I don't recognize the black bourgeoisie as different from any other exploited people. They are living in a fantasy world, and the main thing is to instill consciousness, to point out their real interests, their objective and true interests, just as our white progressive and radical friends have to do in the white community.

How do you go about raising the level of consciousness in the black community? Educationally, I mean. Do you have formal programs of instruction?

Well, we saw a need to formalize education because we didn't believe that a haphazard kind of learning would necessarily bring about the best results. We also saw that the so-called halls of learning did nothing but miseducate us; they either drove us out or kicked us out. They did me both ways. So what we are trying to do is structure an educational institution of our own.

Our first attempt along these lines is what we call our Ideological Institute. So far we have about fifty students, and these fifty students are very—well, may I say very unique students, because all of them are brothers and sisters off the block. What I mean is that they are lumpen proletarians. Most of them are kickouts and dropouts; most of them left school in the eighth, ninth, or tenth grade. And those few who stayed all the way didn't learn how to read or write, just as I didn't learn until I was about sixteen. But now they are dealing with dialectics and they are dealing with science—they study physics and mathematics so that they can understand the universe—and they are learning because they think it is relevant to them now. They will relate this learning back to the community and the community will in turn see the need for our program. It's very practical and relates to the needs of the people in a way that makes them receptive to our teachings and helps open their eyes to the fact that the people are the real power. They are the ones who will bring about change, not us alone. A vanguard is like the head of a spear, the thing that goes first. But what really hurts is the butt of the spear, because even though the head makes the necessary entrance, the back part is what penetrates. Without the butt, a spear is nothing but a toothpick.

What about Malcolm X University? Would you say that it has value?

The whole issue is: Who is in control? We, the Black Panther Party, control our Ideological Institute. If the people (and when I say "the people," I mean the oppressed people) control Malcolm X University, if they control it without reservation or without having to answer for what is done there or who speaks there, then Malcolm X University is progressive. If that is not the case, then Malcolm X University, or any university by any other name, is not progressive. I like its name, though. [Laughter]

The thing I don't understand is: If unity of identity is going to exist in revolutionary intercommunalism then what will be the contradictions that produce further change? It seems to me that it would be virtually impossible to avoid some contradictions.

I agree with you. You cannot avoid contradictions, you cannot avoid the struggle of opposite tendencies within the same wholes. But I can't tell you what the new opposites will be because they are not in existence yet. See what I mean?

I guess so. But how does all that fit in with your idea of a unified identity?

Well, in the first place, we do not deal in panaceas. The qualitative leap from reactionary intercommunalism to revolutionary intercommunalism will not be the millennium. It will not immediately bring into being either a universal identity or a culture that is essentially human. It will only provide the material base for the development of those tendencies.

When the people seize the means of production, when they seize the mass media and so forth, you will still have racism, you will still have ethnocentrism, you will still have contradictions. But the fact that the people will be in control of all the productive and institutional units of society—not only factories, but the media too—will enable them to start solving these contradictions. It will produce new values, new identities; it will mold a new and essentially human culture as the people resolve old conflicts based on cultural and economic conditions. And at some point, there will be a qualitative change and the people will have transformed revolutionary intercommunalism into communism.

We call it "communism" because at that point in history people will not only control the productive and institutional units of society, but they will also have seized possession of their own subconscious attitudes toward these things; and for the first time in history they will have a more rather than less conscious relationship to the material world—people, plants, books, machines, media, everything—in which they live. They will have power, that is, they will control the phenomena around them and make it act in some desired manner, and they will know their own real desires. The first step in this process is the seizure by the people of their own communities.

Let me say one more thing, though, to get back to your question. I would like to see the kind of communism I just described come into being, and I think it will come into being. But that concept is so far from my comprehension that I couldn't possibly name the contradictions that will exist there, although I am sure that the dialectics will go on. I'll be honest with you. No matter how I read it, I don't understand it.

But I still don't see where the contradictions are going to come in.

I can't see them either because they are not in existence yet. Only the basis for them is in existence, and we can't talk about things in the blue, things we don't know anything about. Philosophers have done that too much already.

You are talking about this ideology of intercommunalism as part of the program of the Black Panther Party and telling us that the idea is to strive for unity of identity. Yet a few minutes ago you mentioned that the Party only accepts blacks as members. That sounds like a contradiction to me.

Well, I guess it is. But to explain it I would have to go back to what I said earlier. We are the spearhead most of the time, and we try not to be too far ahead of the masses of the people, too far ahead of their thinking. We have to understand that most of the people are not ready for many of the things that we talk about.

Now many of our relationships with other groups, such as the white radicals with whom we have formed coalitions, have been criticized by the very people we are trying to help. For example, our offer of troops to the Vietnamese received negative reaction from the people. And I mean from truly oppressed people. Welfare recipients wrote letters saying, "I thought the Party was for us; why do you want to give those dirty Vietnamese our life blood?" I would agree with you and call it a contradiction. But it is a contradiction we are trying to resolve. You see, we are trying to give some therapy, you might say, to our community and lift their consciousness. But first we have to be accepted. If the therapist is not accepted, then he can't deliver the message. We try to do whatever is possible to meet the patient on the grounds that he or she can best relate to, because, after all, they are the issue. So I would say that we are being pragmatic in order to do the job that has to be done, and then, when that job is done, the Black Panther Party will no longer be the Black Panther Party.

That brings up a related question in my mind. How do you view the struggles of women and gay people right now? I mean do you see them as an important part of the revolution?

We think it is very important to relate to and understand the causes of the oppression of women and gay people. We can see that there are contradictions between the sexes and between homosexuals and heterosexuals, but we believe that these contradictions should be resolved within the community. Too often, so-called revolutionary vanguards have tried to resolve these contradictions by isolating women and gay people, and, of course, this only means that the revolutionary groups have cut themselves off from one of the most powerful and important forces among the people. We do not believe that the oppression of women or gays will end by the creation of separate communities for either group. We see that as an incorrect idea, just like the idea of a separate nation. If people want to do it, all right; but it won't solve their problems. So we try to show people the correct way to resolve these problems: the vanguard has to include all the people and understand their defects.

on the defection of Eldridge Cleaver from the Black Panther Party and the defection of the Black Panther Party from the Black community: April 17, 1971

The Black Panther Party bases its ideology and philosophy on a concrete analysis of concrete conditions, using dialectical materialism as our analytical method. As dialectical materialists we recognize that contradictions can lead to development. The internal struggle of opposites based upon their unity causes matter to have motion as a part of the process of development. We recognize that nothing in nature stands outside of dialectics, even the Black Panther Party. But we welcome these contradictions because they clarify and advance our struggle. We had a contradiction with our former Minister of Information, Eldridge Cleaver, but we understand this as necessary to our growth. Out of this contradiction has come new growth and a return to the original vision of the Party.

Early in the development of the Black Panther Party I wrote an essay titled "The Correct Handling of a Revolution." This was in response to another contradiction: the criticisms raised against the Party by the Revolutionary Action Movement (RAM). At that time RAM criticized us for our aboveground action: openly displaying weapons and talking about the necessity for the community to arm itself for its own self-defense. RAM said that they were underground and saw this as the correct way to handle a revolution. I responded to them by pointing out that you must establish your organization aboveground so that the people can relate to it in a way that will be positive and progressive for them. When you go underground without doing this you bury yourself so deeply that the people can neither relate to nor contact you. Then the terrorism of the underground organization will be just that—striking fear into the hearts of the very people whose interest the organization claims to be defending because the people cannot relate to them and there is nobody there to interpret their actions. You have to set up a program of practical action and be a model for the community to follow and appreciate.

The original vision of the Party was to develop a lifeline to the people by serving their needs and defending them against their oppressors, who come to the community in many forms, from armed police to capitalist exploiters. We knew that this strategy would raise the consciousness of the people and also give us their support. Then, if we were driven underground by the oppressors the people would support us and defend us. They would know that in spite of the oppressors' interpretations our only desire was to serve their true interests, and they would defend us. In this manner we might be forced underground but there would be a lifeline to the community that would always sustain us because the people would identify with us and not with our common enemy.

For a time the Black Panther Party lost its vision and defected from the community. With the defection of Eldridge Cleaver, however, we can move again to a full-scale development of our original vision, and come out of the twilight zone which the Party has been in during the recent past.

The only reason that the Party is still in existence at this time, the only reason that we have been able to survive the repression of the Party and the murder of some of our most advanced comrades, is because of the Ten-Point Program—our survival program. Our programs would be meaningless and insignificant if they were not community programs. This is why it is my opinion that as long as the Black community and oppressed people are found in North America, the Black Panther Party will last. The Party will survive as a structured vehicle because it serves the true interests of oppressed people and administers to their needs. This was the original vision of the Party. The original vision was not structured by rhetoric nor by ideology but by the practical needs of the people. And its dreamers were armed with an ideology that provided a systematic method of analysis of how best to meet those needs.

When Bobby Seale and I came together to launch the Black Panther Party, we had observed many groups. Most of them were so dedicated to rhetoric and artistic rituals that they had withdrawn from living in the twentieth century. Sometimes their analyses were beautiful but they had no practical programs that would translate these understandings to the people. When they did try to develop practical programs, they often failed because they lacked a systematic ideology which would help them make concrete analyses of concrete conditions and gain a full understanding of the community and its needs. When I was in Donald Warden's Afro-American Association, I watched him try to make a reality of community control through Black capitalism. But Warden did not have a systematic ideology, and his attempts to initiate his program continually frustrated him and the community. They did not know why capitalism would not work for them since it had worked for other ethnic groups.

When we formed the Party, we did so because we wanted to put theory and practice together in a systematic manner. We did this through our basic Ten-Point Program. In actuality it was a Twenty-Point Program, with the practice expressed in "What We Want," and the theory expressed in "What We Believe." This program was designed to serve as a basis for a structured political vehicle.

The actions we engaged in at that time were strictly strategic actions for political purposes. They were designed to mobilize the community. Any action which does not mobilize the community toward the goal is not a revolutionary action. The action might be a marvelous statement of courage, but if it does not mobilize the people toward the goal of a higher manifestation of freedom it is not making a political statement and could even be counterrevolutionary.

We realized at a very early point in our development that *revolution is a process*. It is not a particular action, nor is it a conclusion. It is a process. This is why when feudalistic slavery wiped out chattel slavery, feudalism was revolutionary. This is why when capitalism wiped out feudalism, capitalism was revolutionary. The concrete analysis of concrete conditions will reveal the true nature of the situation and increase our understanding. This process moves in a dialectical manner and we understand the struggle of the opposites based upon their unity.

Many times people say that our Ten-Point Program is reformist, but they ignore the fact that revolution is a process. We left the program open-ended so that it could develop and people could identify with it. We did not offer it to them as a conclusion, we offered it as a vehicle to move them to a higher level. In their quest for freedom and in their attempts to prevent the oppressor from stripping them of all the things they need to exist, the people see things as moving from A to B to C; they do not see things as moving from A to Z. In other words, they have to see first some basic accomplishments in order to realize that major successes are possible. Much of the time the revolutionary will have to guide them into this understanding, but he can never take them from A to Z in one jump because it is too far ahead. Therefore, when the revolutionary begins to indulge in Z, or final conclusions, the people do not relate to him. Therefore he is no longer a revolutionary if revolution is a process. This makes any action or function which does not promote the process non-revolutionary.

When the Party went to Sacramento, when the Party faced down the policemen in front of the office of *Ramparts* magazine, and when the Party patrolled the police with arms, we were acting at a time (1966) when the people had given up the philosophy of non-violent direct action and were beginning to deal with sterner stuff. We wanted them to see the virtues of disciplined and organized armed self-defense rather than spontaneous and disorganized outbreaks and riots. There were police-alert patrols all over the country, but we were the first *armed* police patrol. We called ourselves the Black Panther Party for Self-Defense. In all of this we had political and revolutionary objectives in mind, but we knew that we could not succeed without the support of the people.

Our strategy was based on a consistent ideology, which helped us to understand the conditions around us. We knew that the law was not prepared for what we were doing and policemen were so shocked that they didn't know what to do. We saw that the people felt a new pride and strength because of the example we set for them, and they began to look toward the vehicle we were building for answers.

Later we dropped the term "Self-Defense" from our name and just became the Black Panther Party. We discouraged actions like Sacramento and police observations because we recognized that these were not the things to do in every situation or on every occasion. We never called these revolutionary actions. The only time an action is revolutionary is when the people relate to it in a revolutionary way. If they will not use the example you set, then no matter how many guns you have your action is not revolutionary.

The gun itself is not necessarily revolutionary because the fascists carry guns, in fact they have more guns. A lot of so-called revolutionaries simply do not understand the statement by Chairman Mao that "Political power grows out of the barrel of a gun." They thought Chairman Mao said political power *is* the gun, but the emphasis is on "grows." The culmination of political power is the ownership and control of the land and the institutions thereon so that we can then get rid of the gun. That is why Chairman Mao makes the statement that "We are advocates of the abolition of war, we do not want war; but war can only be abolished through war, and in order to get rid of the gun, it is necessary to take up the gun." He is always speaking of getting rid of it. If he did not look at it in those terms, then he surely would not be revolutionary. In other words, the gun by all revolutionary principles is a tool to be used in our strategy; it is not an end in itself. This was a part of the original vision of the Black Panther Party.

I had asked Eldridge Cleaver to join the Party a number of times. But he did not join until after the confrontation with the police in front of the office of *Ramparts* magazine, where the police were afraid to go for their guns. Without my knowledge, he took this as *the* Revolution and *the* Party. But in our basic program it was not until Point 7 that we mentioned the gun, and this was intentional. We were trying to build a political vehicle through which the people could express their revolutionary desires. We recognized that no party or organization can make the revolution, only the people can. All we could do was act as a guide to the people because revolution is a process that moves in a dialectical manner. At one point one thing might be proper, but the same action could be improper at another point. *We always emphasized a concrete analysis of conditions*, and then an appropriate response to these conditions as a way of mobilizing the people and leading them to higher levels of consciousness.

People constantly thought that we were security guards or community police. This is why we dropped the term "Self-Defense" from our name and directed the attention of the people to the fact that the only way *they* would get salvation was through *their* control of the institutions that serve the community. This would require that they organize a political vehicle which would keep their support and endorsement through its survival programs of service. They would look to it for answers and guidance. It would not be an organization that runs candidates for political office, but it would serve as a watchman over the administrators whom the people have placed in office.

Because the Black Panther Party grows out of the conditions and needs of oppressed people *we are interested in everything the people are interested in*, even though we may not see these particular concerns as the final answers to our problems. We will never run for political office, but we will endorse and support those candidates who are acting in the true interest of the people. We may even provide campaign workers for them and do voter-registration and basic precinct work. This would not be out of a commitment to electoral politics; however, it would be our way of bringing the will of the people to bear on situations in which they are interested. We will also hold such candidates responsible to the community no matter how far removed their offices may be from the community. So we lead the people by following their interests, with a view toward raising their consciousness to see beyond limited goals.

When Eldridge joined the Party it was after the police confrontation, which left him fixated with the "either-or" attitude. This was that either the community picked up the gun with the Party or else they were cowards and there was no place for them. He did not realize that if the people did not relate to the Party then there was no way that the Black Panther Party could make any revolution, for the record shows that the people are the makers of the revolution and of world history.

Sometimes there are those who express personal problems in political terms, and if they are eloquent then these personal problems can sound very political. We charge Eldridge Cleaver with this. Much of it is probably beyond his control because it is so personal. But we did not know that when he joined the Party; he was doing so only because of that act in front of *Ramparts*. We weren't trying to prove anything to ourselves. All we were trying to do, at that particular point, was to defend Betty Shabazz. But we were praised by the people.

Under the influence of Eldridge Cleaver the Party gave the community no alternative for dealing with us except by picking up the gun. This move was reactionary simply because the community was not prepared to do that at that point. Instead of being a cultural cult group we became, by that act, a revolutionary cult group. But this is a basic contradiction because revolution is a process and if the acts you commit do not fall within the scope of the process then they are non-revolutionary.

What the revolutionary movement and the Black community need is a very strong structure. This structure can only exist with the support of the people and it can only get its support through serving them. This is why we have the Service to the People Program—the most important thing in the Party. We will serve their needs so that they can survive through this oppression. Then when they are ready to pick up the gun, serious business will happen. Eldridge Cleaver influenced us to isolate ourselves from the Black community so that it was war between the oppressor and the Black Panther Party, not war between the oppressor and the oppressed community.

The Black Panther Party defected from the community long before Eldridge defected from the Party. Our hook-up with White radicals did not give us access to the White community because they do not guide the White community. The Black community does not relate to them, so we were left in a twilight zone where we could not enter the Black community with any real political education programs; yet we were not doing anything to mobilize Whites. We had no influence in raising the consciousness of the Black community and that is the point where we defected.

We went through a free speech movement in the Party, which was unnecessary, and only further isolated us from the Black community. We had all sorts of profanity in our paper and every other word that dropped from our lips was profane. This did not happen before I was jailed because I would not stand for it, but Eldridge's influence brought it about. I do not blame him altogether; I blame the Party because the Party accepted it.

Eldridge was never fully in the leadership of the Party. Even after Bobby was snatched away from us, I did not place Eldridge in a position of leadership because he was not interested in that. I made David Hilliard administrator of programs. I knew that Eldridge would not do anything to lift the consciousness of the comrades in the Party, but I knew that he could make a contribution and I pressed him to do so. I pressed him to write and edit the paper, but he wouldn't. The paper did not even come out every week until after Eldridge went to jail. But Eldridge Cleaver did make great contributions to the Black Panther Party with his writing and speaking. We want to keep this in mind because there is a positive and negative side to everything.

The correct handling of a revolution is not to offer the people an "either-or" ultimatum. Instead we must gain the support of the people through serving their needs. Then when the police or any other agency of repression tries to destroy the program, the people will move to a higher level of consciousness and action. Then the organized structure can guide the people to the point where they are prepared to deal in many ways. This was the strategy we used in 1966 when the people related to us in a positive way.

So the Black Panther Party has reached a contradiction with Eldridge Cleaver, and he has defected from the Party because we would not order everyone into the streets tomorrow to make a revolution. We recognize that this is impossible because our dialectical ideology and our analysis of concrete conditions indicate that declaring a spontaneous revolution is a fantasy. The people are not at that point now. This contradiction and conflict may seem unfortunate to some, but it is a part of the dialectical process. The resolution of this contradiction has freed us from incorrect analyses and emphases.

We are now free to move toward the building of a *community structure* that will become a true voice of the people, promoting their interests in many ways. We can continue to push our basic survival programs, we can continue to serve the people as advocates of their true interests, we can truly become a political revolutionary vehicle which will lead the people to a higher level of consciousness so that they will know what they must really do in their quest for freedom. Then they will have the courage to adopt any means necessary to seize the time and obtain that freedom.

statement: May 1, 1971

The original vision of the Black Panther Party was to serve the needs of the oppressed people in our communities and defend them against their oppressors. When the Party was initiated we knew that these goals would raise the consciousness of the people and motivate them to move more firmly for their total liberation. We also recognized that we live in a country which has become one of the most repressive governments in the world; repressive in communities all over the world. We did not expect such a repressive government to stand idly by while the Black Panther Party went forward to the goal of serving the people. We expected repression.

We knew, as a revolutionary vanguard, repression would be the reaction of our oppressors, but we recognized that the task of the revolutionist is difficult and his life is short. We were prepared then, as we are now, to give our all in the interest of oppressed people. We expected the repression to come from outside forces which have long held our communities in subjection. However, the ideology of dialectical materialism helped us to understand that the contradictions surrounding the Party would create a force that would move us toward our goals. We also expected contradictions within the Party, for the oppressors use infiltrators and provocateurs to help them reach their evil ends. Even when the contradictions come from formerly loyal members of the Party, we see them as part of the process of development rather than in the negative terms the oppressors' media use to interpret them. Above all we knew that through it all the Party would survive.

The Party would survive because it had the love and support of the people who saw their true interests expressed in the actions of the Party.

The Party would also survive because it would be a political vehicle which continued to voice the interests of the people and serve as their advocates.

The importance of a structured political vehicle has always been apparent to us. When we went to Sacramento, we went for the purpose of educating the people and building of a permanent political vehicle to serve their true interests. In our most recent communication with both the North and South Vietnamese Revolutionary governments, they pointed out that they understood what we were doing and saw it as the correct strategy. They said that a "structured organization is related to politics as a shadow to a man." We recognize that the political machine in America has consistently required Black people to support it through paying taxes and fighting in wars, but that same machine consistently refuses to serve the interests of the Black community. One of the problems is that the community does not have a structured organization or vehicle which serves its needs and represents the people's interest. You can no more have effective politics without a structured organization than you can have a man without his shadow. Oppressed Black people—*the lumpen proletariat*—did not have a structured organization to represent their true interests until the Black Panther Party arose from within the community, motivated by the needs and conditions of the people.

Across the country there have been coalitions of Black people and Black caucuses, but these have not served the people as political vehicles. They have merely served as bourgeois structures to get Black candidates into political office. Once elected, the machinery used to thrust these people into office simply passed out of existence or became ineffective insofar as serving the true interests of the Black oppressed people.

A truly revolutionary vehicle which will survive the repression it encounters daily is made up of a number of characteristics. First of all, there is a small but dedicated *cadre of workers who are willing to devote their full time to the goals of the organization*. Secondly, there is a distinct *organized structure through which the cadre can function*. It is this combination of structure and dedicated cadre which can maintain the machinery for meeting the peoples' needs. In this way a printing press can be maintained to review the events of the day and interpret them in a manner which serves the people. Information can be circulated about daily phenomena to inform the people of their true meaning. Programs of service can be carried out to deliver to the people the basic needs that are not met elsewhere because the lumpen proletariat are the victims of oppression and exploitation. A cadre and a structure, however, are not what make the political vehicle a revolutionary one. It is the revolutionary concepts which define and interpret phenomena, and establish the goals toward which the political vehicle will work. A revolutionary vehicle is in fact a revolutionary concept set into motion by a dedicated cadre through a particular organized structure.

Such a vehicle can survive repression because it can move in the necessary manner at the appropriate time. It can go underground if the conditions require, and it can rise up again. But it will always be motivated by love and dedication to the interests of the oppressed communities. Therefore the people will insure its survival, for only in that survival are their needs serviced. The structured and organized vehicle will guarantee the weathering of the test of internal and external contradictions.

The responsibility of such a political vehicle is clear. It is to function as a machine which serves the true interests of the oppressed people. This means that it must be ever aware of the needs of the communities of the oppressed and develop and execute the necessary programs to meet those needs. The Black Panther Party has done this through its basic Ten-Point Program. However, we recognize that *revolution is a process and we cannot offer the people conclusions*—we must be ready to respond creatively to new conditions and new understandings. Therefore, we have developed our Free Breakfast Program, our Free Health Clinics, our Clothing and Shoe Programs, and our Buses to Prisons Program as well as others, responding to the obvious needs of Black people. The overwhelmingly favorable response to these programs in every community is evidence that they are serving the true interests of the people.

Serving the true interests of the people also means that the political vehicle must stand between the people and the oppressive forces which prey upon them in such a manner that the administrators will have to give the appropriate response. Such articulation requires us to have a political organ which will express the interests of the people and interpret phenomena for them. Again, the existence of such a political vehicle is justified only so long as it serves the true interests of the people.

Serving the true interests of the people, however, does not mean that the vehicle is simply a reflector of public opinion, for the opinions of the people have often been molded and directed against their true interests by slick politicians and exploitative educators. Their diversion tactics often lead the people down blind alleys or onto tangents which take them away from their true goals. We can easily see this when we apply the concept of American democracy to the Black community.

Democracy in America (bourgeois democracy) means nothing more than the domination of the majority over the minority. That is why Black people can cast votes all year long but if the majority is against us, we suffer. Then the politicians and educators try to deceive the community with statements such as "It's rule by the majority, but the rights of the minority are protected." If, in fact, participating in the democratic process in America were in the interest of the Black community there would be no need for a Free Breakfast Program, there would be no need for Free Health Clinics or any of the other programs we have developed to meet the people's needs. The rights of the minority are "protected" by the standards of a bourgeois government, and anything which is not in their interest is not permitted. This may be democratic for the majority, but for the minority it has the same effect as fascism. When the majority decreed that we should be slaves, we were slaves—where was the democracy in slavery for us? When the majority decreed that we should pay taxes, fight and die in wars, and be given inferior and racist education against our interests, we got all of these things. Where is democracy for us in any of that? Our children still die, our youth still suffer from malnutrition, our middle-aged people still suffer from sickle-cell anemia, and our elderly still face unbearable poverty and hardship because they reach the twilight period of their lives with nothing to sustain them through these difficult times. Where is the democracy in any of this for Black people? Democracy means only that the majority will use us when they need us and cast us aside when they do not need us. A true understanding of the working and effect of American democracy for Black people will reveal most clearly that it is just the same as fascism for us. Our true interests and needs are not being served.

The political vehicle of the people must be guided by a consistent ideology which represents nothing more than a systematic and organized set of principles for analyzing and interpreting objective phenomena. An ideology can only be accepted as valid if it delivers a true understanding of the phenomena that affect the lives of the people. The development of a wide variety of truths about the community, its internal development, and the external forces surrounding it will lead then to a philosophy that will help orient us toward goals that are in the true interests of the people.

The Black Panther Party was born in a period of stress when Black people were moving away from the philosophy and strategy of non-violent action toward sterner actions. We dared to believe that we could offer the community a permanent political vehicle which would serve their needs and advocate their interests. We have met many foes; we have seen many enemies. We have been slandered, kidnapped, gagged, jailed, and murdered. We know now, more than ever before, that the will of the people is greater than the technology and repression of those who are against the interests of the people. Therefore we know that we can and will continue to serve and educate the people.

on the relevance of the church: May 19, 1971

Since 1966 the Black Panther Party has gone through many changes; it has been transformed. I would like to talk to you about that and about contradictions. I would also like to talk about the Black Panther Party's relationship with the community as a whole and with the church in particular.

Some time ago when the Party started, Bobby and I were interested in strengthening the Black community—rather its comprehensive set of institutions because if there's one thing we lack it is community. We do have one institution that has been around for some time and that is the church. After a short harmonious relationship with the church, in fact a very good relationship, we were divorced from the church, and shortly after that found ourselves out of favor with the whole Black community.

We found ourselves in somewhat of a void alienated from the whole community. We had no way of being effective as far as developing the community was concerned. The only way we could aid in that process of revolution—and revolution is a process rather than conclusion or a set of principles, or any particular action—was by raising the consciousness of the community. Any conclusion or particular action that we think *is* revolution is really reaction, for revolution is a developmental process. It has a forward thrust which goes higher and higher as man becomes freer and freer. As man becomes freer he knows more about the universe, he tends to control more and he therefore gains more control over himself. That is what freedom is all about.

I want now to talk about the mistakes that were made. I hate to

214

call them mistakes because maybe they were necessary to bring about change in the Party, the needed transformation. I am sure that we will have other kinds of contradictions in the future, some that we don't know about now. I am sure they will build up and hurl us into a new thing.

But the church also has been going through phases of development. It too has found itself somewhat isolated from the community. Today, the church is striving to get back into favor with the community. Like the church the Black Panther Party is also trying to reinstate itself with the community.

A short time ago there was an article in the Black Panther paper called "The Defection of Eldridge Cleaver from the Black Panther Party and the Defection of the Black Panther Party from the Black Community." I would like to concentrate now upon the defection of the Party. That is, the larger unit. I hate to place blame upon individuals in our Party particularly since they are always governed by a collective called the Central Committee. Even when I disagree with the Central Committee (and I did much disagreeing and arguing when I was in prison, but I was out-voted), after the vote I supported the position of the Party until the next meeting.

I think, at first, that we have to have some organized apparatus in order to bring about the necessary change. The only time we leave our political machine or our institution altogether is when we feel that we cannot bring about the necessary change through the machine, and the very posture of the organization or the institution will strip us of our individual dignity. I felt that this was true of the Party, and although it could be argued, *I personally thought that the Party should still be held together*. I knew if I left we would have to form a new Party, a new institution, in order to be that spur or that guiding light in the community. Also I would have to contend with new contradictions.

We always say that contradictions are the ruling principle of the universe. I use that word time and time again because I think that it is responsible for much suffering. When things collide they hurt, but collision is also responsible for development. Without contradictions everything would be stagnant. Everything has an internal contradiction, including the church.

Contradiction, or the strain of the lesser to subdue that which controls it, gives motion to matter. We see this throughout the universe in the physical as well as the biological world. We also see this in cultures. Development comes with the phenomenon we call acculturation. That is, two societies meet and when their cultures collide because they have a contradiction, both are modified. The stronger shows less change and the weaker more change. All the time the weaker is attempting to gain dominance over the stronger. But something happens, they both will never be the same again because they have reached a degree of synthesis. In other words, it is all working toward the truth of the trinity: thesis, anti-thesis, synthesis. This principle of contradiction, this striving for harmony, operates in all of our disciplines.

The Black Panther Party was formed because we wanted to oppose the evil in our community. Some of the members in the Party were not refined—we were grasping for organization. It wasn't a college campus organization; it was basically an organization of the grass roots, and any time we organize the most victimized of the victims we run into a problem. To have a Party or a church or any kind of institution, whether we like it or not, we have to have administrators. How an institution, organization, or the Party in this case, functions, as well as how effective it is, depends upon how knowledgeable and advanced in thinking the administrators are. We attempt to apply the administrative skills of our grass-roots organization to the problems that are most frequently heard in the community.

History shows that most of the parties that have led people out of their difficulties have had administrators with what we sometimes call the traits of the bourgeoisie or declassed intellectuals. They are the people who have gone through the established institutions, rejected them, and then applied their skills to the community. In applying them to the community, their skills are no longer bourgeoisie skills but people's skills, which are transformed through the contradiction of applying what is usually bourgeoisie to the oppressed. That itself is a kind of transformation.

In our Party we are not so blessed. History does not repeat itself; it goes on also transforming itself through its dialectical process. We see that the administrators of our Party are victims who have not received that bourgeois training. So I will not apologize for our mistakes, our lack of a scientific approach to use and put into practice. It was a matter of not knowing, of learning, but also of starting out with a loss—a disadvantage that history has seldom seen. That is, a group attempting to influence and change the society so much while its own administrators were as much in the dark much of the time as the people that they were trying to change. In our Party we have now what we call the Ideological Institute, where we are teaching these skills, and we also invite those people who have received a bourgeois education to come and help us. However, we let them know that they will, by their contribution, make their need to exist, as they exist now, null and void. In other words, after we learn the skills their bourgeois status will evaporate once the skills have been applied.

As far as the church was concerned, the Black Panther Party and other community groups emphasized the political and criticized the spiritual. We said the church is only a ritual, it is irrelevant, and therefore we will have nothing to do with it. We said this in the context of the whole community being involved with the church on one level or another. That is one way of defecting from the community, and that is exactly what we did. Once we stepped outside of the church with that criticism, we stepped outside of the whole thing that the community was involved in and we said, "You follow our example; your reality is not true and you don't need it."

Now, without judging whether the church is operating in a total reality, I will venture to say that if we judge whether the church is relevant to the *total* community we would all agree that it is not. That is why it develops new programs to become more relevant so the pews will be filled on Sunday.

The church is in its developmental process, and we believe it needs to exist. We believe this as a result of our new direction (which is an old direction as far as I am concerned, but we'll call it new because there has been a reversal in the dominance in the Central Committee of our Party for reasons that you probably know about). So we do go to church, are involved in the church, and not in any hypocritical way. Religion, perhaps, is a thing that man needs at this time because scientists cannot answer all of the questions. As far as I am concerned, when all of the questions are not answered, when the extraordinary is not explained, when the unknown is not known, then there is room for God because the unexplained and the unknown is God. We know nothing about God, really, and that is why as soon as the scientist develops or points out a new way of controlling a part of the universe, that aspect of the universe is no longer God. In other words, once when the thunder crashed it was God clapping His hands together. As soon as we found out that thunder was not God, we said that God has other attributes but not *that* one. In that way we took for ourselves what was His before. But we still haven't answered all of the questions, so He still exists. And those scientists who say they can answer all of them are dishonest.

We go into the church realizing that we cannot answer the questions at this time, that the answers will be delivered eventually, and we feel that when they are delivered they will be explained in a way that we can understand and control.

I went to church for years. My father is a minister and I spent 15 years in the church; this was my life as a child. When I was going to church I used to hear that God is within us and is, therefore, some part of us: that part of us that is mystical. And as man develops and understands more, he will approach God, and finally reach heaven and merge with the universe. I've never heard one preacher say that there is a need for the church in heaven; the church would negate itself. As man approaches his development and becomes larger and larger, the church therefore becomes smaller and smaller because it is not needed any longer. Then if we had ministers who would deal with the social realities that cause misery so that we can change them, man will become larger and larger. At that time the God within will come out, and we can merge with Him. Then we will be one with the universe.

So I think it was rather arrogant of my Party to criticize the community for trying to discover answers to spiritual questions. The only thing we will criticize in the future is when the church does not act upon the evils that cause man to get on his knees and humble himself in awe at that large force which he cannot control. But as man becomes stronger and stronger, and his understanding greater and greater, he will have "a closer walk with Thee." *Note the song says walk— not crawl.*

So along with the church we will all start again to control our lives and communities. Even with the Black church we have to create a community spirit. We say that the church is an institution, but it is not a community. The sociological definition of a community is a comprehensive *collection* of institutions that delivers our whole life, and within which we can reach most of our goals. We create it in order to carry out our desires and it serves us. In the Black community the church is an institution that we created (that we were allowed to create). The White church warred against us, but finally we won the compromise to worship as a unit, as a people, concerned with satisfying our own needs. The White church was not satisfying our needs in human terms because it felt that we were not human beings. So we formed our own. Through that negative thing a positive thing evolved. We started to organize fraternities, anti-lynching groups, and so forth, but they still would not let our community exist. We came here in chains and I guess they thought we were meant to stay in chains. But we have begun to organize a political machine, to develop a community so that we can have an apparatus to fight back. You cannot fight back individually against an organized machine. We will work with the church to establish a community, which will satisfy most of our needs so that we can live and operate as a group.

The Black Panther Party, with its survival programs, plans to develop the institutions in the community. We have a clothing factory we are just erecting on Third Street, where we will soon give away about three hundred to four hundred new articles of clothing each month. And we can do this by robbing Peter to pay Paul. What we will do is start to make golfing bags under contract to a company, and with the surplus we will buy material to make free clothes. Our members will do this. We will have no overhead because of our collective (we'll "exploit" our collective by making them work free). We will do this not just to satisfy ourselves, like the philanthropist, or to serve, or to save someone from going without shoes, even though this is a part of the cause of our problem, but to help the people make the revolution. We will give the process a forward thrust. If we suffer genocide we won't be around to change things. So in this way our survival program is very practical.

What we are concerned with is the larger problem. Therefore we will be honest and say that we will do like the churches—we will negate our necessity for existing. After we accomplish our goals the Black Panther Party will not need to exist because we will have already created our heaven right here on earth. What we are going to do is administer to the community the things they need in order to get their attention, in order to organize them into a political machine. The community will then look to the Party and look to those people who are serving their needs in order to give them guidance and direction, whether it is political, whether it is judicial, or whether it is economic.

Our real thing is to organize across the country. We have thirty-eight chapters and branches and I would like to inform you that the so-called split is only a myth, that it does not exist. We lost two chapters in that so-called split and I will tell you that the burden is off my shoulders. I was glad to lose them because it was a yoke for me; I was frozen. Even though I couldn't make a move I wouldn't get out of the whole thing then because certain people had such an influence over the Party. For me to have taken that stand would have been individualism. Now we're about three years behind in our five-year plan, but we will *now* move to organize the community around the *survival* programs.

We have a shoe factory that we're opening up on Fourteenth and Jefferson. The machines and everything else were donated. We'll use it to get inmates out of prison because most of us learned how to make shoes in prison. So it will serve two purposes: we can make positions in the shoe factory available and thereby get somebody out on parole; and since the parolees must agree to give a certain amount of shoes away each week, we will have a "right to wear shoes" program. We'll point out that everyone in the society should have shoes and we should not have a situation like the one in Beaufort County, South Carolina, where 70 percent of the children suffer brain damage because of malnutrition. They have malnutrition because of the combination of not enough food and parasites in the stomach. The worms eat up half the food that the children take in. Why? Because the ground is infested with the eggs of the worms and the children don't have shoes to wear. So as soon as we send a doctor there to cure them, they get the parasites again. We think that the shoe program is a very relevant thing, first to help them stay alive, then to create conditions in which they can grow up and work out a plan to change things. If they have brain damage, they will never be revolutionists because they will have already been killed. That is genocide in itself.

We will inform this government, this social order, that it must administer to its people because it is supposed to be a representative government which serves the needs of the people. Then serve them. If it does not do this then it should be criticized. What we will not do in the future is jump too far ahead and say that the system absolutely cannot give us anything. That is not true; the system can correct itself to a certain extent. What we are interested in is its correcting itself as much as it can. After that, if it doesn't do everything that the people think necessary, then we'll think about reorganizing things.

To be very honest I think there is great doubt whether the present system can do this. But until the people feel the same way I feel then I would be rather arrogant to say dump the whole thing, just as we were arrogant to say dump the church. Let's give it a chance, let's work with it in order to squeeze as many contributions and compromises out of all the institutions as possible, and then criticize them after the fact. We'll know when that time comes, when the people tell us so.

We have a program attempting to get the people to do all they will do. It is too much to ask the people to do all they can do even though they can do everything. But that is not the point. The point is how do we get them to do all they *will do* until they eventually get to the place where they will have to be doing all they can.

We organized the Party when we saw that growing out of the Movement was what was called a cultural cult group. We defined a cultural cult group as an organization that disguised itself as a political organization, but was really more interested in the cultural rituals of Africa in the 1100's before contact with the Europeans. Instead of administering to the community and organizing it, they would rather wear bubas, get African names and demand that the community do the same, and do nothing about the survival of the community. Sometimes they say, "Well, if we get our culture back then all things will be solved." This is like saying to be regenerated and born again is to solve everything. We know that this is not true.

Then the Party became just as closed as the cultural cultist group. Many churches are very reactionary and can be described as religious cults. They go through many rituals, but they're divorced from reality. Even though we have many things in common with them, we say they isolate themselves from reality because they're so miserable and reality is so hard to take. We know that operating within reality does not mean that we accept it; we're operating within it so that the reality can be changed. For what we did as revolutionists was abstract, and the people are always real. But we know that reality is changing all the time, and what we want to do is harness those forces that are causing the change to direct them to a desirable goal. In other words developments will continue, but we have no guarantee that they will be developments that allow man to live. We have no guarantee that the bomb won't be dropped, but we know that there are certain ways that we can plan for the new reality. In order to do this we have to take some control over the present. So the people who withdraw, like the religious cultist group, do the same thing as the cultural cultist group.

These are words that we have coined. The Panthers are always coining words because we have to keep defining the new reality, the new phenomena. The old words confuse us sometimes because things have changed so much. So we try to stay abreast by developing or stipulating definitions. The old lexical definitions become so outdated after the qualitative leap (the transformation) that it does not match at all what we are talking about now.

One new word related to what we have been talking about describes something I was guilty of. I was guilty of this when I offered the Black troops to Vietnam. I won't talk about whether it was morally right or wrong, but I will say that anything said or done by a revolutionist that does not spur or give the forward thrust to the process (of revolution) is wrong. Remember that the people are the makers of history, the people make everything in their society. They are the architects of the society and if you don't spur them on, then I don't care what phrases you use or whether they are political or religious, you cannot be classified as being relevant to that process. If you know you're wrong and do certain things anyway, then you're reactionary because you are very guilty. Some of us didn't know. I keep searching myself to see whether I knew we were going wrong. I couldn't influence the Central Committee and maybe I should have risked being charged with an individual violation and said that they didn't know. I think most of them didn't know, so they're not as guilty as I am. I'm probably more guilty than anyone. But anyway, the new word that describes what we went into for a short length of time—a couple of years—is revolutionary cultism.

The revolutionary cultist uses words of social change; he uses words about being interested in the development of society. He uses that ter-minology, you see; but his actions are so far divorced from the process of revolution and organizing the community that he is living in a fantasy world. So we talk to each other on the campuses, or we talk to each other in the secrecy of the night, concentrating upon weapons, thinking these things will produce change without the people themselves. Of course people do courageous things and call themselves the vanguard, but the people who do things like that are either heroes or criminals. They are not the vanguard because the vanguard means spearhead, and the spearhead has to spearhead something. If nothing is behind it, then it is divorced from the masses and is not the vanguard.

I am going to be heavily criticized now by the revolutionary cultists and probably criticized even more in the future because I view the process as going in stages. I feel that we can't jump from A to Z, we have to go through all of the development. So even though I see a thing is not the answer, I don't think it's dishonest to involve myself in it for the simple reason that the people tend to take not one step higher; they take a half step higher. Then they hang on to what they view as the reality because they can't see that reality is constantly changing. When they finally see the changes (qualitatively) they don't know why or how it happened. Part of the reason reality changes around them is because they are there; they participate whether they like it or not.

What we will do now is involve ourselves in any thing or any stage of development in the community, support that development, and try to introduce some insight into it. Then we will work very hard with the people in the community and with this institution so that it can negate itself. We will be honest about this and we hope they are honest too and realize that everything is negated eventually; this is how we go on to higher levels.

I was warned when I got up here that it would be appropriate to have a question-and-answer period, so I guess we should start now because I'm subject to go on and on.

•••

Question: I would like to know in your re-evaluation of your former stance in relationship to the community, in what ways do you expect to merge or bring together the community of the Catholic Church into the Black Panther Party?

Newton: First, we can't change the realities, direct them, or harness their forces until we know them. We have to gather information. We can gather information about the church by experiencing the church. As a matter of fact this is how we gain facts: through empirical evidence, observation, and experience. In order to do this we have to go to the church. You see, the only laboratory in society we have is the community itself, and we view ourselves not only as scientists but also as activists.

Now we say we try to merge theory with practice, so we're going to churches now. I went to church last week for the first time in ten years, I guess. We took our children with us. We have a youth institute, the Samuel Napier Youth Institute. We have about thirty children now and we took them to church and involved ourselves. We plan to involve ourselves in many community activities, going through the behavior the church goes through in order to contribute to the community. We also hope to influence the church, as I'm sure the church will influence us. Remember that we said that even when whole societies and cultures meet they are both modified by each other. And I am saying that the very fact that we're there is the new ingredient in the church, and we know that we will be affected and hope that they will be affected. But I warn you that we hope to have more effect than they.

Just briefly I mentioned our Youth Institute. We have children from three to fourteen years old; most of them have already been kicked out of schools and we have a shortage of facilities because the hardcore Black community is just an aggregate now. People who happen to be Black.

We are teaching them first what I mentioned earlier, bourgeois skills. It is necessary for us to learn these skills in order to understand the phenomena around us, the society. On the other hand, we don't like the way the skills have been used, so we're going to use them a different way. Thirdly, our children are not going to withdraw. I don't like parochial schools; I don't like separate schools, but I think that sometimes you have to use that strategy. For example, the Black Panther Party is a Black organization. We know that we live in a world of many cultures and ethnic groups and we all interconnect in one way or another. We say that we are the contradiction to the reactionary Western values, but we cannot separate because we're here. Technology is too far advanced for us to isolate ourselves in any geographical location—the jet can get there too fast and so can the early-bird TV set—so what we have to do is share the control of these devices.

So far as our children are concerned, the only reason they are at this separate school is because the public schools were not giving them the correct education. They can hardly learn to read and write. I don't want them to end up as I did: I only learned how to read after I was seventeen and that must not happen to them. I've only been reading for about ten years or so and that is not very good—I still don't read very well. Our plan is not to have our children graduate from our school and live in a fantasy. Our effort is to keep them in there just as long as it will take for them to organize the school and make it relevant. In other words we are going to send them back into the wilderness, but we're going to send them with their purse and their scribes with them this time.

When David Hilliard spoke to the National Committee of Black Churchmen that met in Berkeley, he called the preachers who were gathered there a bunch of bootlicking pimps and motherfuckers, a comment that never should have been made public anyway. And he threatened that if the preachers did not come around that the Panthers would "off" some of the preachers. If you're not able to influence the Black church as much as you think, will the Panther Party return to this particular stance?

The Black Panther Party will not take the separate individual stand. We'll only take the stand of the community because we're interested in what the community will do to liberate themselves. We will not be arrogant and we would not have the most rudimentary knowledge if we did not know that we alone cannot bring about change. It was very wrong and almost criminal for some people in the Party to make the mistake to think that the Black Panther Party could overthrow even the police force. It ended up with the war between the police and the Panthers, and if there is a war it needs to be between the community and the reactionary establishment, or else we are isolating ourselves.

As for what David Hilliard said, what he did was alienate you. That kind of alienation put us in a void where blood was spilled from one end of this country to the other, our blood, while the community watched. Our help watched on, you see? But it was more our fault than theirs because we were out there saying that we were going to lead them into a change. But we cannot lead them into a change if they will not go. As a matter of fact, we cannot exist individually if we don't band together to resist the genocide against all of us. So just as I criticize David Hilliard, I criticize myself, because I knew that stuff was going on and I argued against it, but I didn't leave the Party. Finally the change came about.

And so what I am saying is that I understand, and the reason that I didn't leave was that it wasn't an outrage to my humanity, even though I cringed every time. Because I understood that he did it not out of hatred, but love. He did it because he was outraged by the church's inactivity, as you are outraged (not you personally, but you in the plural) at this situation, and he was outraged, of course, because of your isolation. So we are all in the same boat; and when we end up in the same boat that means we are unified.

Black capitalism re-analyzed I: June 5, 1971

This is a dialogue in our continuing discussion of the new thrust of the Black Panther Party, as we begin to carry out the original vision of the Party. When we coined the expression "All Power to the People," we had in mind emphasizing the word "Power," for we recognize that the *will to power is the basic drive of man.* But it is incorrect to seek power over people. We have been subjected to the dehumanizing power of exploitation and racism for hundreds of years; and the Black community has its own will to power also. What we seek, however, is not power over people, but the power to control our own destiny. For us the true definition of power is not in terms of how many people you can control. To us power is, first of all, the ability to define phenomena, and secondly the ability to make these phenomena act in a desired manner.

We see then that power has a dual character and that we cannot simply identify and define phenomena without acting, for to do so is to become an armchair philosopher. And when Bobby and I left Merritt College to organize brothers on the block we did so because the college students were too content to sit around and analyze without acting. On the other hand, power includes action, for it is making phenomena perform in the desired manner. But action without thinking and theory is also incorrect. If the social forces at work in the community have not been correctly analyzed and defined, how can you control them in such a way that they act in a desired manner? So the Black Panther Party has always merged theory and practice in such a way as to serve the true interests of the community.

In merging theory with practice we recognized that it was necessary to develop a theory which was valid for more than *one* time and place. We wanted to develop a system of thinking which was good anywhere, thus it had to be rather abstract. Yet our theory would relate to a concrete analysis of concrete conditions so that our actions would always be relevant and profitable to the people. Yet, at the same time, it had to advance their thinking so that they would move toward a transformation of their situation of exploitation and oppression. We have always insisted on good theory and good practice, but we have not always been successful in carrying this through.

When the Black Panther Party defected from the Black community, we became, for a while, revolutionary cultists. One of the primary characteristics of a revolutionary cultist is that he despises everyone who has not reached his level of consciousness, or the level of consciousness that he thinks he has reached, instead of acting to bring the people to that level. In that way the revolutionary cultist becomes divided from the people, he defects from the community. Instead of serving the people as a vanguard, he becomes a hero. Heroes engage in very courageous actions sometimes, and they often make great sacrifices, including the supreme sacrifice, but they are still isolated from the people. Their courageous actions and sacrifices do not lead the people to a higher level of consciousness, nor do they produce fundamental changes in the exploitation and oppression of the people. A vanguard, however, will guide the people onto higher levels of consciousness and in that way bring them to the point where they will take sterner actions in their own interests and against those who continue to oppress them. As I've said previously, revolution is a process, not a conclusion. A true revolutionist will not only take courageous actions, he will also try to advance the people in such a manner that they will transform their situation. That is, by delivering power to the people the true revolutionist will help them define the social phenomena in their community and lead them to the point where they will seize the time and make these phenomena act in a desired manner.

Therefore, as revolutionaries we must recognize the difference between what the people can do and what they will do. They can do anything they desire to do, but they will only take those actions which are consistent with their level of consciousness and their understanding of the situation. When we raise their consciousness, they will understand even more fully what they in fact can do, and they will move on the situation in a courageous manner. This is merging your theory with your practices.

Point 3 of the original Ten-Point Program of the Black Panther Party is "We want an end to the robbery by the CAPITALISTS of our Black Community." *That was our position in October 1966 and it is still our position.* We recognize that capitalism is no solution to the problems we face in our communities. Capitalist exploitation is one of the basic causes of our problem. It is the goal of the Black Panther Party to negate capitalism in our communities and in the oppressed communities throughout the world.

However, many people have offered the community Black capitalism as a solution to our problems. We recognize that people in the Black community have no general dislike for the concept of Black capitalism, but this is not because they are in love with capitalism. Not at all. The idea of Black capitalism has come to mean to many people Black control of another one of the institutions in the community. We see within this characteristic the seeds of the negation of Black capitalism and all capitalism in general. What we must do then is increase the positive qualities until they dominate the negative and therefore transform the situation.

In the past the Black Panther Party took a counterrevolutionary position with our blanket condemnation of Black capitalism. Our strategy should have been to analyze the positive and negative qualities of this phenomenon before making any condemnation. Even though we recognized, and correctly so, that capitalism is no solution or answer, we did not make a truly dialectical analysis of the situation.

We recognized that in order to bring the people to the level of consciousness where they would seize the time, it would be necessary to serve their interests in survival by developing programs which would help them to meet their daily needs. For a long time we have had such programs not only for survival but for organizational purposes. Now we not only have a breakfast program for schoolchildren, we have clothing programs, we have health clinics which provide free medical and dental services, we have programs for prisoners and their families, and we are opening clothing and shoe factories to provide for more of the needs of the community. Most recently we have begun a testing and research program on sickle-cell anemia, and we know that 98 percent of the victims of this disease are Black. To fail to combat this disease is to submit to genocide; to battle it is survival.

All these programs satisfy the deep needs of the community but they are not solutions to our problems. That is why we call them survival programs, meaning survival pending revolution. We say that the survival program of the Black Panther Party is like the survival kit of a sailor stranded on a raft. It helps him to sustain himself until he can get completely out of that situation. So the survival programs are not answers or solutions, but they will help us to organize the community around a true analysis and understanding of their situation. When consciousness and understanding is raised to a high level then the community will seize the time and deliver themselves from the boot of their oppressors.

All our survival programs are free. We have never charged the community a dime to receive the things they need from any of our programs and we will not do so. We will not get caught up in a lot of embarrassing questions or paperwork that alienate the people. If they have a need we will serve their needs and attempt to get them to understand the true reasons why they are in need in such an incredibly rich land. Survival programs will always be operated without charge to those who need them and benefit by them.

In order to carry out such programs we have always needed money. In the past we received money from wealthy White philanthropists, humanitarians, and heirs to the corporate monopolies. At the same time we were engaging in a blanket condemnation of the small victimized Black capitalists found in our communities. This tactic was wrong since we receive the money for our survival programs from big White capitalists, and we freely admit that.

When we say that we see within Black capitalism the seeds of its own negation and the negation of all capitalism, we recognize that the small Black capitalist in our communities has the potential to contribute to the building of the machine which will serve the true interests of the people and end all exploitation. By increasing the positive qualities of the Black capitalist we may be able to bring about a non-antagonistic solution of his contradiction with the community, while at the same time heightening the oppressed community's contradiction with the large corporate capitalist empire. This will intensify the antagonistic contradiction between the oppressed community and the empire; and by heightening that contradiction there will subsequently be a violent transformation of the corporate empire. We will do this through our survival programs, which have the interest of the community at heart.

We now see the Black capitalist as having a similar relationship to the Black community as the national (native) bourgeoisie have to the people in national wars of decolonization. In wars of decolonization the national bourgeoisie supports the freedom struggle of the people because they recognize that that it is in their own selfish interest. Then when the foreign exploiter has been kicked out, the national bourgeoisie takes his place and continues the exploitation. However, the national bourgeoisie is a weaker group even though they are exploiters.*

Since the people see Black capitalism in the community as Black control of local institutions, this is a positive characteristic because the people can bring more direction and focus to the activities of the capitalist. At the same time the Black capitalist who has the interest of the community at heart will respond to the needs of the people because this is where his true strength lies. So far as capitalism in general is concerned, the Black capitalist merely has the status of victim because the big White capitalists have the skills, make the loans, and in fact control the Black capitalist. If he wants to succeed in his enterprise the Black capitalist must turn to the community because he depends on them to make his profits. He needs this strong community support because he cannot become independent of the control of the corporate capitalists who control the large monopolies

The Black capitalist will be able to support the people by contributing to the survival programs of the Black Panther Party. In con-

---

* Presently the bourgeoisie is in a weaker position now than it was when it was freed from colonialism. Under Reactionary Intercommunalism (such as in Europe) the bourgeoisie is in control of a smaller unit (community) than it was before. Not only does this make it weaker, it also makes a non-antagonistic transformation of their contradiction more likely since the objective interests of the bourgeoisie are in many way similar to the interests of poor people.

tributing to such programs he will be able to help build the vehicle that will eventually liberate the Black community. He will not be able to deliver the people from their problems, but he will be able to help build the strong political machine which will serve as a revolutionary vanguard and guide the people in their move towards freedom.

Our re-analysis of Black capitalism and its relationship to the community from the perspective of dialectical materialism, and our practical understanding of the needs of the community and the attitudes of the people toward Black capitalism, leads us to a new position. Black businesses that have the interests of the community at heart will be able to contribute to the people through the community programs of the Black Panther Party. These free programs will help the community to survive and thus deter the genocide which is always a threat to our existence here.

In return for these contributions the Black Panther Party will carry advertisements of these businesses in our paper and urge the community to support them. We will never sell advertising space in the paper, but we will give space in return for contributions to the survival programs, which are given free to the community. In this way we will achieve a greater unity of the community of victims, the people who are victimized by the society in general, and the Black capitalists who are victimized by the corporate capitalist monopolies. In this way we will increase the positive qualities of Black capitalism until they dominate the negative qualities, and exploitation will no longer be the reality which the community reluctantly accepts.

The community will see those who support their survival and patronize their places of business. At the same time the community will also criticize those who refuse to participate in their survival programs, and turn their backs on them. If the establishment tries to come down hard on those businessmen who support the survival programs, then the community will recognize this as another form of oppression and will move to strongly defend their supporters. In that way the consciousness of the people and the level of the struggle will be advanced.

There is no salvation in capitalism, but through this new approach the Black capitalist will contribute to his own negation by helping to build a strong political vehicle which is guided by revolutionary concepts and serves as a vanguard for the people. In a way our new position has the simplicity and completeness of a mathematical formula. When the Black capitalist contributes to the survival programs and makes a contribution to the community, the community will give him their support and thus strengthen his business. If he does not make any contribution to the survival of the community, the people will not support him and his enterprise will wither away because of his own negligence. By supporting the community, however, he will be helping to build the political machine that will eventually negate his exploitation of the community, but also negate his being exploited and victimized by corporate capitalism.

So we will heighten the contradiction between the Black community and corporate capitalism, while at the same time reducing the contradiction between the Black capitalist and the Black community. In this way Black capitalism will be transformed from a relationship of exploitation of the community to a relationship of service to the community, which will contribute to the survival of everyone.

uniting against a common enemy: October 23, 1971

W hat does the Black Panther Party mean when we say that we are revolutionary intercommunalists? In a few words, we believe that the world's people form a collection of communities, all dominated or controlled, either directly or indirectly, by the United States, by those few who rule the United States. The most common definition for a nation (as opposed to a community) is a group of human beings who have in common their own land or territory, economic system, culture (or way of day-to-day living), language, etc. At one time men from one nation would go out, and through warfare, conquer other nations. The conquerors would bring under their control the resources, the people, perhaps everything that was sovereign or sacred to the other nation. A variety of things would result: a government of the conquering nation might be established on the territory of the conquered nation; the foreign language may be imposed upon the people; the name of the nation might be changed; or most importantly, the economy of the conquered nation would be fully controlled by the conquerors.

Sometimes a nation is very small; sometimes, very large. But in this way, through these wars, the earth's people have over a very long period of time become divided up according to "national" boundaries, in varying ways at different times in history. These wars of conquest have changed world maps, or what one land mass is called. Sometimes one would look at a certain area and it might have a different name or boundary line, depending upon the date of the map (and sometimes, who printed it). We can remember such terms as the Roman Empire, the Ottoman Empire, the Byzantine Empire. We can remember Columbus "discovering" America (or, as he thought, India); and certainly some changes in national sovereignty have been made since then.

Today, things are different. The entire earth's land mass is known to man. The twentieth century's two world wars have complicated things even more as to the national question. Technology is so advanced that places about which we had only heard in the past are immediately reachable in person. Today a person can travel completely around the world in less than a day's time. If we bring all these past and present facts together with other information the world begins to look a little different. What else do we need to remember: that in the area of technology, the United States is the most highly advanced country; that a territory as large as China, containing within its boundaries one quarter of the entire earth's population, cannot either lay claim to its own former province, Taiwan, or participate in an organization supposedly representative of all "nations" in the world, the United Nations; that most former empires, such as France, Germany, Italy, Britain, have lost their former holdings (the French have been run out of Vietnam and Algeria; the British, out of India; the Germans, out of Russia and Poland; the Italians, out of Ethiopia, etc.). The point is that only one country stands as the sovereign stronghold, dominating and threatening the sovereignty of all other people and lands—it is the United States Empire. No people, no land, no culture, no national economy is safe from the long arm of the last remaining empire.

The situation is this: a people can look only backwards, to history, to really speak of its nation. We call these former nations communities. All these territories exist under the threat of being brought into or, in fact, being a part of the United States Empire. Some of the territories are liberated, such as China, the northern halves of Korea and Vietnam, or Albania. But the weapons of conquest, the war weapons produced by modern technology, are in the hands of the United States. Not even a liberated territory can lay claim to sovereign control of its land, economy, or people with this hanging over its head.

We Black people in the United States have always lived under this threat in our communities inside the United States. United States government control of our communities is not difficult to understand. For most of us it is difficult to imagine our lives without such domination.

We have never controlled a land that was ours. We have never controlled our economy. We know of one culture, that as slaves. We know of one language, that of the slavemaster. Our sovereignty was not violated, for we United States Blacks were never a sovereign nation. It is true that we were snatched from African shores. The present fact is that we cannot ask our grandparents to teach us some "native" tongue, or dance or point out our "homeland" on a map. Certainly, we are not citizens of the United States. Our hopes for freedom then lie in the future, a future which may hold a positive elimination of national boundaries and ties; a future of the world, where a human world society may be so structured as to benefit all the earth's people (not peoples).

To achieve this end, we struggle here inside the United States to get rid of our oppression. Others struggle inside their territorial boundaries to get rid of oppression. The more territory we liberate in the world, the closer we will come to an end to all oppression The common factor that binds us all is not only the fact of oppression but the oppressor: the United States Government and its ruling circle. We, the people of the world, have been brought together under strange circumstances. We are united against a common enemy. Today the philosophy of revolutionary intercommunalism dictates that the survival programs implemented by and with the people here in America and those same basic People's Survival Programs being implemented in Mozambique by the Mozambique Liberation Front are essential to bringing about world unity, from Africa to the Black community inside America, developing and uniting against a common enemy. That enemy has rolled up into one large hand the power of the world. If we get rid of this enemy in a united common struggle it will be easy to transform this unity into a common scheme of things. We are not separate nations of men to continue the pattern of fighting amongst ourselves. We are a large collection of communities who can unite and fight together against our common enemy. The United States' domination over all our territories equals a reactionary (in opposition to the interests of all) set of circumstances among our communities: Reactionary Intercommunalism. We can transform these circumstances to all our benefit: Revolutionary Intercommunalism.

On the continent of Africa there are people who look like us. They are Black. We are brothers because our struggle is common. We have both suffered under White racism and under oppression. This is why we should not let the reactionaries of the world be the only ones communicating across the waters and masses of land. We have a common interest to serve, and therefore, we can learn from each other. What happens here affects our brothers in Africa; what happens in Africa affects us. The United States has seen to this. But this is good. We can learn to fight together, though separated.

There is a place in Africa called Mozambique. It lies on Africa's eastern shore, in the southern portion of the continent. It is a rich land, like most in Africa. In 1498 (six years after Columbus' famous "discovery") the Portuguese invader (if you remember, your elementary school books credit him as an "explorer") Vasco da Gama violated the shores of Mozambique. The rest of the troops landed seven years later, in 1505. From that point on the Portuguese have dominated the economy and lives and the culture of the Mozambican people. Their national language became, and still is, Portuguese. To this day, the Portuguese lay claim to Mozambique, referring to "Portuguese" Mozambique.

This, of course, is not in agreement with our brothers and sisters in Mozambique. Mozambique is their home. They are not the invaders. Of course, the people of Mozambique have made many attempts throughout their long history of Portuguese colonial oppression to rid themselves of their chains. However, the most powerful and successful struggle is presently being waged under the guidance of the revolutionary organization FRELIMO (Front for the Liberation of Mozambique). The people support FRELIMO, for FRELIMO is of the people and is organizing struggle in the true interest of all the people. This great effort really began when FRELIMO was organized in 1962, primarily through the efforts of Dr. Eduardo Mondlane. In 1964 the first attack upon the Portuguese was launched by FRELIMO forces, which were by then organized and trained. Since then, armed struggle has been waged heroically by the Mozambican people under FRELIMO. This has resulted in the liberation of three key areas: Tete Province, Niassa Province, and the Mueda Plateau. The ridiculous fact is that the Portuguese deny this. They deny the reality that they will eventually be pushed out of Mozambique (like the United States in Vietnam or in our Black and other oppressed communities). Portuguese premiere Marcello Caetano (who replaced fascist dictator Salazar) and

his "official" governor General Eduardo De Oliveira, inside Mozambique, have consistently denied that their troops are being destroyed,
their planes shot down.

Caetano denies that FRELIMO membership alone is more than
10,000; that one quarter of Mozambique is liberated territory; that
liberated zones have a population of one million people (of a total population of nine million). He wishes to deny the fact that the people
are fighting for and winning their freedom. Our brothers in Mozambique know differently. When I was in China earlier this month, I
had the opportunity to receive and subsequently report to the people
firsthand, accurate information. I met with the president of FRE-
LIMO, Comrade Samora Moises Machel, former chief of the army.
President Machel gave a clear picture: not only have three major areas
been liberated, but FRELIMO has established over 200 primary
schools, hospitals, and other programs to serve the interest and needs
of the people. Recently (in 1968) an entire detachment of women
fighters was formed. It was around that time that while denying their
losses, the racist, fascist Portuguese government called upon their old
friends to help destroy the struggle. In these past two years the United
States, Britain, France, and Germany have played an openly active role
in attempting to destroy the people's struggle for liberation. The
United States, of course, "helps" most, providing Boeing-707 planes
to bomb the people with napalm and all the other life-destroying
material the United States can come up with. President Machel told
us that in 1970 alone over 128,000 troops of the combined forces
attacked, and 63,000 tons of bombs were viciously rained upon the
people. However, President Machel said, "We destroyed the soldiers;
we shot down the planes."

These successes have certainly not been easy. From within and from
without, the people of Mozambique have suffered. After giving guidance to FRELIMO for nearly seven years, Eduardo Mondlane was
assassinated by the enemy. In February of 1969, while in his home (in
Tanzania), he opened a box that was part of his morning mail. Upon
opening the box a bomb exploded in his face and killed him. Naturally, the Portuguese used even the treachery of this murder to try to
deceive the people. Soon after this, Caetano's government issued statements that a "left-wing faction" of FRELIMO had murdered their leader.

As is familiar (or should be to us by now) the Portuguese attempted to install their own "Man" to lead FRELIMO. They tried to push a native Mozambican, Lazaro Kavandame, popular among the people as the leader of the large (200,000 population) Makonde tribe, into leadership of FRELIMO. As a lackey for Portugal, Kavandame began issuing statements like, "Listen to me well. There must not be a single Makonde chief sending soldiers to war." He was telling the people not to fight for what was theirs. Also, the former Vice-President of FRELIMO, Uriah Simango, was pushing to take over. They were both eventually defeated.

Today, FRELIMO, under the wise leadership of President Machel, is guiding the People of Mozambique toward greater and final victory. But today, naturally, the attacks of the combined forces of the United States, Portugal, Germany, France, and Britain are even more fierce: constant bombings and many ground attacks take place. However, there is a more intricate, but ultimately more vicious, plan in the making, headed primarily by the United States. They plan to build, for the Portuguese, a large hydroelectric dam. The site for the dam is in the liberated Tete Province in Cabora Bassa, along the Zambesi River, bordering racist Rhodesia. Its purpose is to not only give financial aid to impoverished Portugal but to be used as a key part in a plot with South Africa to launch a political, diplomatic, and military offensive upon all of Africa. A familiar name to us is General Electric. The General Electric Company has spent millions to aid in building the Cabora Bassa Dam. Altogether, the United States and others have agreed to invest 500 million dollars in the dam, which is capable of producing 18.4 billion kilowatts of electricity. Also, in regard to this Cabora Bassa Dam, late FRELIMO President Mondlane once said, "They say it will enable them to settle one million Whites in Mozambique within 10 years…to form a great white barrier across Southern Africa."

If we believe that we are brothers with the people of Mozambique, how can we help? They need arms and other material aid. We have no weapons to give. We have no money for materials. Then how do we help? Or, how can they help our struggle? They cannot fight for us. We cannot fight in their place. We can each narrow the territory that our common oppressor occupies. We can liberate ourselves, learning from and teaching each other along the way. But the struggle is one; the enemy is the same. Eventually, we and our brothers in Mozambique, in all of Africa, throughout the world, can discuss a world without boundaries or national ties. We will have a human culture, a human language, the earth will be all our territory, serving all our interests; serving the interests of all the people.

fallen comrade: eulogy for George Jackson, 1971

George Jackson had genius. Genius is rare enough and should be treasured, but when genius is combined in a Black man with revolutionary passion and vision, the Establishment will cut him down. Comrade Jackson understood this. He knew his days were numbered and was prepared to die as a true believer in revolutionary suicide. For eleven years he insisted on remaining free in a brutal prison system. All along he resisted the authorities and encouraged his brothers in prison to join him. The state retaliated: parole was continually refused; solitary confinement was imposed on him for seven years; threats on his life were frequent—from guards, from inmates who called themselves "Hitler's Helpers," from "knife thrusts and pick handles of faceless sadistic pigs." And finally they murdered him.

In the months before his death everything began to close in. He was one of the few prisoners who was shackled and heavily guarded for his infrequent trips to the visitors' room. Attempts on his life became almost daily occurrences. But he never gave in or retreated. Prison was the crucible that shaped his spirit, and George often used the words of Ho Chi Minh to describe his resistance: "Calamity has hardened me and turned my mind to steel."

I knew him like a brother. At first, I knew him only spiritually, through his writing and his legend in the prison system, when I was at the Penal Colony and he was at Soledad. Then, not long after my arrival, I received through the prison grapevine a request from George to join the Black Panther Party. It was readily granted. George was made a member of the People's Revolutionary Army, with the rank of general and field marshal. For the next three years we were in constant communication by means of messages carried by friends and lawyers and inmates transferred from one prison to another. Despite the restrictions of the prison system, we managed to transmit our messages on paper and on tapes. Among George's contributions to the Party were articles he wrote for *The Black Panther* newspaper, which furthered our revolutionary theory and provided inspiration for all the brothers. In February, 1971, I received this letter from him:

2/21/71

Comrade Huey,

Things are quiet here now, tonight we have discipline and accord, tomorrow all may fly apart again—but that's us.

I have two articles that I would like to be put in the paper, one following the other by a week. The one on Angela first. Then if you approve, I would like to contribute something to the paper every week or whenever you have space for me.

If yes, let me know if there is any area in particular you would like me to cover (comment on).

Then do I comment as observer or participant?

One favor—please don't let anyone delete the things I say or change them around, I don't need an editor, unless what I say is not representative of the Party Line, don't let anyone change a word. When I make an ideological error of course correct it to fit the party's position. And don't let them shorten or condense; if something is too long, part one–part two it.

If you want to use me to say nasty things about those who deserve it, it may be best for me to comment as an observer, that way less contradictions between yourself and people you may have to work with.

You told _____ that you and I had a "misunderstanding" once but that it was cleared up. When was it that we misunderstood each other?

Be very careful of messages or any word that has supposed to have come from me. I really don't recall any misunderstanding.

People lie for many reasons.

Try to memorize my handwriting, that is how all messages will come in the future (if we have a future).

Did you know that Angela and I were married a while back? And

I had almost pulled her all the way into our camp, just before Eldridge made that statement?

I had done so well in fact that C.P. tried to cut our contacts, attacked my sanity in little whispers and looks in conversing with her, and cut off my paid subscription to their two newspapers.

Strange, that they would be afraid of the F.B.I., and not afraid of the Cat. Perhaps they've reached an understanding. Some of them anyway.

Is ____ C.P.? Man, what's happening with her. She has no control at all of her mouth. Or ego.

Arrange for a good contact or write and seal messages with a thumbprint. I have ideas I'd like to leave with you all.

Thanks Brother for helping us. Beautiful, hard, disciplined brothers in here, I'd like to deliver them to you someday.

George

In the last three years of his life Comrade Jackson felt sustained and supported by the Black Panther Party. He had struggled alone for so long to raise the consciousness of Black inmates, and his example encouraged thousands who were weaker and less intrepid than he. But the price he paid in alienation and reprisals was fearsome. Within the Party he was no longer alone; he became part of a burgeoning and invincible revolutionary liberation movement. In his second book, *Blood in My Eye*, he expressed this faith: "The Black Panther Party is the largest and most powerful political force existing outside establishment politics. It draws this power from the people. It is the people's natural, political vanguard."

George asked the Party to publish his first book, *Soledad Brother*, but in the difficult negotiations between go-betweens and without direct contact, the arrangements fell through. To make sure this mistake would never happen again, he left his estate and all his writings to the Party. More important, he bequeathed us his spirit and his love.

George's funeral was held in Oakland on August 28, 1971—exactly one week after his murder—at St. Augustine's Episcopal Church, pastored by Father Earl Neil. A crowd of about 7,000 friends gathered to pay their last respects to our fallen comrade, and the Black Panther Party had a large contingent of comrades on hand to handle the crowd and protect the Jackson family. I arrived at the church shortly before the funeral cortege. The second-floor sanctuary was empty, but from the window I could see the crowd stretching for more than a block in each direction, filling every available space and closing off the streets to motor traffic.

A number of Black Panthers sat talking quietly downstairs. Occasionally they relieved the comrades who were controlling the crowd and directing traffic outside. The children from the Intercommunal Youth Institute were there, and although they had been in the building since early morning, they did not complain of weariness. The children felt the loss of George deeply; when they had learned of his death the previous week, all of them had written messages of condolence to his mother. They loved George, and in their faces I could see their determination to grow up and fulfill his dreams of liberation.

Tensions were high. We had received many threats the previous week, from prison guards, from police, and from many others, stating that the funeral would not be held, and if it was, there would be cause for more funerals of Black Panthers. We were ready for anything. The comrades were angry about the threats, and they were righteously angry about the continued oppression of the poor and Black people who live in this land. You could see it in their faces, in their measured, firm strides, in their clenched fists, and in their voices as they greeted the hearse with shouts of "Power to the People" and "Long Live the Spirit of George Jackson."

When the funeral cortege arrived, Bobby and I prepared to meet the people in it as they entered the door of the church. It was the first time Bobby and I had shared a public platform in over four years, but there was no cause for rejoicing. We said nothing to each other; we knew only too well what the other was thinking.

As the casket bearing the body of Comrade George was brought into the sanctuary, a song was playing—Nina Simone singing "I Wish I Knew How It Would Feel to Be Free." Inside the church the walls were ringed with Black Panthers carrying shotguns. George had said that he wanted no flowers at his funeral, only shotguns. In honoring his request we were also protecting his family and all those who were dedicated to carrying on in his spirit. Any person who entered that sanctuary with the purpose of starting some madness would know that he did not stand a chance of going very far. In death, even as in life, George thought about the best interests of his companions.

Father Neil made a short but powerful statement about the lesson of George Jackson's death, that Black people would have to get off their knees and take their destiny in their own hands. Bobby read some of the many messages from around the world, Elaine Brown sang "One time's too much to tell any man that he's not free," and I delivered the eulogy, which went in part:

> George Jackson was my hero. He set a standard for prisoners, political prisoners, for people. He showed the love, the strength, the revolutionary fervor characteristic of any soldier for the people. He inspired prisoners, whom I later encountered, to put his ideas into practice and so his spirit became a living thing. Today I say that although George's body has fallen, his spirit goes on, because his ideas live. And we will see that these ideas stay alive, because they'll be manifested in our bodies and in these young Panthers' bodies, who are our children. So it's a true saying that there will be revolution from one generation to the next. This was George's legacy, and he will go on, he will go on into immortality, because we believe that the people will win, we know the people will win, as they advance, generation upon generation.
>
> What kind of standard did George Jackson set? First, he was a strong man, without fear, determined, full of love, strength, and dedication to the people's cause. He lived a life that we must praise. No matter how he was oppressed, no matter how wrongly he was done, he still kept the love for the people. And this is why he felt no pain in giving up his life for the people's cause. . . .
>
> Even after his death, George Jackson is a legendary figure and a hero. Even the oppressor realizes this. To cover their murder they say that George Jackson killed five people, five oppressors, and wounded three in the space of thirty seconds. You know, sometimes I like to overlook the fact that this would be physically impossible. But after all George Jackson is my hero. And I would like to think that it was possible; I would be very happy thinking that George Jackson had the strength because that would have made him superman. (Of course, my hero would have to be a superman.) And we will raise our children to be like George Jackson, to live like George Jackson and to fight for freedom as George Jackson fought for freedom.
>
> George's last statement, the example of his conduct at San Quentin on that terrible day, left a standard for political prisoners and for the prisoner society of racist, reactionary America. He left a standard for the liberation armies of the world. He showed us how to act. He demonstrated how the unjust would be criticized by the weapon. And

this will certainly be true, because the people will take care of that. George also said once that the oppressor is very strong and he might beat him down, he might beat us down to our very knees, he might crush us to the ground, but it will be physically impossible for the oppressor to go on. At some point his legs will get tired, and when his legs get tired, then George Jackson and the people will tear his kneecaps off....

So we will be very practical. We won't make statements and believe the things the prison officials say—their incredible stories about one man killing five people in thirty seconds. We will go on and live very realistically. There will be pain and much suffering in order for us to develop. But even in our suffering, I see a strength growing. I see the example that George set living on. We know that all of us will die someday. But we know that there are two kinds of death, the reactionary death and the revolutionary death. One death is significant and the other is not. George certainly died in a significant way, and his death will be very heavy, while the deaths of the ones that fell that day in San Quentin will be lighter than a feather. Even those who support them now will not support them in the future, because we're determined to change their minds. We'll change their minds or else in the people's name we'll have to wipe them out thoroughly, wholly, absolutely, and completely.

ALL POWER TO THE PEOPLE.

All words are inadequate to express the pain one feels over a fallen comrade. But in a poem my brother Melvin came closer than anyone in voicing our feelings about the loss of George Jackson:

We Called Him the General

The sky is blue,
Today is clear and sunny.
The house that George once
lived in headed for the
grave,
While the Panther spoke
of the spirit.
I saw a man move catlike
across the rooftops,

Glide along the horizons,
Casting no shadow,
only chains into the sea,
using his calloused hands
and broken feet to
smash and kick down
barriers.
The angels say his name
is George Lester Jackson—
El General.

on Pan-Africanism or communism: December 1, 1972

The historic maneuverings that have led to the continued oppression of U.S. blacks and other people of color throughout the world have dealt an intricate and greatly complex problem that we must now face. The definition of the problem, however, has become so complicated that solutions cannot be discussed without a careful analysis of the present-day situation in which blacks and poor people are enmeshed.

To address the questions raised by George Padmore in *Communism and Black Nationalism*, we must consider the most fundamental issues and agree upon certain premises. We must agree, for example, that black people inside the United States live in an oppressed state. Furthermore, the primary characteristic of this oppression is economic with racism at its base. From this fundamental point stem other manifestations of oppression in the political, cultural, and social arenas.

Classic definitions of the nature of oppression of U.S. blacks, nevertheless, do not find much applicability beyond this point. Black Americans cannot be said to be colonial subjects, strictly speaking. That would require the invasion of a sovereign territory by a foreign force, whose purpose would be to overtake the land and all that it yields. Instead, blacks in the United States are forced transplants, having been brought from foreign territory as slave labor. It would therefore be somewhat absurd to discuss expelling those controlling forces from a region that was foreign to blacks in the first place.

Karl Marx set forth a basic analysis of the nature of oppression, defining the fundamental issue as economic; or more specifically, the

248

relationship of man to production. According to Marx, the introduction of industrial development leads to the creation of new relationships between men that are based upon industrial growth wiping out the former feudal system. As such, the question of the feudal landlord as he related to the serf or slave in an agrarian society was replaced by the owner-worker relationship and the accumulation of capital. Marx defined these new relationships in terms of classes, speaking of oppression by the owner class, or the bourgeoisie, of the working class, also known as the proletariat.

Marx's analyses could be readily applied to conditions in those regions that had experienced industrial development to the extent that a capitalist class had been created in that region. Such conditions were found in territories populated by non-European or nonwhite peoples. At the time of Marx's writings, black, brown, red, and yellow peoples dominated areas that still maintained an agrarian-based economy. For black people in the United States, conversely, there was little applicable. Although the United States itself was certainly advancing industrially, black people maintained an indirect relationship to all of it. Once "emancipated," U.S. blacks—who were neither owners nor workers in the Marxist sense of the terms—were shoved into ghettos, where they were given neither reparations for years of institutional chattel slavery nor employment in the new industrial state. Racism guaranteed it.

How, then, does the question of Pan-Africanism relate to blacks in relation to communism as outlined by Marx? Mr. Padmore's elaborate discussion on the rejection of communism by blacks in favor of Pan-Africanism describes very accurately the Russian Communist betrayal of African and U.S. blacks. Admittedly, the various collaborations of the Soviets for the salvation of "Mother Russia" were a vicious Machiavellian web that lured in people of color worldwide. However, Mr. Padmore's failure to deal with the unique situation of U.S. blacks, not to mention his neglect of analyzing concretely the African situation, is due to his emotional hatred of Moscow Communists (to whom he was for so long closely tied), but also his emotional, newfound love for the people of his race.

Let us examine the questions he poses with a close eye on the historic placement of his particular analysis; namely, the 1950s. As Mr. Padmore points out, Lenin realized that Marxist theory needed to be applied to actual social conditions. With that in mind, Lenin successfully led the 1917 Revolution with the support of Russia's dark minorities by promising self-determination and autonomous government under the new socialist state. From here, Mr. Padmore points out that the newly formed American Communist Party (1920) used this line to appeal to blacks in America, recognizing the absolute necessity of incorporating the black struggle to advance the Communist Party program. Underscoring the dogma and racism manifested in the concept that through the white-dominated, Russian-directed, Marxist Party, black people could be led to salvation (via groups such as the American Negro Labor Congress or, later, the National Negro Congress, and, even more ridiculously, a black nation inside the U.S.), Mr. Padmore leads one to the conclusion that communism holds no solution to black people's problems. This suggestion could lead easily to the conclusion that if communism is bad for black people, then its antithesis, capitalism, is good.

During the pre–World War II period and throughout the war years, black Americans were pawns on the Soviet chessboard, being led back and forth according to the needs of Moscow: today, oppose Roosevelt, who opposes Hitler, because Stalin has allied with Hitler; tomorrow, support Roosevelt against Hitler, because Hitler has invaded "Mother Russia." All the while, blacks were struggling to eat and survive by entering the system of capitalist endeavor as workers or producers. The Roosevelt New Deal certainly dealt a bad deal to blacks. The President's trumped-up reform programs and the Communist Party of America's sudden Stalin-induced silence on the issue of black civil and human rights excluded many people of color.

With the war's end in 1945, blacks once again saw the spoils going to everyone else. The world was divided up by the victors, but blacks in the United States and Africa—not to mention people of color around the world—had no participation. Can we conclude, then, that imperialism has a color—white? Can we also conclude that because a Russian Communist Party or Communist Party of America failed to fully support the interests of people of color, racism is the prime characteristic of black oppression? Can we further conclude that if colonized blacks unite, sharing among themselves all their wealth, racial oppression will be overcome?

These are serious questions that must be properly reviewed if we are to resolve the problem of black oppression and human exploitation in general. Said Mr. Padmore:

> The time is fast passing when coloured folk will continue to accept their colonial status, which in the modern world signifies racial and national inferiority. If the Western Powers are really afraid of Communism and want to defeat it, the remedy lies in their own hands. First, it is necessary to keep one step ahead of the Communists by removing the grievances of the so-called backward peoples, which the Communists everywhere seek to exploit for their own ends. Secondly, there must be a revolutionary change in the outlook of the colonizing Powers, who must be prepared to fix a date for the complete transfer of power—as America did in the Philippines—and to give every technical and administrative assistance to the emerging colonial nations during the period of transition from internal self-government to complete self-determination. Fortified with the knowledge that, regardless of their stage of development, full responsibility will be theirs on the agreed date, the colonial peoples will throw their full energies into making the experiment a success. Only responsibility can develop the latent potentialities of a subject people, as events in the Gold Coast have shown. None of the members of the present All-African Cabinet in the West African colony had any experience in governing prior to taking office in 1951.

Historically, colonial wars and other aggressive maneuverings led African nations to become colonial subjects of various European powers. The Allied victory in WWII pulled the United States' Depression-era economy out of the red, placing American rulers in positions of unprecedented global prominence. This period is crucial in understanding our present situation. For it was due to the American victory at war that the spoils—including land territories formerly held by other imperialist countries—were rewarded to the U.S., thrusting the country into its present "almighty" position among world powers. The crucial implication of this new U.S. dominance is the relation created between the United States' rulers and the rest of the world. Essentially, a qualitative change began to evolve: dominance of the global economy by the United States of America.

The so-called socialist world, representing the needs and aspirations of the oppressed, now had a more formidable force with which to deal.

The classic contradiction outlined by Marx between a native or colonial bourgeoisie and the oppressed of a nation was turned into a very different contradiction. The liberation of China, Cuba, and Algeria that succeeded WWII and followed the general line of territorial liberation determined by socialist construction would also be transformed in nature: that is, could socialist construction be meaningful in view of the decline of the would-be British, French, or other empires and the rise of the U.S. Super Power?

As Mr. Padmore notes, the First Workers State, with its European and American offshoots, had begun to betray its historic task of supporting the oppressed. The doctrines of Marx were well received among white minorities, fitting classically into the Marxian mold around industrial owners and workers. However, as the dogma of Moscow had not been useful to the Chinese, it could find no home in the rest of the world of color. Perhaps there was the added factor of centuries of race superiority coupled with the sudden and shocking inability of the European "greats" to lay claim to all the world that caused such insensitivity to the undeveloped, nonindustrial world of color on the part of Moscow-directed, "communist" citizens of the "civilized world." Certainly, there was a betrayal of silence by the American Communists toward blacks at the crucial point when the United States rose above the imperialist crowd. The essential question is how shall the liberation of blacks in the U.S. or in Africa—or people of color throughout the world—be effected?

Another fundamental question is what does liberation mean? Mr. Padmore puts certain concepts before us in relation to the liberation of blacks: Pan-Africanism or communism. The brilliant Dr. Kwame Nkrumah, having identified and warned his people of the deviant dangers in neocolonialism, called for a united Africa. The unity that Dr. Nkrumah called for carried the demand of solidarity based upon certain principles: specifically, pooling resources from all separate countries of Africa into an all-African treasury to produce the industrial and technological development that could ensure Africa true economic and political independence. This in turn would allow for a fair distribution of wealth to every African along socialist lines.

Nkrumah had seen that a functional definition of the economic and political situation in Africa defied the notion of separate, independent nations within the continent. He had seen that within the African nation-ranks, black men had risen to leadership of independent states but who were no more than comprador agents for the United States. He knew that as long as these small states remained separate, capitalist ideology, and thereby the continued exploitation of the people, could always creep back into Africa and thwart the real control by the people over their lives. Nkrumah's dream, however, was cut short at the hands of the U.S. by a CIA-directed coup.

With these facts in mind, let us take a careful look at America. The economic power of the U.S. rulers is so great that there is no denying its effects upon the rest of the world. This economic power is manifested in the concentration of production capabilities and raw materials in the hands of American forces. What the United States cannot obtain and develop, it can synthesize in its technological laboratories.

Looking further at the situation, let us consider black Americans. Tied only historically to Africa, they can lay no real claim to territory in the U.S. or Africa. Black Americans have only the cultural and social customs that have evolved from centuries of oppression. In other words, U.S. blacks form not a subjugated colony but an oppressed community inside the larger boundaries. What, then, do the words "black nationalism" concretely mean to the U.S. black? Not forming anything resembling a nation presently, shall U.S. blacks somehow seize (or possibly be "given") U.S. land and expect to claim sovereignty as a nation? In the face of the existent power of the United States over the entire world, such a notion could only be fantasy that could lead to the extinction of a race.

What does "Pan-Africanism" mean to the black African who did not live Nkrumah's dream, but lives in the real nightmare of U.S. economic/military might? For what does a national flag actually mean when Gulf Oil is in control? Or if Gulf Oil is expelled, what happens if the "nation" cannot supply for its own needs?

The oppressed people of the world face a serious dilemma: the Chinese people are as threatened by the American Empire, just as blacks globally and people in South America are similarly threatened. Even Europe bends to the weight of the United States, yielding theoretical national sovereignty.

The answer lies in facing the matter at hand. Pan-Africanism, as defined by Mr. Padmore, is hardly the issue. It is not only outdated, it sets back the liberation of all oppressed people. It leaves room for exploitative endeavor by men. It suggests both an all-Africanized version of capitalist economic distribution in a world where capital and its power lie tightly in the hands of the U.S. rulers, and it fails to encompass the unique situation of black Americans. Further, with Mr. Padmore's rejection of the fundamental tenets of communism due to misapplication, his Pan-Africanism paves the way for Moscow's own reactionary line of peaceful coexistence with the "former" oppressors:

> In this connection of aid to Africa, if America, the "foremost champion and defender of the free world" is really worried about Communism taking root in Africa and wants to prevent such a calamity from taking place, I can offer an insurance against it. This insurance will not only forestall Communism, but endear the people of the great North American Republic forever to the Africans. Instead of underwriting the discredited system of Colonialism by bolstering up the European regimes, especially in North, Central and South Africa, with military and financial aid, let American statesmen make a bold gesture to the Africans in the spirit of the anti-Colonialist tradition of 1776.
>
> ...Once confidence, trust, and mutual respect are established between African leaders and their European advisers, there is nothing to prevent the rapid economic and social advancement of Africa. It is a continent of great potentialities. In planning its welfare and development certain basic principles should be observed. For example, the main sector of the national economy should be State controlled, since there is not enough local capital available to undertake large-scale enterprises. But the rest should be left to private initiative.
>
> ...Pan-Africanism looks above the narrow confines of class, race, tribe and religion. In other words, it wants equal opportunity for all. Talent to be rewarded on the basis of merit.

Solutions cannot come in a few words. Let us return, however, to the basic, functional definitions. If it is agreed that the fundamental nature of oppression is economic, then the first assault by the oppressed must be to wrest economic control from the hands of the oppressors. If we define the prime character of the oppression of blacks as racial, then the situation of economic exploitation of human being by human being can be continued if performed by blacks against blacks or blacks against whites. If, however, we are speaking of eliminating exploitation and oppression, then the oppressed must begin with a united, worldwide thrust along the lines of oppressed versus oppressor. We must seize the machinery of power and through the unity of struggle begin the task of redistributing the world's wealth. Without the unity of all oppressed people, the world shall remain in a state of reaction, with everyone yielding to the whim of the U.S. rulers.

the technology question: 1972

K nowing how to struggle is the essence of winning. Recognizing ills is fundamental; recognizing how to overcome ills is mandatory. If we acknowledge the U.S. rulers as the prime oppressors, not only of America's internal masses but also of the world's people, then we must decipher the phenomena that allow for world domination so that it can be overcome.

To clearly discuss this crucial issue—crucial to the survival of us all— we have only to observe the form that this U.S. world domination takes. Consider the U.S. protein industry for example. The U.S. capitalists can yield more milk, cattle, and heifers than anyone, because of advancements in the biological and husbandry sciences. With such advancements, man is becoming less dependent upon the natural forces of nature. This particular example alone demonstrates how the crucial issue of our time is the control of technology.

Technological advancements have been gained through expropriation from the people, including slavery proper but also chattel slavery followed by wage slavery. With this expropriation, a reservoir of information was created so that Americans could produce the kinds of experimental agencies and universities that created the information explosion. Every serious thinker knows that scientific and technological developments do not grow in a straight line. They develop exponentially by leaps and bounds.

We thus see that it is because of the expropriation of the world that the technology exists, and the reactionary intercommunalists—the U.S. capitalists/imperialists—are able to dominate world markets. They set the pace, enabling themselves to discredit socialism and communism via foreign aid made available—or unavailable, as the case may be—

to developing countries. American capitalists discredit wars of liberation, especially the establishment of what we call provisional revolutionary governments, by pouring in the very bounty they stole into the puppet administrations they set up. This is why they keep talking about "Vietnamization"; because, they say, "We will supply them." They *can* supply them.

It is for these reasons that I always make reference to a Latin phrase: *trespass de bonis asportatis*. In the old English law, this referred to a particular kind of trespass that included the expropriation of someone else's goods. Usually, it was a charge made against landlords, who had illegally seized a tenant's possessions. The landlord might ship these belongings to a storage facility or distribute the tenant's articles as he saw fit. In many respects, this is precisely what the U.S. rulers have done with the goods of the people of the world; not with the lock and key of the landlord, but with the gun. This abundance of bounty from robbery has built a monster of technology. In the future, however, this will be good for *us*, because the same supercapitalists will be our supply sergeants. We will feed India, and all of Africa will spring up as one breadbasket.

Yet this leads us to the question: Why does Africa need contributions from a small continent like North America? Simply put, it is the result of the technology question. If so-called revolutionists would start thinking in terms of this relationship, they would see that Africa *will* blossom and spread her wings, but only spread her wings when we learn to get from her natural resources a maximum yield. With the poor land in the United States, American capitalists produce more than Africa is producing now. However, this phenomenon develops only *after* they break the people and expropriate the raw materials and wealth. At that point, the technology is applied, at leisure, to the spoils. The loot is abstracted and removed to the technological institutes.

Another question arises: Why do the tyrants fight? They fight simply because of the need of the ruling, reactionary circle of the United States to sell the products of their technology to more and more people for capital gains. Consequently, they fight in Vietnam not for the land or for the raw materials found there. Rather, they fight *because they need the people!* Western capitalists need people in order to have buyers at too-high prices for their now overexpanding market. As socialism spreads inexorably, human resources are applied in order to uplift and benefit *all*, which cuts out the middle man, the capitalist. The capitalists therefore will not stand for it, because once he is cut out, the whole exploitive warfare state is doomed. If you do not have a buyer for all of the consumer goods that you produce, then what is the purpose of producing more? The monopolist wants himself as the only producer, and he wants the entire world as his consumer. If he cannot sell to you, then he will fight any force that resists him in order to push his product upon you. He will perform this task in an attempt to make it impossible for you to resist: that is, to make you an offer you cannot refuse.

The situation is a technology question, because the answer to the dilemma lies in the control of that vehicle to which we have all contributed through the exploitation of our lives and labor. Asia, Africa, and Latin America, in particular, could have shared with their brethren in the Western world. They would have been willing to share.

Historically, the land question was an important question. But at this point, they have taken what they need from most of the lands. Now, it is only a matter of capitalizing upon the advancements, the "interest" made from their original robbery.

How do we settle it? The settlement does not lie with the liberation of territory, per se, even though we do not stand against that. The Black Panther Party would certainly support the liberation of any territory by those with the correct vision or ideology. We would not support, however, the liberation of territory strictly for the purpose of allowing a national bourgeoisie to take the place of the colonizer. Besides, the national bourgeoisie cannot even exist without relying upon the Empire. He needs trade; he needs support to keep him intact, or else the people will struggle again. Therefore, if it is a question of liberating a geographical location in order to free the people, then that struggle must be waged with the idea that freeing the land will free the people only to the degree that they will not have to consume what they do not want to consume, and to the degree of providing the people with the ability to make strong coalitions to develop their resources and technology. This would position everyone to enact the actual overthrow of that force that oppresses all of us. When the people unite for that purpose—to gain the strength necessary to move against the reactionary control of the technology, in order to expropriate it and then make it available to all—then the question of liberating land will be placed in proper perspective.

If the question of liberating land is not placed in this context, then those who struggle run the risk of engaging in meaningless battle and, worse, failure. The most devastating war of our time is the Vietnam conflict. If we look closely at the meaning of this war, we might ask what does "Vietnam will win" mean? It is inevitable that U.S. military force will be expelled from Vietnamese soil, the ultimate alternative being the complete genocide of the Vietnamese people. Projecting this inevitability, let us consider the question of "socialist construction" in Vietnam, which necessarily includes the developing of the Vietnamese market in relation to world trade. As far as the country's future ability to trade and sell on the market, it is a very dismal picture, especially when you compare it to the state of California, and what that state can overproduce and sell abroad for a lesser price. The cost to the nation or territory with less technology—to produce, to refine, and to ship—would obviously be greater than the cost for such a process to one in possession of advanced means. Thus, even with the liberation of land, the Vietnamese will remain dependent. There is an undeniable interconnection to everything among all the territories in the world. That is why we say that there are no longer nations; there are only communities under siege by the reactionaries. This is where we get the term *reactionary intercommunalism*.

The picture I draw is not a very pretty image. As for the people in Vietnam, I would predict that, after the so-called liberation, the average per capita income will likely be much lower than the lowest echelon in the United States. Of course, the American people look at that situation and remark that our Empire, with its overexpanded capitalism, is better than what they arranged for themselves over there. Further, it might be said that we could have built more hospitals and schools for them. Sadly, this is the truth. However, the sadness is due not only to the overexpansion of capitalism, which turned into imperialism and then into an Empire with its reactionary intercommunalism, but to Americans themselves enjoying a higher quality of life than everybody else, at the expense of everybody else.

The only way to really liberate Vietnam, if not the whole world, is to crush the U.S. reactionary ruling circle, thereby making the technological vehicle available to everyone. This is what the concept of "peaceful coexistence" means: peaceful co-optation. If the freeing of the land is part of a people's strategy, then I have no criticism. If national liberation wars are just strategies to mobilize the unconscious peasants or workers, I would agree with that, too. However, if the people are laboring under fantasies that they will be liberated through troop or arms withdrawal with the U.S. reactionary ruling circle staying intact, then they are living in romantic finalism. By their own conclusion, they will condemn their very liberty, because the United States does not need their territory. That is not the question. The people of the oppressed territories might fight on the land question and die over the land question. But for the United States, it is the technology question, and the consumption of the goods that the technology produces!

The picture becomes even more grim in the face of the open agreements recently made between the two most powerful countries in the world: the United States and the Soviet Union. Arms and trade agreements between these two monsters can only make clearer the predicament that the world's people face, especially the people of the Third World. This ultimate compromise on the part of the First Workers State presents an even more difficult situation for those engaged in so-called national liberation struggles. They must ask, "Does peaceful co-existence socialism work?"

Russia's first mistake came in the form of an incorrect analysis: that socialism could co-exist peacefully with capitalist nations. It was a blow to the communities of the whole world that led directly to the crippling of the people's ability to oppose capitalist/imperialist aggression and aggression's character. Remember, the capitalists claim that as soon as you agree to accept their trade and fall under their economic ideology, then they will agree to have peaceful co-existence.

The Russians allowed this to happen through naïveté or treachery. Regardless of how this came about, they damaged the ability of the Third World to resist. They could have given the Third World every technique available to them long ago. With the high quality of Soviet development at a time when the United States was less advanced than it is today, the Russians could have built up the necessary force to oppose imperialism. Now, all the they can do is whimper like whipped dogs and talk about peaceful co-existence so that they will not be destroyed. This presents the world with the hard fact that the United States is the only state power in the world. Russia has become, like all other nations, no more than a satellite of the United States. American rulers do not care about how much Russians say that they are the Soviets, as long as Ford can build its motor company in their territory.

In reference to this, I would like to quote two statements:

> Wherever death may surprise us, it will be welcome, provided that this our battle cry reaches some receptive ear, that another hand stretch out to take up weapons, and that other men come forward to intone our funeral dirge with the staccato of machine guns and new cries of battle and victory.
>
> Let the flag under which we fight represent the sacred cause of redeeming humanity, so that to die under the flag of Vietnam, of Venezuela, of Guatemala, of Laos, of Guinea, of Colombia, of Bolivia, of Brazil, to name only the scenes of today's armed struggles, be equally glorious and desirable for an American, an Asian, an African, or even a European.
>
> Each drop of blood spilled in a country under whose flag one has not been born constitutes experience for those who survive to apply later in the liberation struggle of their own country, and each nation liberated is a step toward victory in the battle for the liberation of one's own country: Each and every one of us will pay on demand his part of sacrifice, knowing that altogether we are getting ever closer to the new man whose figure is beginning to appear.
>
> —CHE GUEVARA

> It is our goal to be in every single country there is. We look at a world without any boundary lines. We don't consider ourselves basically American. We are multi-national; and when we approach a government that doesn't like the United States, we always say, "Who do you like; Britain, Germany? We carry a lot of flags."
>
> —ROBERT STEVENSON
> Ford's Executive President for
> Automotive Operations, *Business Week*

We have difficulties selling a progressive political line to not only the hard hats but also to blacks. It is because the evil of the reactionary ruling circle is often hard to pinpoint. It becomes more difficult when those people in the proletarian group, those who are fully employed, are happy just to have a job with a higher wage than anyplace in the world. The U.S. ruling circle has succeeded in what Hitler attempted to do. His vision was to rob Peter to pay Paul, even though he used the Jews at that time, like white Americans used blacks, to build the state. He expropriated from the Jews right in their own country, making other Caucasians hate them. This was all done as a forward thrust to shackle the world, and, in turn, raise the economy of Germany. The average German supported the Nazis, because Hitler was giving them something they had never had before. And they were not concerned at what expense.

Although the United States participated in Hitler's defeat, American capitalists took up the same *Weltanschaung*, the same line. They have raised the standard of living, using the same method Hitler instituted, beginning with the generals and "crooks-in-arms," what we call our military contractors, or our military states such as "California-Lockheed." As U.S. capitalists began raising the standard of living for everybody, they even became somewhat disinterested in their own political line. They may even disguise their fascist moves by making big circuses of political administrators in the arena of human rights. Still, the capitalist keeps the shackles on the workers. The situation becomes highly complex, for the U.S. capitalist has been able to spread out his entire operation. You put together his machinery in parts, thus you are not building a bomb, you are building a transistor. They raise the standard of living through transistors in order to further rip-off/sell its goods to the workers and the people of the world. This began with industrial advancement, going arm-in-arm with forcing people to buy.

As Hitler accommodated the German people with the idea that he would start to minimize the forward assault (offensive; aggressive wars), because that would get them into trouble, so the U.S. capitalist will accommodate "stop" the war, as long as he still controls all the world. The Empire will make the people of the world adjust themselves to whatever kind of exploitation is required for consumption, because he is building a gigantic technological empire, starting with the advancements in the latest war equipment. Just as the German people saluted "Heil Hitler!" we now have the average U.S. worker, the hard hat, waving the American flag.

What would Hitler have done? "Let's stop the crucifixion of the Jews." The United States will stand for civil rights, and "stop the crucifixion of blacks," because now the imperialists can let blacks share in it. The U.S. capitalists will say, "We will continue to rip-off Southeast Asia; we'll continue ripping off Latin America and Africa." With the acceptance of the sharing will come the end of our whole political-type ideological war, because the people of this nationalist empire will have a bid in the shackling of the whole world. This is the reason why politics at this stage is so complicated. For in reality, it is non-politics. It does not matter who takes over, as long as the people with the big interest, those that get the big money, can pay off enough people to keep them quiet. Franklin Delano Roosevelt did it in World War II. He delivered a job and a guaranteed income based on the war effort. Everybody rallied to the war. Americans, black and white, who had hated the government only two years before that, turned right around and saluted.

At present, however, corporate America can boast that if you are a Communist, you can run for president. What they will not add is that this is so because the president is relatively unimportant. The technological question is unopposed—as far as who benefits from it, because we all do on one level or another—that so it becomes very difficult to deal with. It is difficult for us to move against that mythical, politically reactionary ruling circle, or to point out the target, because it relates back to the statement that we have to deal with in the end, that "Ye, who is not guilty, cast the first stone." It is difficult to cast the stone, because those holding the stone can say, "Will I be out of a job; I'm looking for a job. Will I join the forces that cannot hire me at all? Will I be fired from General Motors?"

The problem, finally, is at what point will the centralization, coupled with the welfare state, no longer be useful in its reactionary form? Moreover, how long will it take the people to see it? Americans are in a position of dependency on the people outside the U.S., those who are getting ripped off. How long will the U.S. imperialists have the ability to pull the masses? They have already shot down the First Workers State. Now it seems that even the Second Workers State is threatened. The world is in a predicament, and we do not have a world policy. We, the people, do not have a worldview. Why is Ford one of the biggest philanthropic foundations in the world? Is it because they are kindhearted? If you go to Ford, you can get almost any kind of program you want, in relation to social welfare or a job program. You show them anything that makes sense, and as long as you do not oppose the economic principle of the United States, they will fund it. We just read Ford's policy statement, "We carry many flags .... We don't even consider ourselves America.... We consider ourselves multi-national.... We don't respect boundary lines ...."

American leaders under the right circumstances will support civil rights. Presidents Kennedy, Johnson, and Nixon all stood behind the quickest solution to the so-called problems of racial discrimination. They even promoted equal employment. We have all reaped benefits, whether or not these crumbs were given intentionally, and it is the result of having enjoyed these benefits that U.S. rulers are in the position to allow a little "liberation." Nevertheless, these benefits affect not only the people inside the United States but also the people of the world, including the so-called socialist world. They, too, are bombarded with the same imperialist propaganda, leading socialist people to question the very concept of the new state, the so-called revolutionary socialist state, that cannot provide what the United States can through consumer trade. In fact, there is already a problem within these socialist territories relating to the people's consistent support of the ideology. Even the strength of the people to fight the "introduction" of U.S. capitalists to foreign markets is beginning to crumble.

In other words, a worker in Korea may presently accept the state's drive to work harder, to push production for everybody. The United States government is saying the same thing: "We're producing for everybody; we're giving out the goods." The difference, however, is everybody in America has a television, a car, and a relatively decent place to live. Even the lowest of the low do not live anywhere near the level of the poor of the world. Even the average person, the average "nigger," in the United States does not live as low as the average Chinese. Those who support the so-called socialist states will begin to be swayed by the introduction of a U.S. consumer market into their socialist countries. This becomes an even greater problem, because reactionary intercommunalism would then infect the very people of that part of the world, as well as blacks and other people in this country.

It is a technology people question, and that is why the United States will fight hard for an introduction to new markets abroad.

The U.S. imperialists have a serious problem presently in their efforts to reach that point of commerce. It is why they set up puppet governments; so that when the introduction comes, they will be *able* to pay off those people under the reins of control in the first place. They need a reliable force of compradors, as it were, and cannot afford to pay-off everyone to the point of complete acquiescence. If they can make this first step, they will have the necessary force to keep the people in line. After all, they cannot send U.S. troops everywhere.

The situation in the First Workers State provides the best example of a struggle for sovereign territory deteriorated into a struggle to accommodate the needs and desires of the people with concessions to U.S. technology, its might, and the infiltration, thereby, of imperialist ideology. One need only take a look at the Russian people today—the so-called "socialist people" hopping around for tips. Or consider those people who went through the 1917 Revolution, only to end up dreaming of mink coats and two-car garages.

It is important to realize that there is not so much of a deterioration, for the continuity is not broken. If one recalls Lenin's statement in 1917, when he had had trouble mobilizing a basically peasant country, one can see why and how such a development occurred. In order to move the peasants against the feudal lords, he said something for which many scholars criticize him, because it created a problem for Stalin when he had to try to nationalize the farms. First, Lenin said, "Break thy shackles, want and dread. Bread is freedom; freedom bread." However, even with this slogan, the peasants could not be moved. Finally Lenin said, in essence, "The Land is Ours, Seize the Land." When he said that, the peasants rose up, like a mighty storm. Later, when it was necessary to actualize this, Stalin ended up slaughtering many peasants, because they demanded, "The Land is Ours!" Stalin attempted to make the people understand that it was necessary to collectivize the land in order to build the necessary industrial state. His methods may be criticized but are not the issue here. For it was after Stalin that the Russian state began to fall into its present condition of decay.

With such information, one can begin to realize the dialectics of the entire structure. We would not be in trouble at the moment had liberated territories built up their land and overthrown the United States with proletarian international revolution, intercommunal revolution. It did not happen, and a great deal is dependent upon the American people understanding this complex nature of the matter in order to move forward.

a spokesman for the people: in conversation with William F. Buckley, February 11, 1973

(The following interview was broadcast on the Public Television program Firing Line.*)*

BUCKLEY: Will you explain your concept of revolutionary suicide?

HUEY: ...if I may impose upon you, I'll answer your question, but first, I have a friend who is almost dying for me to ask this question: During the Revolution of 1776, when the United States of America broke away from England, which side would you have been on?

BUCKLEY: I think probably I would have been on the side of George Washington. I'm not absolutely sure because it remains to be established historically whether what we sought to prove at that point might not have been proved by more peaceful means. On the whole, I'm against revolutions, although I think that that revolution will go down as a pretty humane one.

HUEY: You're not such a bad guy after all. My friend will be surprised to hear that.

BUCKLEY: His assumption was what?

HUEY: He was puzzled. He was inclined to believe that you'd have

267

been on the side of the colonizers. But I'm pleased with your answer, and I agree with you. The only revolution that's worth fighting is a humane revolution.

BUCKLEY: Also, one that succeeds.

HUEY: Yes, eventually.

BUCKLEY: I feel that if King George had captured George Washington, he'd have had the right to hang him.

HUEY: According to law.

BUCKLEY: Yes.

HUEY: But revolutions always in some ways contradict some laws. That's why it's called revolution.

BUCKLEY: Well, revolutionary justice is its own justice, isn't it?

HUEY: Yes. Of course it always professes to go under some human right or humane consideration. I think we can judge revolutions on the basis of how much in fact, objectively, people are dealt with in a fair way and are given more freedom. One of my principles is that contradiction is the ruling principle of the universe, that every phenomenon, whether it's in the physical world, the biological world, or the social world, has its internal contradiction that gives motion to things, that internal strain. Much of the time we Homo sapiens don't realize that no matter what conditions we establish, no matter what government we establish, there will also be that internal contradiction that will have to be resolved—and resolved in a rational and just way. Of course that's very vague. Many times we claim actions are revolutionary when really they're not. So I appreciate your answer, and would agree with that part of it.

BUCKLEY: Which part?

HUEY: That the only revolution that is worthwhile, and is a real revolution, and that succeeds, is a humane revolution....

BUCKLEY: Otherwise it's called an insurrection or a mutiny.

HUEY: Or a rebellion, or riot.

BUCKLEY: As I understand it, the generally accepted test of the integrity of a revolution is whether it is established once it has taken place, if the people truly support it.

HUEY: A revolution cannot succeed without the people's support. Changes in authority can be successful, but I think we'd have to have a functional definition, we'd have to stipulate what we mean by *revolution*.

BUCKLEY: Well, there are revolutions every two or three months in Latin America without the people getting involved at all.

HUEY: I'd probably call that a coup d'état. But, by way of definition, I'd reject your definition, but I appreciate your calling a coup d'état a revolution. I can function with that.

BUCKLEY: Fine, and if you want to call a popular revolution a popular revolution, please call it a popular revolution.

HUEY: I'd have to say that revolution would have to be popular or else I wouldn't label it a revolution. So really, we're just dealing in the semantics of what a revolution is made of. We won't have to belabor that. Any rebellion that establishes a new authority, if you would like to call that a revolution, then I could entertain it because it's just a word anyway. In governments, changes in relationships between people and authority and institutions, I'd say many forms are taken....

BUCKLEY: What would you call the thing that ousted King Farouk?

HUEY: I wouldn't call it a revolution.

BUCKLEY: Even though an entirely new order was brought in?

HUEY: Yes. With coup d'état it's common that an entirely new order is brought in.

BUCKLEY: Not necessarily. Sometimes a coup d'état takes away one colonel and puts in another colonel.

HUEY: Sometimes. But other times a coup d'état establishes an entirely different relationship between the institutions and the people in a particular place.

BUCKLEY: In which case it's revolutionary.

HUEY: I said I could function with that definition, if you insist. But to me, *revolution* carries a special connotation. Of course this is only my subjective feeling about it. If I have to distinguish between those changes of power, in my own way of thinking, I would call one a flower and the other a skunk.

BUCKLEY: I grant that you have considerable authority in your movement. But I'm not sure that you have the authority to impose your own terminology.

HUEY: I agree that your definition is not necessarily a lexical definition. I already granted that if you wanted to stipulate that as the definition of revolution, I'll entertain it…. I'm not attempting to stipulate a new definition. There are authorities I could cite that would call a revolution a very special thing. One authority would be the scholar philosopher Chairman Mao Tse-tung. He would only call a people's movement, and the overthrow of the authority by the proletarians, a revolution. But I wouldn't support Chairman Mao against you in saying that that is the only definition. Unfortunately, with the English language or rather the American language (that's a little different from the English language) it, (revolution), becomes a pretty vague thing. You have so many lexical definitions that directly contradict each other. I don't think we should belabor our audience who has the authority to define a particular phenomenon.

BUCKLEY: As you no doubt know, the word people, the term *popular support,* is used by Chairman Mao, as you refer to him in your book, with some sense of proprietorship. That is to say, he always talks about "the people." But the people are in fact never consulted about anything. They have never been consulted about Chairman Mao, about any of his regulations, or about any of his foreign policy.

HUEY: I differ with you. I think that too much of the time, because of our cultural differences, we only consider being consulted within the scope of what we feel being consulted is. For instance, in the West, as well as in Latin America, people say there's no democracy in Cuba because they' re not putting the ballot in the box. So therefore people are not consulted. On the other hand, Fidel Castro says that the people are consulted in an even more severe way; that the authority is put to the acid test. The acid test is that for a long time the people can be fooled, but they can't be fooled and misused all of the time. The test would be the doom of authority through armed revolution. That is the way the people are consulted in the final analysis.

BUCKLEY: I don't know what you're talking about, and I don't think you do either.

HUEY: Well, you can only speak for yourself. I'll be more clear. I'm going to explain a principle. The principle is how the people are consulted in a democratic society. I'm saying that Westerners have a particular definition of what democracy is about, and I can appreciate that definition. Here in the West it is felt that the only time the people are given democratic rights is when they can put the ballot in the box. You vote for a particular person within a particular framework. What I'm saying is that sometimes people are heard, people participate, and it could be called democracy, because what matters is who defines democracy. In the West much of the time if you're not allowed to vote by putting the ballot in the box and choosing an administrative person, if this does not take place, then in the West, we're inclined to say there's no democracy. This is not necessarily true, if democracy is defined as all of the people getting a fair share and a fair deal of whatever wealth there is and some control over their administrators. But here you can only vote within the scope of the definition of the institutions and the authorities that control them.

BUCKLEY: Democracy consists not only of being permitted to vote but in being permitted to organize an opposition so as to discover whether people are latently on your side. There is no practice of democracy, as commonly understood, in Cuba. The assumption that an organization is democratic or otherwise the leader would be overthrown is naive.

HUEY: There's one fallacy in what I think you would consider a democracy. You could only organize in opposition within the scope defined by the authorities that have control anyway. And this is true in the socialist society as well as in the capitalist society.

BUCKLEY: Give me an example.

HUEY: The example is this: In this society you are not allowed to organize in opposition against the authority through armed resistance with intent to overthrow the government.

BUCKLEY: We call that rebellion.

HUEY: By law. But you've already agreed that if you had lived in 1776, you probably would have chosen Washington. This definitely would have been against the law. I'm saying that when we talk about organizing opposition against government in this world, nothing that I know about has the audacity at this point to allow anyone to organize in opposition against the authority any way they like.

BUCKLEY: I don't understand you. If you want to organize in opposition in the U.S. short of killing people—

HUEY: Hold it right there. "Short of killing people." Why do you say that?

BUCKLEY: Well, because those are the rules.

HUEY: That's just what I'm saying, You have to operate within a limited scope.

BUCKLEY: The rules of democracy are that the art of persuasion has to be practiced short of assassination.

HUEY: I understand that. There is also the same principle operating in socialist or communist countries.

BUCKLEY: Give me an example, where?

HUEY: Well, let's choose the People's Republic of China.

BUCKLEY: Tell me one authority on—

HUEY: We could start with Chou En-lai. I spoke with him in the People's Republic of China. I had six hours of private talks with him, and I had many hours of talks with responsible members of the Central Committee of the Chinese Communist Party. I was shocked. I suddenly realized how brainwashed I had been by Western thought. As I sat there, it was said that all state administrations are oppressive to someone. And he started to explain that the capitalist state, that the people who own the capital, are a minority; they oppress the majority through exploitation. He said that in the national state, sometimes a whole nation will oppress the rest of the world with their state national administration, so they're still a minority oppressing the majority of the world's people, the way the Hitler regime attempted to do, and the way this [American] regime attempts to do. What I thought was so shocking was that he said,

"While you have state administration, we expropriate from the people. If the people in this country earn ten dollars an hour, we only give them eight. The difference between us and the capitalist state is that our expropriation is different. We don't have private ownership, so we would give the two dollars that we expropriated from the people back for their own welfare. The capitalist state gives it to themselves, into their pockets. Therefore, the people are still not free as we would like. However, we work for the dissolution of a State—for our own disappearance."

When he said that, I realized that he was saying that he is working for the end of the communist regime in China. I thought that was very honest. That was a statement that led me to believe that if he's working for the dissolution of the state, then opposition could arise to work to wither away territorial boundary lines.

BUCKLEY: I'm attempting to pin down a point and I'm losing track of it. I said, "Who agrees with you?" and you said "Chou En-lai." And then you proceeded to tell me what Chou En-lai said to you.

HUEY: I can tell you of other people: Comrade Tung, Comrade Li; you wouldn't know the difference. I named a person that you're probably familiar with. They say that you're well read and you are conscious of world events, so I only named one of the officials in China so that you could identify him. I doubt if you've been to the villages, the countryside of China. Have you?

BUCKLEY: Yes, I did go. Are you aware of the messages that Chou En-lai sent to Allende [the president of Chile]?

HUEY: Yes, I saw the letter.

BUCKLEY: And you remember that he said that he does not believe that Marxism can be ushered in by a parliamentary democracy? You know that Chou En-lai, in that particular statement, said that he does not believe in the right to organize an opposition that is contrary to the dialectics of Marxism.

HUEY: I would like to make this clear, for the audience and for you: I don't know about Chou En-lai, but I'm not a Marxist. I think the whole concept that Marx tried to lay down as a scholar, a historian, a philosopher, has been distorted. People became priests of Marx. I am not. I think that Marx was a scientist. He tried to point out a very advanced method of analyzing phenomena; it is called dialectical materialism. You can't usher in dialectical materialism because that is the whole order and process of the universe. In other words, I explained one of the principles, that contradiction is the ruling principle of the universe; it gives motion to matter.

Contradictions based upon internal strife seem to give it the ability to move and to be transformed. Societies, people, and my fellow revolutionaries, who think that you can usher in a social order through any sort of ideological proclamation are very wrong. The society itself strains itself to fight against colonialism, such as America did with England. After that a situation arises with workers, unions. There is the struggle against the owners of the factories, and you can come up with another type of order, which is much different from the formalities of the ballot. You don't know where it's really going to progress to until you become such a scientist of the people that you can harness the forces that are in operation and set them in a direction that is most desirable.

BUCKLEY: Why don't we get a little more concrete, if you don't mind; let's talk about the Black Panther movement.

HUEY: I like to argue theory with you probably better than factual things.

BUCKLEY: I'm a little more interested in factual things.

HUEY: I think you're very fictitious. I was inclined to believe that you were a thinker, somewhat of a scholar, and a theoretician, but I'm usually wrong about those sort of things.

BUCKLEY: I'm also a yachtsman, which doesn't mean that we're here to discuss boats.

HUEY: I don't know anything about the facts of boats, I couldn't talk to you about that, but I know something about theory.

BUCKLEY: Let's talk about your Party. Why did you feel it necessary to expel Eldridge Cleaver?

HUEY: He was not expelled. He left the Party, and we thought that it was a good time for him to leave because in organizations, parties, companies, there are very bright, articulate people. They often have great influence upon others, and people are impressed. When a person comes in who is articulate, bright, and eloquent, and because of the oppression he's gone through, he becomes somewhat sick, his great influence over the whole administration can lead the whole organization down the drain.

BUCKLEY: By doing what? What was it that "lead you down the drain"?

HUEY: Well, when the Party started in October 1966, in Oakland, we had the occasion, as a strategy, to arm ourselves in a police-alert patrol. We followed the police, we were very careful to follow city ordinances, gun regulations, state law, and our constitutional rights. But we realized that it wasn't the principle of revolution or the armed principle of our Party, to take the gun and make the gun the only thing that could fight a revolution. So, it was a strategy that was mistaken after I went to prison.

We realized that we had to treat the issues that the people were most concerned about. After I went to prison, with this influence, and much of the respect that I personally gave him, he led us astray. So, it was my fault also. The media enjoyed the sensationalism of the gun. In many ways, we set ourselves up for the murder we received. We had to deal with the objective situation to see what changes could be made; the changes I saw that I could support, because there are some changes that I don't support, and I wouldn't call them revolutionary changes. I'm not a leader, I'm an organizer.

BUCKLEY: So you think that your organizing talent would result in a victory over Eldridge Cleaver, not your theoretical ability.

HUEY: Well, if Eldridge Cleaver was able hypothetically to organize the people, then that would mean that history would denounce me and justify him, or history would justify my way of doing things, or my influence in the Party, because really it's the Party that really makes things move. I'm influential, and I have a vote, and my vote is probably worth more influence than many other comrades, but I work for that to be changed, as they become more organized, more clear, and gather expertise in organizing.

It wouldn't be a fight. I can't conceive of a fight between Eldridge and myself for leadership or anything. If the Party said that they think that Eldridge Cleaver is correct, then I'll bow out. The biggest problem is that I don't think that Eldridge will come back. But, hypothetically, if he were to come back, I think the media would drop him quickly, because we have an affectionate name for him: we call him an M.F., or media freak. The media created this kind of ghost split that supposedly occurred within the Party. They listened to him and then give a kind of credence to Eldridge Cleaver as a representative of a small Party or large faction. But we can't ever find any small cult, Party, or anything. However, as soon as the news reporters come in and put the cameras up and start talking, they have created what I call a media organization. It's a little different than a paper organization, but we live in a pushbutton world now.

BUCKLEY: Well, given your organizing talent and your theoretical position, why is that?

HUEY: No, I said I would like to think of myself somewhat as an organizer with some expertise, but I'm not very good really. If I were good, America would be changed tomorrow, or yesterday, but we're still struggling on precinct levels, making many turns and many maneuvers.

BUCKLEY: Yes, I know that you're struggling.

HUEY: Well, I couldn't be that good, because I'm saying from objective evidence that there are not too many changes that I desire that have been made as rapidly as I desired. However, everything is in a constant state of transformation. America's certainly changed; the situation in the country is different from what it was in 1619. I have to acknowledge that. I have to acknowledge contributors to the people's struggle such as Martin Luther King or John Brown, Denmark Vesey, Nat Turner. I have to acknowledge people who have contributed to change in America.

BUCKLEY: Well, who said you didn't? I don't know what you're up to.

HUEY: I'm only up to this: I'm saying that we all play a part in attempting to change things so that we will not have the physical clash that causes the inevitable death of men. I reject violence; there's no need for it and violence will no longer have to exist. I think that the death of any man diminishes all of us, because we're involved with humanity. I would like to admit to you that I don't have the answer to even start to resolve the contradictions in this country, so that we can have that new order. But I do have a desire, a desperate desire, to reach the other shore. And I think that each day, each minute, whether we know it or not, we're slowly, in this world, arriving at another level. Some other relationship between all of us, whether you define yourself philosophically as a conservative, as a progressive, as a reactionary, or as a revolutionist.

BUCKLEY: Mr. Simpson from Trinity College.

MR. SIMPSON: I've enjoyed the exploration of Mr. Newton's concepts. I thought what you said was quite clear.

HUEY: Well, it seems that Mr. Buckley is the only dunce around here so far.

MR. SIMPSON: But I'm even more interested in getting a little more practical and down to present social policies in the cities, in the inner cities; the continuing and ever-occurring crisis in the inner cities, where large numbers of people are trapped in a cycle of poverty. I want to know whether either of you can suggest and agree upon a social policy for the inner city that would lead to the reduction of tensions and new levels of communication?

HUEY: First, I would like to make this very clear, so that Mr. Buckley and I don't go off onto another tangent. I saw, crystal clear, how we can start to reduce the kinds of conflicts that we're having in this country. I saw an example of that in China. This is not China, that is a different culture. Their history is different, therefore the transformation there will be different. Things will take a different shape. What I saw was this: when I went there, I was very unenlightened and I thought that I knew something about China. I thought, as it has been said so often, that China would be a homogeneous kind of racial/ethnic territory. Then I found that 50 percent of the Chinese territory is occupied by a 54 percent population of national minorities, large ethnic minorities. They speak different languages, they look very different, they eat different foods. Yet, there is no conflict. I observed one day that each region—we call them cities—is actually controlled by those ethnic minorities, yet they're still Chinese.

BUCKLEY: Would that include the Tibetans?

HUEY: Yes, there was a big conflict for so long—

BUCKLEY: Yes, they called it genocide.

HUEY: Well, all right then. You talk about genocide. If the Chinese were wrong then, they're in the barrel with the rest of us—with England as well as America, in your genocide against blacks. The whole Western world has crucified over 50 million blacks alone. America took part in this. You can call that genocide. I'm talking about a general condition in China where ethnic minorities I've observed control their whole regions. They have a right to have representation in the Chinese Communist Party. At the same time they have their own principles. You talked about organizing opposition. You cannot vote to organize an opposition to reinstate private ownership there any more than you can organize an opposition to take away private ownership in this country. So, it's what you choose. I happen to choose the way they go about it, all right?

BUCKLEY: I thank you, Mr. Simpson, for listening to this illusive reply to the problems of the inner city.

HUEY: Did I get too theoretical again?

BUCKLEY: Well, Mr. Simpson will explain it to you later....

HUEY: Then I will say this: The cities in this country could be organized like that, with community control. At the same time, not black control so that no whites can come in, no Chinese can come in. I'm saying there would be democracy in the inner city. The administration should reflect the population of the people there.

BUCKLEY: No capitalists, like Lin Piao? Mrs. Holland?

HUEY: You say that Lin Piao is a capitalist?

BUCKLEY: I was teasing you.

MRS. HOLLAND: In reading through most of the earlier Panther material, religion was not emphasized, or rather was deemphasized. Have you and the members of your Party rethought about the relevance of religion in the culture of black people of America?

HUEY: I think that with any people, religion is almost a necessary thing to engage in. I'm a very religious person. I have my own definition of what religion is about, and what I think about God and so forth. As I analyze religion, I find that we are all talking about the same God, the person or thing in nature that we do not know, that we do not understand, that we do not control, but that somehow affects us. In Webster's dictionary they say that this too could be defined as ignorance. You don't know God, but you know there's something there. You didn't create yourself, so you must have been created.

I find it hard to tell a person, "Don't believe in God" and also tell him, "Pretend that you know everything, all the answers." So no matter what religion it is—whether Judaism, Christianity, or Islam—God is always that "thing": the unknown, the unknowable. I say that it's ignorance. It's ignorance when you don't know, and it's wisdom when you do. My father has been a minister ever since I can remember, and he used to always tell me, "You know, the church is the heart of men and God grows from within." So as we eliminate our ignorance, and our God stops being ignorance and becomes wisdom and he grows within us, then we will really know who God is. We will see that we walk with him, that we talk with him, that we will find ourselves. We will know that our pipes have been in our mouths all the time. We'll know really who we are, and we'll know who God is. We'll find that he's the "all," which is a nonsense term because man only knows events in between the beginning and the end. Both of those are words that maybe Mr. Buckley can define, but I can't. We know there's something outside of events that we don't understand.

BUCKLEY: Mr. Moots?

MR. MOOTS: I have a question for you, Mr. Buckley. Much of the emphasis on modern research, perhaps the concern of students here, has been viewing the Panthers in the last two or three years and seeing a great deal of metamorphosis that has taken place. Probably we have many more questions for Mr. Newton about where the Panthers stand now compared with the past. I would like to ask you if you have undergone a metamorphosis in your own appraisal? Some of your earlier statements about the Panthers were rather strong. I was curious about your present appraisal.

BUCKLEY: My judgment has been publicly made of the Panther

movement. It was made on the examination of its literature. I've read the Panther paper and described its contents and its publication. But I don't think that it's an historical exaggeration to say that the Black Panther Party, to the extent that one could infer its thoughts from these declarations, was based on its need to despise the white race.

MR. MOOTS: Could I suggest an example. In one piece, I believe it was in *Look* magazine, you disagreed strongly with Dick Gregory, who had indicated that the militant stance, symbolism, and rhetoric functionally could actually displace violence, if you see what I mean. Could you perhaps accept that as a phenomenon?

BUCKLEY: Yes.

MR. MOOTS: Of a positive good that the Panthers have…?

BUCKLEY: Yes, yes, I could. Unfortunately, as much could be said of the Ku Klux Klan. Dick Gregory gave an example to me that you may not remember about a black woman who felt intimidated. This was about two or three years ago, and she called the Black Panther headquarters and they sent someone to look out for her. And he was armed. On the basis of the assurance that she got from his presence, she did calm down, and recovered her stability. And there is an impression that people can perform that kind of a function, armed in that kind of a way. I have no doubt that the Black Panthers did it.

HUEY: I would like to say this, and I'm sorry if I interrupt, but when people equate the Black Panther Party with the Ku Klux Klan and White Citizens Council, I get upset. The point is that dialogue, dialectical struggle, or struggle through words—this would be what I hope will be the next advance man will make; that he will put down the club. But I think there are certain difficulties to face before that point. I think that things don't just happen, they start. But as long as there's a special economic interest one has to support, an authority that one must support, then he creates a rhetoric that he uses in order to sell ideas to a group, an army, or a henchman. I think that this kind of dialogue would be inflammatory and cause much violence. I think that rhetoric ran amok in the Black Panther Party while the leadership was under the influence of Eldridge Cleaver. It caused murders of many of our people. It laid the foundation so that even the black community could say, "Oh, see those bad guys are out there, you see, they always want violence and robberies and so forth." This kind of rhetoric can provoke physical conflict. Dialogue itself carries no virtue unless it's pointed in a direction to resolve a problem. You see?

MR. MOOTS: What about the role today of the Panthers? You indicate in your *To Die for the People* that one of the first priorities is education. But you don't actually define that. Do you mean political education, the use of the media, or do you mean formal education? For example, would you have advice for the black students here today?

HUEY: Most of us have been taught, we've been programmed by our schools and universities, to think in categories. That's very different from thinking dialectically. Many, many things are in play at the same time, but we think of *education* to refer to formal knowledge perhaps or maybe political education. When I say *education* I mean a raising of the consciousness of the people so that external stimuli will bombard the human organism and from that process a person will begin to have some sort of awareness of what is going on. I agree with Sigmund Freud in that the first step in controlling what's wrong with you in relation to the social forces is to know what you're dealing with. When I say *education* I mean it in the broadest sense of the word. Technical education—we're living in a very technical world now, thanks to the West—is a contribution to humanity. I don't like the way they arrive at it, I accuse them of trespassing. They took away other people's goods and they dominated other people as their very own, and certain people were able to inherit without ever working at all—such as my friend here [Buckley]. They [Westerners] protect that interest of the right to inheritance. I say that being educated is to be conscious and know as much as you possibly can so that we can start dealing with this garbage pile we call society.

BUCKLEY: For the record, while you were relaxing in jail, I was working.

HUEY: Maybe you call working, running your mouth on these TV programs. I don't see any calluses on your hands.

BUCKLEY: I was writing all those books you didn't read.

HUEY: Is that right? From what I understand of the books, it didn't take too much time to do that. They're very much like your conversation here. I'm only joking with you, because I really enjoy talking with you. No, truly, I think you're very entertaining, and I like the hot kind of debates in which we have to struggle to get to the seed, you know? So, I'm sorry if I was hard to take. You've proven yourself to be the gentleman everyone says you are, in spite of all the other criticisms.

Eldridge Cleaver: he is no James Baldwin, 1973

Eldridge Cleaver's prison masterpiece, *Soul on Ice*, was a manifesto of its time. The book is riddled with powerful insights and contradictions typical of the transitional period of the 1960s. It is a link in that long chain of prison literature brought to its zenith in the 1970s by George Jackson. George Jackson was Eldridge Cleaver's dream come true. Since his release from prison, Cleaver has been acting out his own nightmares. The essay on James Baldwin in *Soul on Ice* is an angle of refraction into the springs of that nightmare.

The essay to which I refer, "Notes on a Native Son," is a classically ambivalent attack on Baldwin, his politics, and most of all his sexuality. There are passages of stabbing relevance and malevolence:

> Baldwin says that in Wright's writings violence sits enthroned where sex should be. If this is so, then it is only because in the North American reality hate holds sway in love's true province. And it is only through a rank perversion that the artist, whose duty is to tell us the truth, can turn the two-dollar trick of wedding violence to love and sex to hate—if, to achieve this end, one has basely to transmute rebellion into lamblike submission—"You took the best," sniveled Rufus, "so why not take the rest?" Richard Wright was not ghost enough to achieve this cruel distortion. With him, sex, being not a spectator sport or panacea but the sacred vehicle of life and love, is itself sacred.
>
> Of all Black American novelists, and indeed of all American novelists of any hue, Richard Wright reigns supreme for his profound political, economic, and social reference.... But, ah! "O masters," it is Baldwin's work which is so void of a political, economic, or even a social reference. His characters all seem to be fucking and sucking

in a vacuum. Baldwin has a superb touch when he speaks of human beings, when he is inside of them—especially his homosexuals—but he flounders when he looks beyond the skin; whereas Wright's forte, it seems to me, was in reflecting the intricate mechanisms of a social organization, its functioning as a unit.

Baldwin's Christian survival tactic of love is shredded mercilessly. Christian love and passive homosexual love are mere functions of each other, and the scandal of turning the other cheek in racist America is a madness to Cleaver. He writes:

> Rufus Scott, a pathetic wretch who indulged in the white man's pastime of committing suicide, who let a white bisexual homosexual fuck him in his ass, and who took a Southern Jezebel for his woman, with all that these tortured relationships imply, was the epitome of a black eunuch who has completely submitted to the white man. Yes, Rufus was a psychological freedom rider, turning the ultimate cheek, murmuring like a ghost, "You took the best so why not take the rest," which has absolutely nothing to do with the way Negroes have managed to survive here in the hells of North America! This all becomes very clear from what we learn of Erich, the arch-ghost of Another Country, of the depths of his alienation from his body and the source of his need: "And it had taken him almost until this very moment, on the evening of his departure, to begin to recognize that part of Rufus' great power over him had to do with the past which Erich had buried in some deep, dark place: was connected with himself, in Alabama, when I wasn't nothing but a child; with the cold white people and the warm black people, warm at least for him.

Beneath the glinting surface of the criticism there is always a paranoid position that must be explained because of the sad and virulent scenario Cleaver set in motion when he put down the pen for the sword—or pretended that he did.

In a telling passage, Cleaver throws light on Baldwin and the "deviant" tradition so threatening to the incarcerated revolutionist:

> Somewhere in one of his books, Richard Wright describes an encounter between a ghost and several young Negroes. The young Negroes rejected the homosexual, and this was Wright alluding to a classic, if cruel, example of an ubiquitous phenomenon in the black ghettos of America: the practice by Negro youths of going

"punk-hunting." This practice of seeking out homosexuals on the prowl, rolling them, beating them up, seemingly just to satisfy some savage impulse to inflict pain on the specific target selected, the "social outcast," seems to me to be not unrelated, in terms of the psychological mechanisms involved, to the ritualistic lynchings and castrations inflicted on Southern blacks by Southern whites. This was, as I recall, one of Wright's few comments on the subject of homosexuality.

But that is precisely the buried meaning of Cleaver's essay! Ostensibly concerned with James Baldwin, Cleaver is "punk-hunting."

In 1967, Cleaver was invited to a special dinner for James Baldwin, who had just returned from Turkey, and he in turn invited me. When we arrived, Cleaver and Baldwin walked into each other, and the giant, six-foot-three-inch Cleaver bent down and engaged in a long, passionate French kiss with the tiny (barely five feet) Baldwin. I was astounded at Cleaver's behavior because it so graphically contradicted his scathingly written attack on Baldwin's homosexuality in his article "Notes on a Native Son." I later expressed my surprise to Cleaver, who pleaded that I not relay this incident to anyone. I did not understand then but now realize that Baldwin ("The Native Son"), who had neither written nor uttered a word in response to Cleaver's acid literary criticism, had finally spoken. Using nonverbal communication, he dramatically exposed Cleaver's internal contradiction and "tragic flaw"; in effect, he had said, "If a woman kissed Cleaver she would be kissing another woman, and if a man kissed Cleaver, he would be kissing another man."

In *Soul on Ice* Cleaver quite accurately explains that "self-hatred takes many forms; sometimes it can be detected by no one, not by the keenest observer, not by the self-hater himself, not by his most intimate friend." Baldwin, in Cleaver's eyes, is a "self-hater" and a "homosexual." Cleaver states, "I, for one, do not think homosexuality is the latest advance over heterosexuality on the scale of human evolution. Homosexuality is a sickness, just as are baby-rape or wanting to become the head of General Motors." Cleaver forgets to mention that Baldwin makes no attempt to conceal his homosexuality and thereby escapes the problems of the repressed homosexual.

Yes, Baldwin is an admitted homosexual, but he is not a depraved madman. Can Cleaver say the same? Does Baldwin's *open homosexuality* threaten Cleaver's *repressed* homosexuality, which manifests itself in violence against women? The lady doth protest too much, methinks. The problems, difficulties, and internal conflict that Cleaver has within himself—because he is engaged in denial of his own homosexuality—is projected onto an eternal *self* (Baldwin) in order to defend his own threatened ego. He attempts to project his own femininity onto someone else and to make someone else pay the price for his guilty feelings. Cleaver embraces supermasculinity, pretends to despise Baldwin as a "punk," while admitting that he (Cleaver) is a rapist. One must despise (and/or envy) women in order to be driven to degrade and ravish them.

What does Cleaver think of women? Better yet, what does he think of those black masses that he accuses Baldwin of despising? By his own admission:

> I became a rapist. To refine my technique and *modus operandi*, I started out by practicing on black girls in the ghetto—in the black ghetto where dark and vicious deeds appear not as aberrations or deviations from the norm, but as part of the sufficiency of the evil of a day—and when I considered myself smooth enough, I crossed the tracks and sought out white prey. I did this consciously, deliberately, willfully, methodically—though looking back I see that I was in a frantic, wild, and completely abandoned frame of mind.
>
> Rape was an insurrectionary act. It delighted me that I was defying and trampling upon the white man's law, upon his system of values, and that I was defiling his women—and this point, I believe, was the most satisfying to me because I was very resentful over the historical fact of how the white man has used the black woman. I felt I was getting revenge. From the site of the act of rape, consternation spreads outwardly in concentric circles. I wanted to send waves of consternation throughout the white race.

He "practiced" on black women in order to acquire perfection for his rape of white women. This implies not only envy of the female principle but contempt for blackness, combining the elements of self-hatred and repressed sexual needs. Cleaver degrades black women twice, first by rape and second by viewing it as a *dress rehearsal*. By practicing on blacks he expresses his admiration for whites. He in fact pays white women a childish compliment: He ascends the heights to their vaginas by stepping on the bodies of black women!

The irony of Cleaver and his flaw is his self-hatred and his sexual insecurity; his pitiful need for a clear love-hate dichotomy, his need for a clear-cut male-female dichotomy, and his need to be a superhero. Cleaver's criticism of Baldwin rests upon his secret admiration of Baldwin and upon his ambition to become Baldwin in a literary sense. In order to become Baldwin, he must topple and consume him. He had to find in Baldwin a tragic flaw, and it follows that he finds in his hero the things that he cannot, due to built-in totems and taboos, accept in himself (that is, his lack of absolute masculinity and his infantile character). He finds it necessary to make a vicious, apolitical attack upon the psychosexual condition of Baldwin in an effort to appear the superstud and to steal Baldwin's fire. He elevates himself on Baldwin's shoulders. Cleaver once said to me, "*Soul on Ice* is my *Fire Next Time*."

If only this failed revolutionist had realized and accepted the fact that there is some masculinity in every female and some femininity in every male, perhaps his energies could have been put to better use than constantly convincing himself that he is everyone's superstud. How confused and tortured he must be to equate homosexuality, baby-rape, and the desire to become the head of General Motors. But Cleaver's imagination is not healthy. It is paranoid and self-condemning; it is consumed by a need to be female and white. He is no Baldwin, no Genet.

Part Four

The Last Empire

BY THE MIDDLE 1970s the Black Panther Party had reached a crossroads. Just as the civil rights movement associated with Martin Luther King, Jr., had been forced to reassess its purpose following its landmark legislative victories in the 1960s, the Black Panthers found that portions of our platform had been integrated into the American political mainstream.

As this closing section suggests, Intercommunalism was Huey's defining ideology throughout the latter years of the Black Panther Party. Both "Who Makes U.S. Foreign Policy"? and "The Dialectics of Nature" underscore his ever-increasing interest in the United States "empire," especially its organized methods for crushing political dissension. Additionally, Huey's writings of this period begin to assume an explicitly academic tone new to his body of work. Whereas flashes of rhetoric often predominate in his early pieces, Huey's readings in the areas of philosophy and natural sciences inspired a series of intellectually dense considerations of issues such as gender and human evolution.

Further research in this area was interrupted, however, in 1974 when, in order to avoid prosecution on charges of pistol-whipping his tailor and murdering a prostitute, Huey and party comrade and later wife Gwen Fountaine fled to Cuba. Acquitted of all charges in 1977, Huey entered the University of California, Santa Cruz, upon his return home. His doctoral dissertation, "War Against the Panthers: A Study of Repression in America," became the most detailed summation of the FBI's campaign to end the Black Panther Party ever published when it was printed posthumously as a book in 1996. The Freedom of Information Act made formerly classified government documents available to the general public of the post-Watergate era. Huey thereby accessed over eight thousand 250-page volumes of never-before-released "intelligence" reports to chronicle J. Edgar Hoover's fifteen-year "war" on the Panthers. As the excerpted "Response of the Government to the Black Panther Party" demonstrates, the Bureau's intention was to criminalize the politics of dissent at all cost.

Although *War Against the Panthers* is the last book of Huey's writing produced during his lifetime, he remained politically active during the 1980s. He lectured frequently on the black liberation movement and global affairs, as well as participating in various grassroots social-justice causes until his death in 1989.

who makes U.S. foreign policy?: 1974

The ideals enshrined in the Declaration of Independence recognize the right of nations to self-determination. Any oppressed people may, in the spirit of the American Revolution, forcibly overthrow the institutions of their oppressors in order to secure for themselves the rights to "life, liberty, and the pursuit of happiness." Yet the record shows that as the United States has assumed its role of dominant world power, it has consistently opposed the major social revolutions of our times. In violation of the principle of self-determination, the U.S. has intervened militarily, diplomatically, and economically to crush or to cause grave setbacks to these revolutions, whether in Russia, Mexico, China, Cuba, Greece, or Vietnam.

Nowhere has this pattern of policy been more evident than with the American intervention in Vietnam. In 1945, the Democratic Republic of Vietnam was established in a document modeled on the American Declaration of Independence. The Republic was at first recognized by the former colonial power, France. But when that power sought to reassert control of its former colonial territory by establishing a puppet regime in Saigon, it found support in U.S. policy. Not only did Washington support France's illegitimate war of conquest through economic and military aid, but Washington itself took over the struggle to defeat the Vietnamese Republic when the French failed. Indeed, more than twenty years after the proclamation of Vietnam's Declaration of Independence, the Vietnamese peasants are still being assaulted by the U.S. armed forces in what must be the most ruthless and destructive intervention on historical record.

Such counterrevolutionary expeditions are of course standard U.S. Cold War policy, despite the unprecedented ferocity and unparalleled savagery of this execution. As already noted, it forms a consistent pattern with other U.S. interventions in Santo Domingo, Cuba, Guatemala, the Congo, the Middle East, China, Greece, and elsewhere during the Cold War years, and in Russia, Mexico, Cuba, China, and other countries earlier in the century. Indeed, counterrevolutionary intervention, which is at the heart of the Cold War and its conflicts, has been a characteristic of U.S. foreign policy ever since the United States embarked on a course of overseas economic expansion following the closing of the geographical frontier more than seventy years ago.

How is this counterrevolutionary policy, which runs directly counter to the high ideals of the American republic, to be explained? How is it to be explained that the largest "defense" program of any nation in history (and of the United States in particular, which, prior to the postwar decades, never maintained a peacetime conscription army) is organized around the unprecedented concept of counterinsurgency? These questions can only be answered if it can be shown that there is a group wielding predominant power in the American polity; a group whose interests not only run counter to America's high ideals but who can impose its own interpretation of the American tradition onto the framework of policy making in the state. If it can be shown that there is an expansionist, militaristic class among the plurality of competing interest groups that enjoys a predominance of power and therefore can establish its own outlook as a prevailing ideology, then an explanation of both the paradoxical character of American policy and the sources of the Cold War conflicts can be seen.

Such a "ruling class" can, in fact, be readily shown to exist: its locus of power and interest is in the giant corporations and financial institutions that dominate the American economy, and more broadly, the economy of the entire Western world. "In terms of power," writes one corporate executive and former U.S. policy maker, "without regard to asset positions, not only do five hundred corporations control two-thirds of the nonfarm economy, but within each of that five hundred a still smaller group has the ultimate decision-making power. This is, I think, the highest concentration of economic power in recorded history." Further, "since the United States carries on not quite half of the manufacturing production of the entire world today, these five hundred groupings—each with its own little dominating pyramid within it—represents a concentration of power over economies which makes the medieval feudal system look like a Sunday school party." As this observer points out, many of these corporations have budgets, and some of them have payrolls that affect a greater number of people than most of the hundred-odd sovereign countries of the world. Indeed, the fifty largest corporations employ almost three times as many people as the five largest U.S. states, while their combined sales are over five times greater than the tax revenue collected by the states.

In the final analysis, it is the dependence of men individually and collectively on the corporately organized and controlled economy that provides the basis for the corporate domination of U.S. policy, especially U.S. foreign policy. The basic fulcrum of corporate power is the investment decision, one that is effectively made by a small group of men relative to the economy as a whole. This decision includes how much the corporations spend, what they produce, where the products are to be manufactured, and who is to participate in the process of production. But this is not the whole extent of the power of the corporate investment decision. In the national economy the small oligarchy of corporate and financial rulers, who are responsible to no one, determine the level of output and employment for the economy through their investment outlays.

As Keynes observed, the national prosperity is excessively dependent on the confidence of the business community. This confidence can be irreparably injured by a government that pursues a course of policy inimical to business interests. In other words, basic to the political success at the polls for any government or its specific programs will be the way the government's policies affect the system of incentives on which the economy runs: a system of incentives that is also the basis of the privileges of the social upper classes.

This does not mean, of course, that the business community as such must prefer a particular candidate or party for that candidate or party to be victorious. It means, much more fundamentally, that short of committing political suicide, no party or government can step outside the framework of the corporate system and its politics by embarking on a course that threatens the power and privileges of the giant corporations. Either a government must seize the commanding heights of the economy at once (that is, initiate a course of social revolution), or run things more or less according to the priorities and channels determined by the system of incentive payments to the corporate controllers of the means of production. This is an unspoken but well-understood fact conditioning politics in capitalist countries, which explains why the pattern of resource allocation—the priority of guns over butter, of highway construction over schools and hospitals—is so similar in all of them. It also explains why, despite the congressional and parliamentary enactment of progressive tax laws in all these countries, the spirit of the law has been thwarted everywhere. And nowhere has the significant redistribution of income promised by these democratically ratified statutes taken place.

The sheer economic pressure that the corporations can exert over the policies of democratically elected governments is lucidly manifest in the experience of the Wilson Labour government in England. While owing its office to labor votes and labor money, this government was forced by "the economic situation," (that is, domestic and international capital), to pursue precisely the policies that it had condemned as anti-labor while in opposition. Of course, under normal conditions, particularly in the United States where no labor party exists, the corporations have less subtle means at their disposal for ensuring policies conducive to their continued vigor and growth. The means by which the upper classes maintain their privileged position and vested interests in countries where universal suffrage prevails vary with the differing traditions, social institutions, and class structures of the countries involved. They vary also with their historical roles. Thus, as the United States has replaced Britain as the guardian power and policeman of the international system of property and privilege, the corporate ruling class has less often been able to entrust policy to indirectly controlled representatives and has more often had to enter directly the seats of government itself.

In the postwar period, the strategic agencies of foreign policy—the State Department, the CIA, the Pentagon, and the Treasury, as well as the key ambassadorial posts—have all been dominated by representatives and rulers of America's principal corporate financial empires. In addition, all the special committees and task forces on foreign policy guidelines have been presided over by the men of this business elite, so that on all important levels of foreign policymaking, "business serves as the fount of critical assumptions or goals and strategically placed personnel." While the corporate-based upper class in general occupies a prodigious number of positions in the highest reaches of the "democratic" state, it need not strive to occupy all the top places to impose its own interpretation of the national interest on American policy. Precisely because the prevailing ideology of U.S. politics in general, and of the federal government in particular, is corporate ideology, reflecting the corporate outlook and interests, and because the framework of articulated policy choices lies well within the horizon of this outlook, political outsiders may be tolerated and even highly effective in serving the corporate system and its programs.

There are additionally two principal methods by which corporate ideology comes to prevail in the larger political realm. In the first place, it does so through the corporate (and upper-class) control of the means of communication—and the means of production of ideas and ideology of its strength. In a class-divided society under normal (that is, nonrevolutionary) conditions, the national interest vis-à-vis external interests is inevitably interpreted as the interest of the dominant or ruling class. Thus, in a corporate capitalist society, the corporate outlook as a matter of course becomes the dominant outlook of the state in foreign affairs. This is not to say that there is never a conflict over foreign policy that expresses a conflict between corporations and the state. Just as there are differences among the corporate interests themselves within a general framework of interests, so there are differences between the corporate community outside the state and the corporate representatives and their agents in the state, resulting from the difference in vantage and the wider and narrower interests that each group must take into account. But here, too, the horizon of choice, the framework of decisive interests, is defined by the necessity of preserving and strengthening the status quo order of corporate capitalism and consequently the interests of the social classes most benefited by it.

What, then, is the nature of corporate ideology as it dominates U.S.

foreign policy? What is its role in the development of the Cold War? As a result of the pioneering work of Professor William Appleman Williams, these questions can be answered precisely and succinctly. The chief function of corporate ideology is, of course, to make an explicit identification of the national tradition and interest—the American Way of Life—with its own particular interest. This identification is accomplished by means of an economic determinism, that takes as its cardinal principle the proposition that political freedom is inseparably bound up with corporate property: that a "free enterprise" economy is the indispensable foundation of a free polity, where *free enterprise* is defined to coincide with the status quo order of corporate capitalism, not with an outdated system of independent farmers and traders.

Starting from this basic premise, the ideology articulated by American policymakers since the nineteenth century maintains that an expanding frontier of ever-new and accessible markets is absolutely essential for capitalist America's domestic prosperity. Hence, the extension of the American system and its institutions abroad is a necessity for the preservation of the American, democratic, free-enterprise order at home. Originally formulated as an "open door" policy, both to prevent the closing of the external frontier by European colonialism and to ensure American access to global markets, this policy has led to the preservation and extension of American hegemony and the free enterprise system throughout the so-called "free world." From Woodrow Wilson's First World War cry that the world must be made safe for democracy, it was but a logical historical step to Secretary of State Byrnes's remark at the close of the Second World War that the world must be made safe for the United States. This is the core of America's messianic crusade: that the world must be made over in the American image (read: subjected to the American corporate system) if the American Way of Life (read: the corporate economy) is to survive at home.

If expansion (and militarism) had held the key to American prosperity or security, the postwar period would undoubtedly have realized Secretary of State Byrnes's ambitious goal. In the last stages of the war and the first of the peace, the United States successfully penetrated the old European empires (those of France, Great Britain, and the Netherlands); assumed control of Japan and its former dependencies; and extended its own power globally to an unprecedented degree. By 1949, the United States had liens on some four hundred military bases, while the expansion of direct overseas investments was taking place at a phenomenal rate. Whereas U.S. foreign investments had actually declined from $7.9 to $7.2 billion between 1929 and 1946, they increased an incredible eightfold to more than $60 billion between 1946 and 1967. It is this global stake in the wealth and resources of the external frontier that forms the basis of the U.S. commitment to the worldwide status quo, even though it may not always provide the whole explanation for particular commitments or engagements. This commitment to the internal status quo in other countries renders Washington's expansionist program not the key to security but the very source of Cold War conflict.

The expansion of corporate overseas investment has not produced beneficial results on the whole, and the corporate status quo is a status quo of human misery and suffering in almost every region.

> No one acquainted with the behavior of western corporations on their pilgrimages for profit during the last fifty years can really be surprised that the…explosions now taking place (in the underdeveloped world) are doing so in an anti-American, anti-capitalist, anti-western context. For many years these continents have been happy hunting grounds for corporate adventurers, who have taken out great resources and great profits and left behind great poverty, great expectations and great resentments. Gunnar Myrdal points out that capitalist intervention in underdeveloped countries thus far has almost uniformly had the result of making the rich richer and the poor poorer.
> —W. H. Ferry, *Irresponsibilities in Metrocorporate America*

This has indeed been the undeniable historical consequence of capitalist corporate expansion, even though this is not what one is led to believe by the orthodox theorists and academic model builders who function so frequently as the sophisticated apologists of the American Empire and the policy of counterrevolutionary intervention necessary to maintain it. In the writings of such theorists, the expansion of America's monopolistic giants and their control of the markets and resources of the poverty-stricken regions is presented as entailing the net export of capital to these capital-starved areas, the transfer of industrial technologies and skills, and the flow of wealth generally from the rich world to the poor.

From this point of view, revolutions that challenge the presence and domination of foreign corporations and their states in the underdeveloped world are misguided, sinister in intent, or contrary to the real needs and interests of the countries involved. Indeed, for those who maintain this view, revolutions are regarded as alien-inspired efforts aimed at subverting and seizing control of the countries in question during periods of great difficulty and instability prior to the so-called takeoff into self-sustaining growth. This is the argument advanced by W. W. Rostow, former director of the State Department's Policy Planning Staff and the chief rationalizer of America's expansionist counterrevolutionary crusade. In fact, this view rests neither on historical experience, which shows the presence of foreign capital and power to have had a profoundly adverse effect on the development potential of the penetrated regions, nor on a sound empirical basis.

Far from resulting in a transfer of wealth from richer to poorer regions, the penetration of the underdeveloped world by the imperialist and neo-imperialist systems of the developed states has had the opposite effect. As a result of direct U.S. overseas investments between 1950 and 1965, for example, there was a net capital flow of $16 billion to the United States. Similarly, when looked at in their political and economic settings, the much-heralded benefits of the advanced technologies transplanted into these areas (but under the control of international corporations), also tend to be circumscribed and even adverse in their effects. Regarded in terms of its impact on total societies rather than on particular economic sectors, the operation of opening the backward and weak areas to the competitive penetration of the advanced and powerful capitalist states has been nothing short of a catastrophe. For as Paul Baran showed in his pioneering work *The Political Economy of Growth*, it is precisely the penetration of the underdeveloped world by advanced capitalism that has in the past obstructed its development and continues in the present to prevent it. Conversely, it has been primarily the ability of a select few countries to escape from the net of foreign investment and domination that has made countries such as Japan exceptions to the rule. Professor Gunder Frank and others have continued the work that Baran initiated, showing how foreign capitalist investment produces the pattern of underdevelopment (or "growth without development," as it is sometimes called) that is the permanent nightmare of these regions. The crisis of reactionary intercommunalism has now inevitably given rise to the concept of "revolutionary intercommunalism."

dialectics of nature: 1974

> The subject of our discussion is the Ocean, which was described in olden times as immense, infinite, the father of created things, and bounded only by the heavens; the Ocean, whose never-failing waters feed not only upon the springs and rivers and seas, but upon the clouds, also, and in certain measure upon the stars themselves; in fine, that Ocean which encompasses the terrestrial home of mankind with the ebb and flow of its tides and which cannot be held nor enclosed, being itself the possessor rather than the possessed.
>
> —Grotius

The revolutionary, dialectical materialist, or intercommunalist perceives both the problem and the solution of environmental disaster differently from the Establishment of Western scientific reformers. Where the Establishment sees individual human nature and technological progress as the engine of destruction, the dialectical materialist looks on the ecological spoilation and traces the poisonous spoor back to the strongholds of reaction and capital; calls the pollution for what it is—war against nature, against people, against the race itself, against the unborn.

In his book *The Frail Ocean*, Wesley Marx supplies us with a particularly ugly model of pollution. To the resource-poor Anglo-American Empire the following is meant to symbolize the total confusion of responsibility and solution to what is in reality a complex ecological crisis that has become a function of the superindustrial West.

No other natural phenomenon on this planet—not even mountains five miles high, rivers spilling over cliffs, or redwood forests—evokes such reverence as the sea. Yet this same "all-powerful" ocean now proves as slavishly subservient to natural laws as a moth caught by candlelight or a rose seed blown into the Atlantic. The ocean obeys. It heeds. It complies. It has its tolerances and its stresses. When these are surpassed, the ocean falters. Fish stocks can be depleted. The nurseries of marine life can be buried. Beaches can erode away. Seawater, the most common substance on this planet and the most life-nourishing, can be hideously corrupted. It can host substances that in the stomachs of oysters or clams are refined into poisons that paralyze porpoise and man alike.

Or as it became appallingly clear on March 18, 1967, an entire ocean region can suddenly find itself in direct jeopardy. The Atlantic Ocean off the southern tip of Great Britain sparkled deep blue, unsullied by running whitecaps or shadowing storm clouds. Guillemots, auks, redshanks, herons, and Penzance fishermen dipped into this blue world, drawing succor from its life-giving energy. At Land's End, hotel owners ordered new carpets to greet London's annual summer pilgrimage to the Cornish coast. Since the sapping of its tin mines and fertile lands, the magnet of ocean beaches alone keeps Cornwall from sinking into economic depression. (Characteristically, Marx passes over the tin and land depletions. This is an example of one-dimensional analysis, and fatal to any solution.)

As the world discovered, the spilled cargo of one ship twenty miles away managed to shatter this serenity as no gale could do. The cargo of the reef-gashed *Torrey Canyon* was a liquid one, totaling thirty-six million gallons, ordinarily a raindrop in the vast solution of the ocean. But the ocean cannot absorb oil very efficiently. Within three days, slicks the color of melted chocolate sprawled over one hundred square miles of ocean, a moving quagmire that ensnared seabirds by the thousands. The slicks, with their chirping cargo of flightless birds, rolled up on the golden beaches of Cornwall. Land's End smelled like an oil refinery. Like the oil-fouled birds, the oysters, clams, and teeming inhabitants of tidepools found themselves encased in a straitjacket of Kuwait crude. Three weeks later, and some two hundred miles away, the pink granite coast of Brittany received the same greasy absolution from la marée noire. Silently, without the fanfare of howling winds and crashing waves, this oil-stricken ocean was coating the coastlines of two countries with havoc.

Great Britain, perhaps history's most famous maritime nation, swiftly mobilized its forces. RAF jets dropped napalm bombs on the slicks to fire them into oblivion. It was like a grand military campaign. (JENKINS TELLS OF PLAN TO USE THE VIETNAM HORROR BOMB, proclaimed an extra edition of the London *Daily Mirror*.) But the open ocean, heeding its own laws, dispersed the spilled oil into a slick solution that, as a reporter on the scene for the *Economist* noted, is "incombustible by anything short of the fires of hell." From napalm bombs, the campaign accelerated to include a fleet of thirty warships armed with chemical detergents. Yet the detergent fleet could hardly cope with the extent of the slicks, and those that they did manage to emulsify drifted down into the ocean depths to asphyxiate schools of fish. Great Britain retreated to its shores, and Tommies, along with children using garden spray cans, began deploying detergent on the beaches. Ironically, the detergent created a milky liquid more toxic to shellfish that Kuwait crude, and much of the muck had then to be shoveled up. Meanwhile, in makeshift hospitals, bird lovers, their hands clawed red, cleaned terrified oil-smeared seabirds with talcum. The nation that started out to napalm the fireproof sea was hand-cleansing its beaches and its birds—and waiting for the next high tide. The British prime minister, who had called out the RAF, tried to cheer up Cornwall's worried hotel and shop owners, their livelihood suddenly threatened. "I am not canceling my holiday in that part of the world," said Harold Wilson reassuringly.

Some hotelkeepers canceled their carpet orders; others rolled up their carpets, while one more inventive owner prohibited the wearing of shoes in his hotel. When oil from a Liberian tanker grounded in international waters and controlled by an American company smears your rugs, whom do you sue? Today marine bacteria, the only creatures that can stomach Kuwait crude, busily feast on the remains of the slicks.

Professor Marx goes on to tell us that the stresses on the ocean are ceaselessly intensifying. As land resources shrink, the world's population and its expectations expand. Indeed, the functions of land on a congested planet that consists largely of water may narrow to one: providing living space for man. Already we contend with orange groves and cattle ranches for elbow room. The continuing depletion and/or usurpation of land resources raises the need for a new storehouse of energy to keep the Technological Revolution fueled with food, water, pharmaceuticals, gas, and minerals. Barring cultivation of the universe, the ocean emerges as that vital storehouse.

Today the "society where none intrudes" is being penetrated by submarines equipped with nuclear reactors and rockets, by oceanographers with silken deip nets, by oil-drill islands built to hurricane specifications, and by scuba divers clad in pastel neoprene suits. "A complete three-dimensional realm for the military, commercial, scientific and recreational operations of man," exults Seabrook Hull, a new-style ocean admirer, in his book *The Bountiful Sea*. A "sea of profit," gloats a Wall Street broker. Even the Boy Scouts offer a new merit badge for oceanography.

The challenge of the ocean is international as well as national in scope. As marine technology generates more activities and ambitions, nations must learn how to preserve marine resources as well as their respective tempers. Nutrition experts promote the ocean as a food locker for future survival, but the high-seas fishery competition seems little related to effective conservation or food distribution. The ocean promises to be the ultimate challenge to nations to coexist on a watery planet whirling through space. An indication of the ultimate seriousness of this challenge is that three estranged world powers—the United States, mainland China, and Russia—now share the common border of the Pacific Ocean, perhaps the planet's richest resource.

Marx concludes elegantly that a rather ominous question emerges. Byron claimed that "Man marks the earth with ruin." Many of our hills, valleys, and rivers—even the air we breathe—today testify grotesquely to the accuracy of this pessimism. Are we perhaps fated to mark the ocean with ruin, to plunder, pollute, and contend until we have a ghost ocean bereft of all but the voice of its waves?

Wesley Marx, like other official and semi-official experts, points to the ocean as a last refuge for the world's exploding population (of course, they call for birth control by the State along with all other ecological reforms). These experts mention in passing that the U.S. Navy, Atomic Energy Commission (AEC), and various huge multinational corporations may undermine, somewhat, bold environmental reform. These same experts argue for moderation on the part of the navy from turning the sea into a hostile arena bristling with atomic submarines and other instruments of "defense."

In the end, the experts hope, forlornly, that a traditional human love of the sea will, somehow, mystically overcome the powers of consumption, greed, and war.

Without dwelling on the horrors of environmental pollution (exploitation for profit), it is easy to contrast the dialectical analysis of the crisis with the traditional wisdom of the experts, some without being aware, and the regulatory agencies who have sold out in advance of this struggle for survival for both humans and nature.

Let us take up a factor of that spilled oil off the English coast, and see the interrelationship of a part of this energy crisis.

Most of our energy reserves are on public land: more than half of our oil and natural gas reserves, 40 percent of our coal and uranium, 80 percent of our oil shale, and 60 percent of our geothermal resources. Within the past year, hundreds of thousands of acres of offshore oil and gas reserves, oil shale and lands in Colorado, and geothermal sites in California have been turned over to Exxon & Company.

This is in addition to the hundreds of thousands of acres of western coal rights that were leased to the same corporation in the years prior to 1973. A study by the Federal Power Commission found that eight major corporations already lease 74 percent of the available oil and gas reserves on federal land.

Example: Washington is literally giving away an estimated six hundred million barrels of oil from shale to a few giants. A consortium of Gulf and Standard of Indiana stands to gross more than $40 billion on the oil shale tract it has leased. The way the game is played, the government will wind up giving the consortium money.

While dishing out the loot to the favored, Nixon is impounding $11.8 billion voted by Congress for "housing, health, welfare and water pollution controls," says the *Christian Science Monitor*. This is because he has "a fundamentally different approach to the problem of community life," to use his own words.

While Nixon proposes to cut $800 million from welfare costs, he gears up the Pentagon budget with new weapons systems whose total cost could run upwards of $100 billion. (A Joint Economic Committee study shows the Pentagon wants to increase its take in the new budge by $12.4 billion, from $82.6 billion to $95 billion.)

Human beings are the component left out of the survival equation by the environmentalists (except in generalized "underdeveloped" nation statistics, and as objects of blame for the whole mess, in the industrialized countries, and, of course, as suicidal breeders in the colonies). Because of oil politics, coal is once again receiving attention. The politics of coal? One hundred thousand killed in the American mines by the "economies" of the owners and the "regulatory" agencies they control.

The preferred method of extracting the shale is strip mining. That means roughly one million acres (the area of Massachusetts, New Jersey, and Delaware together) could be torn out. *Eighty percent of that is public land.* The mined rock is then to be crushed and cooked at nine hundred degrees Fahrenheit, which produces low-grade raw oil, which then must be upgraded to be usable.

Great quantities of coal are needed for the cooking process. It will be strip-mined elsewhere in the West. Greater quantities of water are needed—one estimate is three to six barrels for each barrel of oil—and this is country where water is already short.

Once oil is shipped out, the residue will be left behind. There will be about a cubic yard of it for each barrel of oil.

That figures out to many cubic miles of black waste to dispose of. The plan is to pack it into canyons and smooth it off and try to grow vegetation on it. Leaching and runoff from the waste, oil spills, and other water pollution are the inevitable next step.

Besides taking precious water from the Colorado River and its tributaries (which provide water for Los Angeles, and irrigated farming in California), the shale oil industry will poison what water remains. And on top of all this will be the roads, trucks, pipelines, housing developments, sewage, and air pollution that comes when a massive industrial complex is imposed on virtually virgin land.

It is on a scale that makes any previous government giveaway seem trivial. But the horror of it is not to be grasped in the figures alone. That takes seeing the deer and the mountains, feeling the wind and hearing the silence.

To return to the politics of oil: the oil shale deal. A congressional investigator, Rep. Charles Vanik (D-Ohio) calls this a "giveaway, another Teapot Dome." It involves a seventeen-thousand-square-mile area of semi-wilderness in the Rocky Mountains where Colorado,

Utah, and Wyoming meet. A fine, gray rock found here yields oil after specialized processing. The Gulf-Standard bid for "leasing" shale lands was "$210 million for the first tract, with four billion barrels of oil recoverable." "That works out to five cents a barrel," says *The New Republic* (April 6). The world price for oil is around ten dollars and seems due to rise.

The bonus offered by the Interior Department for rapid development would lower the cost to three cents a barrel. However, a 1969 ruling by the IRS permits the 15 percent mineral depletion allowance to be computed not against the value of mined shale but against the more valuable crude that comes out of the retorting process. *Thus for each barrel of oil produced, the companies will get a tax write-off that far exceeds what they will pay the Treasury in royalties.* In addition, they'll enjoy the 7 percent investment credit and an assortment of state-level tax breaks.

This is not enough for the reactionary intercommunalists (by which we mean the total technologizing of monopoly capital beyond the mere brute force of imperialism). An Interior Department official, who has since joined the Atlantic Richfield oil shale operation, proposed that the depletion allowance should be raised to 22 percent, the investment credit to 12 percent, and an accelerated write-off of new plant costs should be thrown in as well.

Oil profits are booming. Sun Oil, for example, reports its first-quarter profits this year were 85 percent higher than a year ago. Exxon, 39 percent; Texaco, 123 percent and Occidental, 148 percent. *The New Republic* points out: "The large oil energy corporations that could sit on inflation are letting it rip. Oil that sold a little more than a year ago at the profitable level of $3.40 a barrel now sells at $5.25 or $10 a barrel. *The gap between the 1973 and 1974 prices represents almost pure profit. The policy of this administration is to put its trust in Big Oil and hope for the best.*" The new energy czar, John C. Sawhill, predicts the price of gas "may increase by another five cents over the next several months," the *Washington Post* reports.

The Guardian says, "The critical question over the next few years is what will be done with these publicly owned energy resources? Will they be given away to the same profit-seeking cartel that created the present 'crisis,' or will they be developed on a nonprofit basis in the public interest?... The most comprehensive alternative yet proposed is a bill by Senator Adlai Stevenson III to establish a Federal Oil and Gas Corporation, patterned after TVA.... [It] would have access to publicly owned oil and gas rights, as well as the power to acquire energy rights on public lands. It would enter into the full range of activity necessary for the exploration, development, refining, transportation and marketing of petroleum and gas products."

But Nixon is almost sure to veto such a bill if it should pass. This is not simply economic philosophy, the "trickle-down theory." It is a tactic borrowed from organized crime, the shakedown, protection racket. Big oil put up five million dollars for CREEP.

It got its money's worth: More than one hundred ex-oil industry employees work for the Federal Energy Office. The administration wants to open up the largest oil reserves, the navy's twenty-four-million-acre tract, to big oil according to the *St. Louis Post-Dispatch*. Major oil companies have been breaking antitrust laws with the knowledge and approval of the Justice Department, witnesses told a House investigating subcommittee.

In 1970 the Justice Department killed an antitrust action against major bidding on offshore lands. Nixon has advised GOP congressional leaders that "he is determined to take natural gas out from under federal regulations, even thought it will drive up the cost of heating homes and fuel plants," Jack Anderson reports. The IRS, when queried about taxes paid by oil companies, refers questions to the American Petroleum Institute, a private lobbying outfit. The administration is asking that private companies get a "guaranteed price" for oil obtained by new methods.

Intercommunalism is founded on the basic concept of the unity of nature underlying and transcending all arbitrary national and geographic divisions. Western science, of course, confirms this obvious concept at the same time as it slaves away in the service of reactionary intercommunalism.

Reactionary intercommunalism perceiving the interrelationship of all natural phenomena, *including all human beings*, seizes upon the phenomena in an attempt to distort the balance in its favor. This exploitation has led to enormous profits and power in the short run. But in a split second, historically, the superindustrial engines of the imperialist, reactionary intercommunalists have come to grief, and even the populations of the Anglo-American Empire itself are in the process of being "nativized" and pauperized in the name of "energy crisis." This crisis is, however, one of capital, not one of energy.

Revolutionary intercommunalism argues that the rising expectations of the Human Rights revolution in the exploited world will violently disrupt the reactionary distortion of the chain of nature in *its* favor. That this process of reversal has already begun is evident in the multiple crises in the reactionary capitals of the West at this hour.

Eve, the mother of all living: 1974

The psychobiologist Mary Jane Sherfrey made two startling discoveries in the mid-1950s. The first was that biological research had clear evidence that life in the uterus begins as female; the fetus was defined by a rudimentary phallus. The surpassing irony of Dr. Sherfrey's discovery was that this elemental fact had been totally ignored, or rather repressed, by biology as it existed under the spell of the "male bias"—and that is the second discovery. The two discoveries are of equal importance: to begin with, that life begins female, and second, that science has repressed and suppressed this twentieth-century heresy.

During the period of pre-science, the assumption had been, predictably, that life began as male, and that a castrated or deformed fetus was born as a female. This atavistic belief was eventually replaced by the idea that life began as a neuter with sex differentiations arriving at a later stage of intra-uterine development. This scientific-sounding proposition gave way under the weight of modern research data, but the new discovery was ignored.

This incredible gap in the scientific dialogue can have only one explanation: that Adam came out of Eve and not the reverse, as we have been taught for millennia. The fairy tale of Genesis is taken lightly at our peril, as Ms. Sherfrey and lately the women's liberation movement have told us. But the conflict between appearance and reality is perhaps more profound than even the women's movement has argued.

The first principle of nature itself seems to be female. Genesis is a startling testament to man's realization of that basic identity. In Genesis we see the ancient Mother Nature co-opted by a patriarchal super-masculine beard of a god. The trauma of female primacy is further

313

denied by making the woman, Eve, a mere extension of the man, Adam, and the issue of *his* body!

The early *gens* and tribes, as far as we can tell, were primarily matriarchal and matrilocal, or at the least, avuncular, with the mother's brother as the power. *All* of the earliest mythology is univocal in the identification of creativity, power, and primacy with the female. Mother Nature and Mother Earth are the universal models for *all* creation, human and metaphysical. But by the time of writing the Bible, woman had suffered her world-historical defeat and man's revenge appears complete.

It is my argument that women were socially supreme as long as the size of population groups was relatively small. Man was ignorant of his role in procreation and so worshiped women and the impenetrable process of birth and renewal that she acted out. The seed, he thought, came from the rain and the wind. This set of fantasies was bound to lead to a slavelike mentality in the man that, combined with his socially inferior status in the *gens*, snakelike, caused him to plot his rebellion and revenge against women and nature itself. A revenge he is still exacting.

Behind the iron reaction formation of the myth of Genesis stands a much older sensuous myth that enshrines woman as the center of creation. Modern chromosomal research echoes the old story of parthenogenesis. Twenty million years ago at the dawn of the Pleistocene there must have existed a basic ambiguity about the process of fertilization. A remnant of this Ur-theory of procreation can be seen in Genesis. The Hebrew word *Ladat* means both "knowledge" and "sexuality" in its broadest sense.

The Tree of Knowledge is a transitional symbol, looking backward to a time when men were not absolutely necessary for the creation of life. Simultaneously, the tree is a maddening symbol of power that men must possess if they are to control the mysterious female. Thus men must destroy the garden and the tree in order to make woman totally dependent on him and his seed. This reverses the power relationship at one stroke. But the existential and race memories of the female paradise where man was a parasitic nonentity throbbed then, as they do now, like unhealed wounds.

In those days "there were giants," Genesis says. No doubt, but by the time of Genesis, the sex of the giants had been changed. And the sacred fruit that reminded men of their eternal biological androgyny was declared forever taboo.

The female could be best overthrown during pregnancy or just after childbirth. When man discovered his role in procreation, he could then attempt indirect coercion by the constant impregnation of the woman, and direct control by the seizure of those goods and symbols that stood for power.

Woman was slowly imprisoned in the very biology that had made her supreme. She bore her fruit in pain, and she became a slave to the now–physically superior male, just as earlier he had been her vassal under the spell of her fecundity.

Men moved swiftly to the necessary dehumanizing of women: she was the snake and the devil, the unclean and the freak of nature—all the identities that man had labored under in a universe that was female in principle. No wound to man's vanity was too small for restitution. Genesis would be hilarious if it were not such frightening evidence of the historical male rage.

Once man was physically and mythologically compensated for his former humiliation, he had to force on women a slave mentality and erase forever any intimations of her former glory. Since the man's exposed and erectile tissue could not *naturally* gratify or answer the complex inner organism of the woman, she had to be desexualized. The age-old whore/madonna strategy was the crude answer to the stinging reminder of female superiority that was before his eyes every day: she was always ready and therefore potent, while he, with his exposed genitalia, was always potentially impotent, and his impotence or inadequacy was called forth precisely by her biological readiness, at almost *any* age!

So man, who could not give birth, began to invent everything else. His "brain children" were all made possible by the art of writing; the exclusion of women from that process meant that she dropped below the level of history to live like an animal in a perpetual drudgery and blows. The "masculine protest" suffered by women, corresponds in many ways to the agony of Black people since the Renaissance.

Now the tables seem to be turning. Modern technology gives women the upper hand once again. She does not need man as a father or a provider or even necessarily as a lover (since her demands for orgasm have created a new epidemic of impotence). Her psychological armor is less paralyzing than that of the fearful male. He must constantly prove his adequacy. In the era of doomsday weapons, his war-loving, chauvinistic, sexist male protests of power have become the scandal of history. Man, who cannot give life, has begun to take it by the billions in our century. He has revenged himself by desecrating Mother Nature and polluting Mother Earth.

The historical defeat of woman came by violence—that must be admitted now. It is only natural, then, that there should be a burning component of violence in the women's movement. The war between the sexes is just that.

Black liberation has something to say to women on the score of revolution and rebellion. The first thing to understand is that black men are enslaved by the white man, just as the white and black women have been. It is therefore futile to try to make black men the enemy of black women. Futile and counterrevolutionary!

The aim of some women to replace men, mechanically, as the master, simply posits another inferior order—men, once again. The "natural superiority" of women does not give them *any* social superiority in this age of technology; they must fight for power with their natural allies: all those who are oppressed by our system of chauvinistic exploitation. Men, except for a handful, are merely "women" to the ruling circle: cannon fodder, taxable objects, cogs in a wheel.

It is *human* liberation that makes a dialectic with every suffering member of the mass of humankind. There is simply not enough power to go around. So men will fight women in the way that whites fight blacks. Women's liberation must transcend the scarcity principle under which it has been operating, must make common cause against the ancient snake of antinatural tyranny; in the house, certainly, but finally, in the White House and other palaces of the West.

And the paradigm for it all began in the Garden of Eden, or rather, the Olduvai Gorge in Africa.

the mind is flesh: 1974

The overthrow of the Cartesian concept of "mind" is a fast-fading victory laurel. A dialectical analysis of "mind," by definition, must subsume the seminal nineteenth-century scientific breakthroughs in biology, anthropology, psychology, and epistemology. Dialectics must reach forward building on this science and its philosophies as represented by existentialism, psychoanalysis, learning theory, and historical materialism. Only dialectics can verify Søren Kierkegaard's memorable theorem that "the mind is flesh." And, we would add, this flesh both evolved and functions in an environment that is modified and partially created by the history and presence of the "mind." Therefore to change the environment is to change the mind at the phenomenal level.

Gilbert Ryle, in his book *The Concept of Mind*, provides a demystification of the mind as the Age of Enlightenment conceived it: the "mind as spirit."

The official doctrine, which hails chiefly from Descartes, goes something like this: With the doubtful exceptions of idiots and infants in arms, every human being has both a body and a mind. Some would prefer to say that every human being is both a body and a mind. His body and his mind are ordinarily harnessed together, but after the death of the body his mind may continue to exist and function.

Human bodies exist in space and are subject to the mechanical laws that govern all other bodies in space. Bodily processes and states can be inspected by external observers. So a man's bodily life is as much a public affair as are the lives of animals and reptiles, and even the careers of trees, crystals, and planets.

But minds do not exist in space, nor are their operations subject to mechanical laws. The workings of our minds are not witnessable by other observers; their careers are private. Only I can take direct cog-

317

nizance of the states and processes of my own mind. A person therefore lives through two collateral histories, one consisting of what happens in and to his body, the other consisting of what happens in and to his mind. The first is public, the second private. The events in the first history are events in the physical world, those in the second are events in the mental world.

It is customary for man to express this bifurcation of his two lives and of his two worlds by saying that the things and events that belong to the physical world, including his own body, are external, whereas the workings of his own mind are internal. This antithesis of outer and inner is of course meant to be construed as a metaphor, since minds, not being in space, could not be described as being spatially inside anything else, or as having things going on spatially inside themselves. But lapses from this good intention are common, and theorists are found speculating how stimuli, the physical sources of which are yards or miles outside peoples' skin, can generate mental responses inside their skulls, or how decisions framed inside their craniums can set into motion their extremities.

Underlying this partly metaphorical representation of the bifurcation of a person's two lives there is a seemingly more profound and philosophical assumption. It is assumed that there are two different kinds of existence or status: What exists or happens may have the status of physical existence, or it may have the status of mental existence.

There is thus a polar opposition between mind and matter, an opposition that is often brought out as follows: material objects are situated in a common field, known as "space," and what happens to one body in one part of space is mechanically connected with what happens to other bodies in other parts of space. But mental happenings occur in insulated fields, known as "minds," and there is, apart maybe from telepathy, no direct causal connection between what happens in one mind and what happens in another. Only through the medium of the public physical world can the mind of one person make a difference to the mind of another. The mind is its own place and in his inner life each of us lives the life of a ghostly Robinson Crusoe. People can see, hear, and jolt one another's bodies, but they are irremediably blind and deaf to the workings of one another's minds and inoperative upon them.

The consensus of Western science is, of course, that the mind is the brain. Variations on this theme represent various competing schools of psychology and psychobiology. All of this, however, dialectical materialism subsumes and then sets itself against. The dialectical approach tries to distinguish at once between the brain and the "mind," to take the quotation marks, provisionally, off of the construct "mind."

The argument concerning inherent versus environmental phenomena in the mind-brain is at least as old as Socrates. Dialectics, of course, considers this but one more tautology or false argument.

There is an article by the great biologist Theodosius Dobzhansky, in the 1960 volume *Hundert Jahre Evolutionsforschung*, to the effect that the theory of preformation in evolution—which amounts to denying evolution in favor of a purely endogenous unfolding, predetermined once and for all—is "irrefutable" in principle and that all one can do with it is show where it is useless. But if one attaches any importance at all to the influence of environment, even by means of some purely structural selection, it becomes very hard to view as deducible the sort of evolutionary history that then emerges. Of course, he makes it clear that environmental influence is exerted by means of selection, although this selection never becomes operational except at some precise moment and "has no foreknowledge of the future." But the genes, according to him, act rather like the members of an orchestra, not like soloists, so that, as he has emphasized elsewhere (*American Naturalist*, November–December 1956), selection operates not upon separate characteristics but upon overall reactions, both of the polygenic kind (concurrent action of the genes) and the pleiotropic kind (modification of a single gene with repercussions on two or more characteristics). What decides success or failure is, moreover, not only the final phenotypic state reached, but all the stages along the line. On the other hand, variability is due not simply to mutations but, above all, to genetic recombinations; it will be remembered that Dobzhansky originated the "hypothesis of balance" (1955), according to which the adaptive norm is an arrangement of a number of genotypes, multiple heterozygotes predominating. The vital factor is then seen to be the internal equilibrium of the genetic pool with what Lerner has called the "genetic homeostasia." The important part played by equilibrium is stressed as much by Wallun (1957) and others as by Dobzhansky and Spassky in their classic experiment.

Jean Piaget and Erik Erikson have given us models of a genetic agenda that suggest a philosophy of mind-brain-body; trust, creativity, generativity, joy, and their opposites, *depending on the environment of the ego.* It is well to recall here Freud's little-remembered dictum: "When I say ego, I mean the body ego."

What are the parameters of the discussion of the mind? Dialectics argues a spatial reference (intercommunalism), the plasticity of the ego: the racial potential to overcome alienation at all orders of abstraction. Temporarily, we argue the historical materialism of the species: that the mind-brain-body evolved in tandem, coeval and concomitant.

The apes, after two and a half million generations, lived their lives much the same as did their earliest ancestors. They remained stooped, languageless, cultureless, static. But they were loving and generally peaceful.

Then a remarkable thing happened. Out of one of their lines, man was born. And though basically loving, he has become the only known creature massively destructive of his own kind. By contrast with the apes, men have accumulated all that our distinctive minds have learned in 3 percent as many generations. For man was born only eighty thousand generations ago.

Almost everything known as civilization has been devised by the most recent 0.5 percent of man's generations.

For example, agriculture and the possibility of living in settled communities were invented only five hundred generations ago.

Recorded history is only two hundred generations old.

The Golden Age of Greece lived but one hundred generations ago.

The entire span of the scientific era is encompassed by the last twenty generations.

The mind of man has been subjected to his own scientific study for only the last three generations.

The era of nuclear power is only a little more than one generation old.

The awareness of the possibility of universal abundance is less than one generation old.

That we have come so far in the human agenda in so few reproductive cycles, particularly in the last twenty, and especially in the last three, makes the only emotional posture appropriate to a human being one of considered confidence. Another way to grasp the dimension of man's achievement is to imagine its two million years compressed into a single lifetime, of, say, fifty years.

After shivering through darkness into middle-aged adulthood, at the age of thirty-seven, men fully tamed fire.

Only after forty-nine and three-quarters years of wandering as hunters did they settle down to till the ground, harvest crops, domesticate animals, weave rough cloth.

Six weeks ago some men invented writing. Three weeks ago the Greek carried literature, art, and philosophy to a pinnacle that set standards for the succeeding weeks. They also devised political democracy for the minority who were free citizens. And Hippocrates laid the foundation for the ethical practice of clinical medicine.

Eighteen days ago Jesus was born and died, and the people of what is now Vietnam began their continuing struggle against invaders. Five days ago the printing press was invented, and Vesalius did his pioneering human dissections. A day and a half later Shakespeare sent his winged words across linguistic and temporal boundaries, and Harvey discovered the circulation of the blood. Thirty-six hours ago Jenner introduced vaccination for smallpox, and the United States became an independent nation dedicated to the extension of democracy, whose people were expected to understand and express their judgment about all matters affecting their mutual future. On the same day the steam engine was invented, Pinel unchained the mental patients, and for the most part men stopped eviscerating in public those who had new ideas of government, or hanging old women accused of traffic with the Devil.

Late yesterday afternoon steamships and railroad trains began hastening about the globe, and Lister introduced antisepsis. This morning Freud launched his daring expedition to the lost inner continent of the unconscious, and the magic of electricity was tamed. At noon today men learned to sail beneath the waves and through the air.

Also around lunchtime a great war was fought to make the world safe for democracy. Six hours ago Fleming discovered penicillin, and another great war was fought, this one to save democracy for the world.

Shortly thereafter, the atom and hydrogen bombs were born. Five hours ago the television industry was born, three and one-half hours ago the war in Korea ended, Americans began to replace the French in Vietnam, and Salk introduced immunization against polio. Less than ninety minutes ago the Nuclear Test Ban Treaty was signed, and President Kennedy was murdered.

Half an hour ago, two astronauts from opposite sides of the earth took astonishing walks in space. We were reminded how tenuous is our mastery of even commonplace technology when half an hour earlier the lights mysteriously went out over the eastern end of the country. And less than a quarter of an hour ago, before most of us watching at home had become aware that our pollutions might destroy our life on earth, two of us celebrated our fifty-first birthday on the moon.

All of civilization spans only one-half of one percent of man's existence. Is this flicker of time a fair trial of so brave an effort?

The attempt must be made to find the balance, the dialectic and analytic relationships, between various orders of abstraction inherent in the mind-brain-body process. The operative word is process and it is the dynamic of process that distinguishes dialectical from traditional methods of analysis.

Concrete examples are called for at this point in the argument.

A great deal is made of the distinctions between personal and race memory as functions of the mind-brain (to which we will add "body"). The terrible anxiety concerning survival in the twentieth century has focused the genius of science, philosophy, and literature on the mind, or the brain, of humankind. Not surprisingly it is the existential novelists (Sartre, Camus, Moravia, and so on) who attempt to make the leap over the abyss, created by the science of the last century, that separates brain and mind; their leap is the beginning of a bridge; the bridge is the human body. The body that is animated by the time lag between the world and the nervous system. Thus, everything is memory, as we know phenomena.

"There is no such thing as *was*—only *is*. If *was* existed there would be no grief or sorrow." Faulkner's reading, with italics applied for emphasis, of the vicissitudes of memory, is magisterial. Memory makes men sick, repression of memory makes men sick, yet, to be well, the sufferer must remember both more and less. This is his psychotherapy.

In some primitive clans, when a child is born, a wooden image is buried in a certain place. This is the *chiringa*, the soul; the *chiringa* that will always be there as a fixed locus of identity surrounded and guaranteed by the earth itself. That is the genesis of the religious identity (*religio* in the sense of "tieing back") that is rooted in earth and soul. Now men are deracinated, denatured, uprooted forever, their souls floating and blown about in the endless wind of history, and any "cure" that cannot minister to this irremediable hurt is nothing more than a straw in that wind. So the soul looks endlessly for its *chiringa*. "Where can I find my home?" asks Nietzsche on his mantic wanderings. Now we all ask that.

One of our failed strategies is, always and everywhere, nostalgia (from *nostos*, "home-going"). But we cannot go home for two reasons. *Was* does not exist anymore, nor did it ever exist as we *choose* to remember it. In fact, we construct this former home out of our own awareness of loss and nothingness, or we project it forward into a heaven. "One day is enough" might have been a motto that modern existentialists have borrowed from one of their mentors, Dostoyevsky. But these big themes of time and inner space flow down this century from a matrix that includes psychoanalysis, existentialism, and dialectical materialism, however hard they try to be opposites of each other. After Freud the unconscious equaled timelessness. One day is enough if only the body could be cauterized of all its secret calls.

What are the laws and logic, as Camus called them, of the body? When Freud spoke of the "I" (ego), he spoke, he said, of the "body I," while Moravia and the others, for their part, seem to be writing of the body's memory. What else could they mean? Certainly there is no such thing as the memory's memory! What but the body can be meant, for what but the body could be the instrumentality of that all-embracing impulse to go home? The body craves again those never-to-be-recaptured caresses and states of childhood, but it also translates into fantasy and projection its abnegations and renunciations. This hidden agenda of yearning and gratification of the flesh is bound to be represented by images, by the feeling of nostalgia, and finally by rebellion. This rebellion, at the deepest level, is the existential revolutionary's field of inquiry. He is pursuing the I, or rather the structure of the I and its relation to Being. Being is comprised of energy in a certain structure called the I. The ideals, projections and sublimations, and atavisms acted out by literary models are the residue of past choices and abnegations. The energy of the "It" (id), the structure of the I, and their always-shifting interrelationship—this is the stuff of Being. The contrariety between the body and its memories (both real and regretted) produces a series of images from which the I selects its memories. The memory is the *chiringa*; unalterable, sanctified history. Looked at in this way, the neurosis is indeed a sacred idiosyncratic religion not to be given up on pain of damnation. It is to this grieving body with its deluded history that the twentieth-century helpers come to make an onslaught on nostalgia, to rescue *personhood* from *personality*, to replace *hiddenness* with *standing open* and being able to *stand it* (to use some of Heidegger's terms that are, for once, clear). This is the new Latin of the existential diagnosis.

Thus, soul-help means body-help in the most generous sense of the term. And the literary physician strives after that seamless web of meaning of the nonliterate aborigine for whom anything not of the here and now is called "in the dreaming." The I stands on the ruins of its choices; the I's choices are chosen from available options; these options are the upshot of environment biology and the nature of the world. This agenda can lead but to alienation of the It and the I if the vital current is broken or no *chiringa* is available. The anodyne for alienation has been, in recent cultures, ratiocination and romanticism: the negative and the positive faces of nostalgia. Nietzsche marked the end of these placebos; it was they, not God, that he canceled. We love and die now within biology and history—the very style of our existence produced by the holy war between these two inexorable forces. Neither God nor Reason may mediate from outside. The Dictionary and the Bible are vacated mythologies.

To live in a "postatheistic" as well as a post-Christian period is to nurture continual anxiety. The idea of Reason or of God must now be freshly invented by Camus and the others. As Buber or Kazantzakis might put it, it is they, Reason and God, who need us! Moravia's protagonists, then, are really gradations of the I, the anomalous flesh caught in its Procrustean tautology: the more one feels life calling in the *sorties* of the *soma*, the more audacious must the project, the *engage-*

ment, become; lest, under the unremitting pressures of finitude, one fall prey to memory, to *nostos,* to that hated "hope" from which the Greeks ran.

If existentialism agrees on anything (and it does), it is that man, as we thought we knew him, has disappeared. It is man that makes a hole in reality when his traditional values and identity have been abrogated. When "moral man" disappears or is wiped out by great events, then the atavist surviving projects his sense of nothingness onto reality and claims that it has vanished or become a hopeless jumble of meaninglessness.

This Mass for our century is given its most downright version by the author of that doomsday book of the everyday, *Being and Nothingness*:

> Freedom in its foundation coincides with the nothingness which is at the heart of man. Human-reality is free because *it is not enough.* It is free because it is perpetually wrenched away from itself and because it has been separated by a nothingness from what it is and from what it will be…. Man is free because he is not himself but presence to himself. The being which is what it is can not be free. Freedom is precisely the nothingness which is made-to-be at the heart of man and which forces human-reality to *make itself* instead of to *be*…. Freedom is not a being; it's *the being* of man—i.e., his nothingness of being.

This is the obligatory and most spectacular of all deductions: man is wholly and forever free. Camus sees "an absurd world where even the moles dare to hope." The wound in the idea of the conscience and of the world caused by the death of the idea of God has been suppurating now for three generations.

An ominous new euphemism—behavior modification—provides a fascinating example of how the superindustrial state, operating on the worldview of the last century, attempts to manipulate the mind-brain (exclusive of the body and the environment) in order to "socialize" modern-day Americans.

Inspired, perhaps, by the Pentagon Papers, someone in the bureaucracy of the federal government has smuggled out a Xeroxed nightmare: a ninety-two-page monograph whose official title is "Development and Legal Regulation of Coercive Behavior Modification Techniques with

Offenders," which is "out of stock," according to the Department of Health, Education and Welfare, which financed its preparation.

The HEW thesis is that social or cultural or, finally, political "rehabilitation" begins inside the nervous system of the citizen. A miniaturized radio transmitter, implanted inside the brain or body, can monitor and transmit the conversations, locations, even the sexual responses of the subject twenty-four hours a day. The report explains that sewed up inside the subject's body along with the transponder would be a radio-controlled electric-shock device. This device could deliver punishment to the "offender" anywhere in the world.

Who are the "offenders" or subjects? The author of the monograph, Professor Ralph K. Schwitzgebel of Harvard University, dwells on homosexuals, but later in the monograph he talks about an "offender's financial matters," and "disputes over financial obligations," and, ominously, "socially troublesome persons."

The paper predicts that "microminiaturization" will permit near-permanent "intra-cranial stimulation." Since the new program would relate to "civil" rather than "criminal" situations, we are assured that the "cruel and unusual punishment" clause of the Eighth Amendment to the Constitution would not present any serious obstacle to implementation of the plan. A euphemism for castration, "sterilization" is given as an example of a technique that is "more likely to be upheld (as a court statute) when it appears to be civil rather than criminal in nature."

A National Security Agency computer specialist has proposed attaching miniature electronic tracking devices to twenty million Americans. The "transponder" would transmit the wearers' locations by radio to a computer and could be used "for arrests following riots or confrontations" and "for monitoring aliens and political sub-groups."

Such devices seem to be the bitter fruits of a rapidly developing field, referred to euphemistically by its adherents as behavioral engineering. Its chief apostle, Dr. Robert Schwitzgebel, twin brother of Ralph, is urging the government to consider increased use of devices "designed to control group behavior." Noting that the government already spends much of its budget on prisons, police, judges, and so forth ("social control hardware"), Schwitzgebel proposes shifting "just a small portion" of the defense budget away from the development of weaponry to "devices for measuring and positively reinforcing desirable behaviors of large groups." The government could easily accomplish this, he added, "because 80 percent of the manufacturing assets in the United States is controlled by about 2,000 of the largest corporations."

Barton L. Ingraham of Berkeley's School of Criminology, suggests that "further control" could be achieved through recent developments in electrophysiology. Not only might "complete and continuous surveillance" of a person who had demonstrated "criminal tendencies" be possible but "automatic deterrence or blocking" of the criminal activity by electronic stimulation of the brain prior to commission of the act is also feasible. Electrical impulses injected into the brain can induce, inhibit, or modify such phenomena as movement, desire, rage, aggression, fear, pain, and pleasure.

At the Yale School of Medicine, Dr. Jose Delgado has implanted radio transceivers into the heads of his experimental animal subjects so that he can monitor and control their activities and emotions from a distant location. Computers have already been tested on subjects in mental "hospitals." The machines are programmed for undesirable behavior and send out inhibitory instructions.

In *Physical Control of the Mind*, Delgado—whose work is also funded in part by the government—predicted that ESB [Electronic Stimulation of the Brain] could become a "master control of human behavior by means of man-made plans and instruments."

Although maintaining law and order through brain control would "require a government with virtually total power," Ingraham sees several things in its favor: (1) it would be "completely effective"; (2) it would obviate the need for "massive changes in the social system"; and (3) it "would be relatively cheap." Thus, it falls out that the "oral modalities" and psychotherapy are for those that can afford to talk to a counselor, whereas the poor enjoy chemotherapy, shock therapy, and "psychosurgery."

And in California, Dr. William W. Herrmann, a "counter-insurgency specialist" for SDC (the System Development Corporation) told the *Los Angeles Times* that a good computer intelligence system would "separate out the...activists bent on destroying the system" and then develop a master plan "to win the hearts and minds of the people."

The Huey P. Newton Reader

The unstated motive of this domestic counterrevolution is nothing less than control of *bodies*. And the techniques are extrapolated world-wide wherever tyranny and the American Empire hold sway.

From the study of these poor souls (the old word for mind-brain-body) in the American laboratory one reckons back to the beginning, to Darwin and his evolutionary voyage:

> While going one day on shore near Wollaston Island, we pulled alongside a canoe with six Fuegians. These were the most abject and miserable creatures I anywhere beheld. On the east coast the natives, as we have seen, have guanaco cloaks, and on the west, they possess seal-skins. Amongst these central tribes the men generally have an otter-skin, or some small scrap about as large as a pocket-handkerchief, which is barely sufficient to cover their backs as low down as their loins. It is laced across the breast by strings, and according as the wind blows, it is shifted from side to side. But these Fuegians in the canoe were quite naked, and even one full-grown woman was absolutely so. It was raining heavily, and the fresh water, together with the spray, trickled down her body. In another harbour not far distant, a woman, who was suckling a recently born child, came one day alongside the vessel, and remained there out of mere curiosity, whilst the sleet fell and thawed on her naked bosom, and on the skin of her naked baby. These poor wretches were stunted in their growth, their hideous faces bedaubed with white paint, their skins filthy and greasy, their hair entangled, their voices discordant, and their gestures violent. Viewing such men, one can hardly make one-self believe that they are fellow-creatures, and inhabitants of the same world. It is a common subject of conjecture what pleasure in life some of the lower animals can enjoy; how much more reasonably the same question may be asked with respect to those barbarians! At night, five or six human beings, naked and scarcely protected from the wind and rain of this tempestuous climate, sleep on the wet ground coiled up like animals. Whenever it is low water, winter or summer, night or day, they must rise to pick shellfish from the rocks; and the women either dive to collect sea-eggs, or sit patiently in their canoes and, with a baited hair-line without any hook, jerk out little fish. If a seal is killed, or the floating carcass of a putrid whale discovered, it is a feast; and such miserable food is assisted by a few tasteless berries and fungi.

Here we may see clearly the subjective misunderstanding of objective phenomenon at the very origin of the modern method: complete ethnocentrism; class blindness; and the seeds of modern, "enlightened" colonization and enslavement. It is these same "half humans" who will have revolutionized the entire human agenda by the middle of the twentieth century. This four-fifths of humankind will rise up in their ghettos, from East to West, to announce their humanity in the name of the wretched of the earth.

It is, then, the task of dialectical materialism to invoke the entire human body in a complete social-historical context whenever the concepts "mind" or "brain" are brought to play in the dialogue of alienation that modern science has become. Our field is real life where each arbitrary order of abstraction (mind-brain-body) is always a function of human flesh and blood. And the sum of these abstractions is the soul. And that the soul and the ego may be congruous when the ego (the "I") and the race are perceived as functions of each other always and everywhere. Thus, dialectical materialism presses, always, toward a structuralism of dynamic process.

In order to take increased responsibility for directing our own biology, consciousness must be improved steadily, diligently applied to understanding the world and controlling ourselves, but resolutely prevented from interfering with activity properly left to automatic behavior.

In order to prevent ourselves from being enslaved by a minority, the majority of us must vigorously insist that new controls of mind not be applied by the few without the prior conscious consent of the many, both as to technique and objective.

If we follow the human agenda methodically, it is conceivable that much will become known about areas that today are totally obscured by bias, such as the possibility of extrasensory perception, survival of the personality after death, and so on. Perhaps long after we have departed, the gradual accumulation of information will shed some light on where and how we went. Personally I would be delighted with a world in which resources were diverted from projects to tyrannize, sell, or annihilate minds onto others designed to prove they can surmount distance or survive the grave. That is, provided all minds were permitted and helped to live freely and fully in the interim.

As we cross the threshold from the past era of scarcity to the future era of abundance, the mind is learning the controls required to remain zestfully engaged with life, throughout increased longevity devoid of drudgery and poverty. It must also learn to generate a new sort of man, capable of preserving, amplifying, and passing to our human or posthuman followers the striving for mastery of reality, while preserving its elements of intellect, character, freedom, and joy. Especially joy, for we are entering some of the most joyous of all the moments of man.

The mind is flesh!

affirmative action in theory and practice: letters on the *Bakke* case, September 22, 1977

(The following letters were sent to Nathaniel S. Colley of the NAACP and to William Coblentz of the Board of Regents of the University of California on the topic of Allan Bakke, a white medical student who charged that affirmative action preferences people of color and is therefore unconstitutional.)

To: Mr. Nathaniel S. Colley, Esquire
Western Regional Counsel
National Association for the Advancement of Colored People

Dear Mr. Colley:

What will a Supreme Court dominated by the racist appointees of an imperial madman decide regarding its previous decision on *Bakke?* The answer is rhetorical. The real questions are whether form is more important than content; does a change in strategy negate a principle; how long will we allow ourselves to play their cruel and usual game?

It is obvious to those with eyes that our people, black people, have suffered, to this day from the first day of chattel slavery in this country, the most outrageous forms of barbarity set upon any single group of people in known history. It is evident that blacks in the United States have been denied—even to this day—by a white-dominated society the most fundamental of human rights. The question of having to reverse a mere trend is piteous in the face of turning over an entire institution of racism.

We must look to win. Do we want to win an argument on the rightness of our plea or do we want to win the issue? We are *right*; but right in this country has usually spelled white. We deserve by decree our forty acres and two mules; but do we have them? We deserve a decent education; and since 1954, have there been any serious changes toward that? We must win any way we can. By any means necessary, pursuing a variety of courses.

The *Bakke* question is not complex. The answers are. Will we ask murderers not to kill? Will we ask racists to deny racism? Will we ask a Supreme Court, that has outraged the civilized world with its many antihuman decisions to become humane, understanding?

I urge, indeed, beg you, my Sisters and Brothers, to reconsider our posture in the *Bakke* case. If the Supreme Court decides on the issue as presented, it will surely find the victim guilty. It will set a nearly irreversible precedent to our disinterest. It will say with the rhetoric of "democratic racism" that to allow minority quotas in schools is a form of "reverse racism." This tragic turnabout will destroy, within a few years, all programs of affirmative action in this country and devastate our little achievements toward full citizenship.

Enclosed is my letter to the University of California Board of Regents. As the letter indicates, only one in five whites even applied to the Davis program. If the program were applied as generally written, it is probable that only a few of them would have been admitted, perhaps not even Bakke himself. If a few whites had categorically fallen into the program, albeit. Better those few than what the Supreme Court can ultimately do: eliminate all or most blacks. With the removal of one concept, the race concept, from the program's language, we will have our program. *It will still be dominated by blacks.* (Who else is more economically and educationally disadvantaged?) My letter to the Board of Regents is a desperate attempt to force the University of California to stop playing its game of saccharin sensitivity and let our people go to school.

Consider this position, please. Consider the withdrawal of the question before the Supreme Court on this basis, lest the inevitable answer make folly of our pathetic lot.

I humbly request your response.

> All Power to the People,
> Huey P. Newton
> President
> Black Panther Party

To: Mr. William Coblentz, Chairman
The Board of Regents of the University of California

Dear Mr. Coblentz:

I write to urge immediate consideration by the University of California toward administering the special admissions program at the medical school of the Davis Campus in a manner consistent with the program's stated purposes and thereby, hopefully, avoiding an opinion in the *Bakke* case now pending before the Supreme Court. I make this request after thoroughly reviewing the opinion of the California Supreme Court and the briefs filed with the United States Supreme Court, as well as after talking with many people concerned about the implications of a ruling either way in the *Bakke* case. It is my conclusion, for reasons I will explain, that the issue posed by the *Bakke* case—that is, the constitutionality of preferential racial quotas—is unnecessary and bitterly divisive to the university and the country at this time.

The twofold purpose of the special admissions program at the Davis medical school is, according to the University, (1) to equalize the opportunity for "educationally or economically disadvantaged" students to obtain a medical education, and (2) to increase the number of doctors who will practice in medically underserved areas. The first goal can be achieved without regard to race, even though a disproportionate number of educationally or economically disadvantaged applicants for medical school are likely to be nonwhite racial minorities. But it is beyond dispute that poor whites, whether they be migrant farmworkers, urban welfare beneficiaries, or Appalachian residents, fit within the category of "educationally or economically disadvantaged." In fact, of the total number of students who applied for the special admissions program at Davis, one in five was white; although since 1969, none but racial minorities, unfortunately, were admitted. Indeed, the university did not even "challenge the trial court's finding that applicants who are not members of a minority are barred from participation in the special admissions program." *Bakke v. Regents of The University of California*, 18 C. 3d 34, 44 (1976). Thus, the practical application of the special admissions program fails to meet its own theoretical standard of assisting "educationally or economically disadvantaged" students; instead, it has obviously only focused on those "disadvantaged" who also happen to be minority. I believe this is a prime example of a program that—at least in terms of the lofty stated purpose of assisting the "disadvantaged"—is constitutional on its face, but not as applied.

Accordingly, I suggest that if the university has not already done so, it immediately administer the special admissions program consistent with its first stated goal and, without regard to race, inform the Court of this fact and urge it to dismiss the case as moot. This will avoid a ruling that is not only factually unnecessary, but puts in political and financial jeopardy numerous programs intended to benefit economically and educationally disadvantaged persons.

With respect to the second stated goal of the special admissions program—that is, increasing the number of doctors who will practice in medically underserved areas—the University can and ought to go further than it has to achieve this aim. Only if we assume that "educationally or economically disadvantaged" persons will practice in underserved areas upon graduation will this goal be achieved. They might, and then again they might not, desire to return to the poverty they can leave behind them after acquiring a medical education. To assure that the present imbalance of physicians throughout California is redressed, I propose that additional points or credits be given to applicants for medical school who will agree to practice in medically underserved areas for a specific period of time upon graduation. This principle is already well established and accepted by the public in similar situations. The military academies and even ROTC (at least the navy) conditioned the public subsidy of a college education upon later military service. Medical education is the most heavily subsidized of all educations, and it does not seem too oppressive to condition its receipt from those who opt for extra credit toward admissions upon their later service for pay in an underserved area. I recognize, of course, that this may raise yet another constitutional issue—the right of a public university to attach such a condition to admission. But I suggest this is politically a far healthier issue to litigate and publicly debate, and at least ought to be put to the test before we reach the divisive one of racial quotas.

The entire debate now raging over *Bakke* and the constitutionality of so-called benign racial classifications reminds me of a story told about my namesake, Huey P. Long. This story was told to me many times by my father, who was from Louisiana, but was also recounted by A. J. Liebling in *The Earl of Louisiana*. During one of his campaigns for reelection as governor, Huey was approached by a group of blacks who were concerned about the massive depression unemployment suffered by the black population of the state. They asked him to do something to relieve their plight. He told them he would but warned them they might not like the way he went about it. Thereupon, Huey began campaign stumping around the state, complaining to audiences that he had been shocked to see black orderlies handling white women patients in some of the state's hospitals. He called for separate hospitals for blacks and, after getting reelected, embarked upon an ambitious and popularly supported construction program for black hospitals, which produced a substantial number of jobs for blacks. Judging by the results, Huey's program was partly benign, an example of color consciousness; but judging by the rhetoric employed—or the means used—it was racist. Only history can judge whether, on balance, this effort of Huey P. Long's to relieve black unemployment was more positive than negative.

History, and not the Court, ought to also judge the value of the special admissions program at the Davis medical school, especially since its purpose is not dependent upon a racial classification.

I have rarely been accused of shirking debate, especially since I believe in the necessity and inevitability of contradiction. See, for example, E. H. Erikson and H. P. Newton, *In Search of Common Ground*

(1973). But the *Bakke* case does not represent a true or necessary contradiction; it is a contrived one that can and should be avoided in the public interest.

I am keenly aware of your personal commitment to public education and equal justice; therefore I am hopeful that you will give these thoughts your immediate attention, share them with the appropriate authorities, and inform the Court of the suggested change in the administration of the special admissions program at Davis that renders *Bakke* moot.

Respectfully,
Huey P. Newton

response of the government to the Black Panther Party: 1980

(A footnoted version of this selection is found in War Against the Panthers: A Study of Repression in America.*)*

Upon Richard M. Nixon's election as president in 1968, the administration addressed itself, in the words of former White House Counsel John Dean, "to the matter of how we can maximize the fact of our incumbency in dealing with persons known to be active in their opposition to our Administration." Stated a bit more bluntly—how we can use the available federal machinery to screw our political enemies.

A "White House Enemies List" was drawn up by officials of the Nixon administration. In its original form, this list contained the names of only a few minority political parties or organizations, among them the Panthers, whom the administration linked with "Hughie [*sic*] Newton," and "George Wallace" of the American Independent Party. Interestingly, though their expressed ideologies were quite opposite, both organizations shared the common feature of having strong grassroots support and active involvement by [their] members, in contrast to the established Democratic and Republican parties. The Enemies List was then incorporated into a detailed plan, commonly known as the Huston Plan, after its White House designated coordinator, Tom Charles Huston. This plan was approved in 1970 by the former director of the FBI, J. Edgar Hoover, in cooperation with the Central Intelligence Agency (CIA), the Defense Intelligence Agency (DIA), and the National Security Agency (NSA). It advocated blanket presidential authorization for such practices as wiretapping, mail covers, and black-

337

bag jobs or break-ins. Its main purported function was to improve inter-agency cooperation among the major intelligence agencies. Although this proposed plan was first approved, but allegedly later disapproved, by President Nixon because J. Edgar Hoover decided not to continue to cooperate, the tactics advocated had already been employed by various federal agencies, particularly the FBI, against the Panthers.

Just why the FBI and other federal law enforcement agencies focused early on the Party as an "enemy" organization is not difficult to understand. At the start of World War II, President Roosevelt directed the bureau to refocus its resources on priorities it had purportedly given up in 1924—the investigation of political organizations and affiliations. Distinctions between foreign espionage and domestic dissident groups became blurred during the height of the war; in fact, "vigilance and caution grew into xenophobia and distrust of anyone who veered noticeably from the political mainstream."

The Cold War followed, with President Truman's establishment of the Federal Employee Loyalty Program. The bureau, having built up a large contingent of agents to guard the nation's internal security, channeled them into loyalty/security investigations. Thus, the FBI took on officially "the role of a kind of ideological security police, an arbiter of what was inside the boundaries of legitimate political discourse and what [was] outside." In the absence of any effective challenge to this role, the bureau continued, essentially unabated.

Not surprisingly, when the Panthers became publicly visible in 1967 and 1968, the FBI felt justified, if not compelled, to devote their full panoply of resources to investigating the organization. In part this was in response to the BPP's ideology. As the chief of the FBI's counter-intelligence program admitted in describing the genesis of the program within the bureau that concentrated on the Panthers:

> We were trying first to develop intelligence so we would know what they were doing [and] second, to contain the threat.... To stop the spread of communism, to stop the effectiveness of the Communist Party as a vehicle of Soviet intelligence, propaganda and agitation.

A more flamboyant assessment was provided by Edward Miller, former assistant director of the FBI in charge of the Intelligence Division, upon his retirement in 1974:

Rome lasted for six hundred years, and we are just coming on to our two-hundredth. That doesn't mean that we have four hundred to go. We have to step back and look at ourselves protectively.... How much of this dissent and revolution talk can we really stand in a healthy country? Revolutions always start in a small way.... Economic conditions are bad; the credibility of government is low. These are the things that the homegrown revolutionary is monitoring very closely. The FBI's attention must be focused on these various situations. If it weren't, the Bureau wouldn't be doing its job for the American people.... The American people don't want to have to fool around with this kind of thing and worry about it; they don't want to have to worry about the security of their country.... We must be able to find out what stage the revolution is in.

The FBI was also aware of and disturbed by the Panther's efforts to build community institutions. Indeed, the one survival program that seemed most laudatory—that of providing free breakfasts to children—was pinpointed by J. Edgar Hoover as the real long range threat to American society. The ostensible reason for this was that children participating in the program were being propagandized, which simply meant they were taught ideas, or an ideology, that the FBI and Hoover disliked. Yet Hoover was not so naive as to believe an overt ideological war was any longer sufficient to garner the support or non-interference necessary for the bureau to destroy the Panthers. A better rationale or cover for the public would have to be employed. This new cover for secret police operations was, as the Huston Plan suggested, a crusade against criminals and terrorists. Now, the administration would fight "crime," not ideologies.

This technique for destroying controversial political organizations is, of course, not new:

History should teach us...that in times of high emotional excitement, minority parties and groups which advocate extremely unpopular social or governmental innovations will always be typed as criminal gangs and attempts will always be made to drive them out.

Internal FBI and other police agency documents make clear this objective of pinning the label "criminal" on the BPP and its leaders, and trying to link criminal activity to the Party's efforts at getting support for various survival programs. A 1974 memorandum to the director of the FBI from the special agent in charge of the San Francisco office stated that the local FBI office

> has continued to follow Newton's and his associates' activities. "...Primarily, the...office has been pursuing Hobbs Act and/or ITAR-Extortion cases on Newton and/or his associates. Although investigations to date, including contacts with other law enforcement agencies,"...*has failed to develop information indicating that Newton and his associates are extorting funds from businesses.... This office is of the opinion that Newton is or has been extorting funds from legitimate businesses...*
>
> In addition to the contacts noted above (i.e., the Alcohol, Tobacco, Tax and Firearms Section of the Department of Justice in Oakland, California, the Oakland Police Department, the Berkeley Police Department and various informants), *the San Francisco Office is selectively contacting pimps and narcotics pushers in the Oakland area in an attempt to develop further intelligence and positive information concerning possible Federal violations on the part of Newton and his associates. This matter will continue to receive vigorous investigative attention.*

Interestingly, the bureau and others seem to feel that any contribution from a business, whether considered legitimate or not, to the BPP survival programs could not be voluntary; it would have to come from extortion. Despite a failure to obtain any evidence of extortion, the bureau continued to hold the opinion that it took place and to try to develop information for a Hobbs' Act prosecution. In 1973, for instance, the assistant attorney general who figured prominently in the Watergate investigations, Henry E. Peterson, wrote the acting director of the FBI regarding Newton and the BPP:

> During the course of filming a movie in Oakland, California, Harvey Bernhard [a film director], was contacted by Huey Newton and Bobby Seale who threatened to picket the filming site unless a $5,000 contribution was made to the Black Panther Party. We note that Bernhard now states that while he gave $5,000 to Newton, he does not feel that he was extorted in any way and that he did not wish to testify.
>
> In light of this, and considering that Max Julian [an actor in the film], who was present when Bernhard met Newton, cannot recall any discussion of money or picketing, there is insufficient evidence to warrant prosecution and further investigation is not warranted.

Extortion was not, of course, the only crime federal law enforcement agencies tried to pin on the BPP. In his book *Agency of Fear*, Epstein described how high-level intelligence officers in the Nixon administration used a narcotics cover to expand domestic counterintelligence operations:

> Under the aegis of a "war on heroin," a series of new offices were set up, by executive order, such as the Office of National Narcotics Intelligence, which, it was hoped, would provide the president with investigative agencies having the potential to assume the functions of "the Plumbers" on a far grander scale. According to the White House scenario, these new investigative functions would be legitimized by the need to eradicate the evil of drug addiction.

The Nixon administration's exploitation of the narcotics menace to justify expansion of federal investigative agencies achieved extraordinary success:

> Between 1968 and 1974, the federal budget for enforcing narcotics laws rose from $3 million to more than $224 million—a seventyfold increase. And this in turn gave the president an opportunity to create a series of highly unorthodox federal agencies.

The utility of a narcotics cover appears in numerous internal law enforcement documents concerning the BPP. Various agencies claim within their reports, in fact, to be investigating narcotics use by Panther leaders, especially Huey Newton. When, for example, Newton and some close friends took a one-week Caribbean cruise for a vacation, the FBI sent at least one clandestine agent, who submitted the following report:

> [An unidentified informant] stated that his company has recently experienced a heavy increase in bookings aboard the "Starward" [the cruise ship taken] by Blacks, and he suspicions [*sic*] that this increase is due in part to the availability of narcotics at Porte Prince [*sic*] and Port Antonio. He stated that his suspicions have been buttressed by the recent confiscation of several pieces of luggage filled with narcotics from a "Starward" passenger.
>
> Inasmuch as reliable sources have identified Newton as a user of cocaine and he is possibly the user of other narcotics, will alert cus-

toms personnel to be on the lookout for narcotics in the possession
of Newton and any of his party upon their return to Miami.

Not content merely to alert Customs, the FBI noted that "the information has been disseminated to State Department and CIA. Copies of attached being furnished to the Department (Internal Security and General Crimes Section) and Secret Service."

Indeed, in April 1973, the FBI requested that "all San Francisco agents be aware of either the purchase or use of cocaine by Huey Newton. Any information obtained in this regard should be immediately furnished to both the OPD [Oakland Police Department] and the appropriate Federal Narcotics agency." Six months later, the bureau seemed less interested in Newton's possible use of cocaine than they were about narcotics dealers he might have been hitting up for contributions to community survival programs.

> Source reports from contacts with various and unidentified Negro dope dealers that the big time dope dealers in the Berkeley and Oakland area are out to get Huey Newton. Source reports that Huey is apparently ripping off certain dealers, pimps and whores for large amounts of money and the talk is that "they" are going to get Huey. Source was instructed to determine some hard facts concerning these rumors and to report same immediately.

By 1973, this process of employing the narcotics and crime covers reached its climax with the creation of a new intelligence superagency, the Drug Enforcement Agency. At the time of its formation, the DEA employed more than 4,000 agents and analysts—including some fifty-three former (or detached) CIA agents and a dozen counterintelligence experts from the military or other intelligence agencies. The DEA had the authority "to request wiretaps and noknock warrants, and to submit targets to the Internal Revenue Service." With its contingent of former CIA and counterintelligence agents, it had the talent to enter residences surreptitiously, distribute "black" (or misleading) information, plant phony evidence, and conduct even more extreme clandestine assignments.

The origin of DEA and its intended purpose are explained by Epstein as follows:

According to [those] familiar with the plan, [G. Gordon] Liddy proposed…to detach agents and specialists who could be relied upon by the White House from the BNDD [Bureau of Narcotics and Dangerous Drugs], the IRS, the Alcohol, Tobacco and Firearms division, and the Bureau of Customs. This new office would operate directly out of the executive office of the president. The beauty of the Liddy plan was its simplicity: it did not even need approval from Congress. The president could create such an office by executive decree, and order all other agencies of the government to cooperate by supplying liaisons and agents. Congress would not even have to appropriate funds, according to those familiar with the Liddy plan: The Law Enforcement Assistance Administration (LEAA), which was located in John Mitchell's Department of Justice, could funnel monies via local police departments to finance these new strike forces. The new office would have wiretappers from the BNDD; Customs agents, with their unique "search authority"; IRS agents who could feed the names of suspects into the IRS's target-selection committee for a grueling audit; and CIA agents for "the more extraordinary missions." In addition, since it would control grants from LEAA, this new office could mobilize support from state and local police forces in areas in which it desired to operate.

The most important feature of the Liddy plan, however, was that the White House agents would act under the cloak of combating the drug menace. Since public fears were being excited about this deadly threat to the children of American citizens and their property, few would oppose vigorous measures even if its agents were occasionally caught in such excesses as placing an unauthorized wiretap. On the contrary, if the dread of drugs could be maintained, the public, Congress, and the press would probably applaud such determined actions. Krogh and the White House strategists immediately saw the advantages to having the new office operate its agents under the emblem of a heroin crusade…and Liddy's option paper, much modified in form to remove any embarrassing illegalities, was sent to the president with the recommendations of Krogh and Ehrlichman.

Finally, in December 1971, the president ordered Ehrlichman and Krogh to create the permanent White House–controlled investigative unit envisioned in the option paper drawn up by Liddy. The new unit was to be known as the Office of Drug Abuse Law Enforcement.

On January 28, 1972, the Office of Drug Abuse Law Enforcement (ODALE), the permanent investigative force which ostensibly would operate against narcotics traffickers, was officially created by an executive order of the President:

Since there was virtually no precedent for an agency like the Office of Drug Abuse and Law Enforcement, [ODALE director Myles J.] Ambrose had to proceed step by step, in assembling his strike forces. The first step was to appoint regional directors who would superintend and select the federal agents and local police on each strike force in each of the thirty-three target cities he selected.... Fifty other lawyers, many of whom Ambrose knew personally, were deployed in instantly created field offices of the new organization. Four hundred investigators were requisitioned from the Bureau of Narcotics and Dangerous Drugs and the Bureau of Customs, and Ambrose requested more than a hundred liaisons from the Internal Revenue Service, as well as specialists from other agencies of the government. This was all accomplished during the first thirty days of existence of this new office, in what Ambrose himself referred to as a "monumental feat or organization.

...The new strike forces had little resemblance to more conventional law-enforcement forces. These highly unorthodox units, which were being controlled from the White House through the president's special consultant Myles Ambrose, included not only trained narcotics and customs officers but also Immigration and Naturalization Service officers; Alcohol, Tobacco and Firearms control agents; probation officers; state troopers; and local police officers.... With the authority of court-authorized no-knock warrants and wiretaps they could strike at will in any of the target cities and against virtually anyone selected as a target. By March 1972, the strike forces had become operational.

There was some resistance to Law Enforcement Assistance Administration officials to using LEAA money to finance ODALE operations. They argued that Congress never intended for LEAA grants to be used to bypass the appropriations process:

So with White House assistance, the new office established a series of local organizations, with such names as "Research Associates," through which grants could be made by LEAA. The money was then channeled back to selected strike forces, with these organizations acting, in effect, as money conduits.

The California conduit for these laundered funds was the Organized Crime and Criminal Intelligence Branch (OCCIB) of the State Department of Justice, which had already been set up in 1970 by California Attorney General Evelle Younger. A report circulated by the OCCIB in 1972 identified among its prime targets the Black Panther Party.

The creation of a new superagency to direct the counterintelligence activities against the BPP and other dissident groups was an indication of how badly the federal government wanted to destroy the Panthers. The successful extent of coordination between law enforcement agencies intent on getting the BPP is not yet clear, largely because documents showing this direction have yet to be discovered. Still, the general method of operation described by Epstein appears to have been employed against the Party, at least if one focuses on just three agencies for which some documented information is available: the FBI, IRS, and CIA.

Within one year of the formation of the Party, the FBI formed a special counterintelligence program dubbed COINTELPRO. The purpose of this program was, in the FBI's own words, to "expose, disrupt, misdirect, discredit, or otherwise neutralize the activities of the Black nationalists." A specific purpose of COINTELPRO was to prevent the rise of a "Messiah," a charismatic Black leader who might "unify and electrify" Black people. Martin Luther King, Jr., was named as a potential Messiah in the FBI's own secret memorandum establishing COINTELPRO, but after the assassination of King in 1968, the FBI shifted its focus to the Party and its leadership, particularly Huey P. Newton.

J. Edgar Hoover, then director of the FBI, publicly stated that the Party constituted "the greatest threat to the internal security of the country . . ." of any organization. Of the 295 documented actions taken by COINTELPRO alone to disrupt Black groups, 233—or 79 percent—were specifically directed toward destruction of the Party. Over $100 million of taxpayers' money was expended for COINTELPRO; over $7 million of it allocated for 1976 alone to pay off informants and provocateurs, twice the amount allocated in the same period by the FBI to pay organized crime informants.

Indeed, while COINTELPRO ostensibly targeted five domestic organizations—the Communist Party, the Socialist Workers' Party, White Hate Groups, Black Nationalist Hate Groups (e.g., the Panthers), and the New Left—it was Blacks, and the Panthers in particular, who received the brunt of the damage. As the Senate Select Committee to Study Governmental Operations found,

The White Hate COINTELPRO also used comparatively few techniques which carried a risk of serious physical, emotional, or economic damage to the targets, while the Black Nationalist COINTELPRO used such techniques extensively.

The vast arsenal of techniques employed by the bureau against the BPP were tried and tested over the years in foreign espionage. As William C. Sullivan, former assistant to the director, stated:

> This is a rough, tough, dirty business, and dangerous. It was dangerous at times. No holds were barred…. We have used [these techniques] against Soviet agents. They have used [them] against us…. [The same methods were] brought home against any organization against which we were targeted. We did not differentiate. This is a rough, tough business.

Specifically, the FBI engaged in or encouraged a variety of actions intended to cause (and in fact causing) deaths of BPP members, loss of membership and community support, draining of revenues from the Party, false arrests of members and supporters, and defamatory discrediting of constructive Party programs and leaders. What follows is an illustrative highlighting of some of these unlawful actions undertaken by the bureau against the BPP.

A major goal of COINTELPRO was to sow dissension within the Party. A 1970 memorandum from Headquarters to the San Francisco field office of the FBI, for example, proposed:

> A wide variety of alleged authentic police or FBI material could be carefully selected or prepared for furnishing to the Panthers. Reports, blind memoranda, LHMs [letterhead memoranda] and other alleged police or FBI documents could be prepared pinpointing Panthers as police or FBI informants; ridiculing or discrediting Panther leaders through their ineptness or personal escapades; espousing personal philosophies and promoting factionalism among BPP members; indicating electronic coverage where none exists; outlining fictitious plans for police raids or other counteractions; revealing misuse or misappropriation of Panther funds, pointing out instances of political disruptive material and disinformation; etc. *The nature of the disruptive material and disinformation "leaked" would only be lim-*

> *ited by the collection ability of your sources and the need to insure the protection of their security.*
>
> Effective implementation of this proposal could not help but disrupt and confuse Panther activities. Even if they were to suspect FBI or police involvement, they would be unable to ignore factual material brought to their attention through this channel. The operation would afford us a continuing means to furnish the Panther leadership true information which is to our interest that they know and disinformation which, in their interest, they cannot ignore.

Obviously, falsely labeling people as informants in any organization carries with it a serious potential risk to the reputation and, in some situations, safety of that person. This is especially true if the combined counterintelligence techniques employed convince the organization that their friends have been imprisoned or harmed because of the targeted informant. Fully aware of this obvious fact, the bureau nonetheless rationalized the placing of "snitch jackets" on innocent people:

> You have to be able to make decisions, and I am sure that labeling somebody as an informant, that you'd want to make certain that it served a good purpose before you did it and not do it haphazardly.... It is a serious thing.... As far as I am aware, in the Black extremist area, by using that technique, no one was killed. I am sure of that.

When asked whether the absence of any deaths was the result of "luck or planning," this same bureau official, George C. Moore, then chief of the Racial Intelligence Section, answered, "Oh, it just happened that way, I am sure." The certitude of Moore's assertion is unfortunately belied by the bureau's own confidential memoranda, more than one of which claimed that the Party murdered "members it suspected of being police informants." Indeed, the FBI worked closely with Connecticut authorities in trying to convict two Party leaders, Bobby Seale and Ericka Huggins, of conspiracy to murder Alex Rackley, an alleged informant. Seale and Huggins were not convicted, but the government's chief witness against them, the person who admittedly participated in Rackley's killing, appears from facts disclosed during and after the trial to have been an agent or informant. At the very least, this person's immediate enrollment in an Ivy League institution after the murder trial, and subsequent employment by the administration of an eastern university, raises serious questions. In any event, the use of snitch-jackets by the bureau was widespread. The Senate Select Committee reports several instances of this technique without any apparent follow-up as to the consequences to the persons wrongly jacketed. Among the instances cited was one in San Diego where a Black Panther leader was arrested by the local police with four other members of the BPP. The others were released, but the leader remained in custody. Headquarters authorized the field office to circulate the rumor that the leader "is the last to be released" because "he is cooperating with and has made a deal with the Los Angeles Police Department to furnish them information concerning the BPP." The target of the first proposal then received an anonymous phone call stating that his own arrest was caused by a rival leader.

Leaders of the BPP were frequently targeted as snitches or sell-outs by the FBI in an effort to discredit or bring harm to them, especially Huey Newton. Upon Newton's release from prison in 1970, for instance, after a court of appeal reversed his conviction for manslaughter in the alleged shooting of an Oakland policeman, a memorandum from the FBI director instructed FBI field offices across the country to formulate COINTELPRO actions directed against Newton. FBI headquarters would direct the campaign; its contours were defined as follows:

> To demythicise [*sic*] Newton, to hold him up to ridicule, and to tarnish his image among BPP members can serve to weaken BPP solidarity and disrupt its revolutionary and violent aims. [COINTELPRO actions] should have the 3-pronged effect of creating divisiveness among BPP members concerning Newton, treat him in a flippant and irreverent manner, and insinuate that he has been cooperating with police to gain his release from prison.

Within a week, the New York FBI field office had drawn up three phony letters, which attempted to discredit Newton. One message, to be mailed to the New York office of the Black Panther Party by the San Francisco FBI field office, read as follows:

Brothers, I am employed by the State of California and have been close to Huey Newton while he was in jail. Let me warn you that this pretty nigger may very well be working for pig Reagan. I don't know why he was set free but I am suspicious. I got this idea because he had privileges in jail like the trustees get. He had a lot of privacy most prisoners don't get. I don't think all his private meetings were for sex. I am suspicious of him.

Don't tell Newton too much if he starts asking you questions—it may go right back to the pigs.

Power to the People

FBI headquarters regarded this anonymous letter as "excellent," but cautioned, "Take usual precautions to insure letters cannot be traced to Bureau. Advise Bureau and interested offices of positive results achieved."

The Philadelphia FBI field office prepared and sent to Newton a fictitious Black Panther Party directive, supposedly prepared by the Philadelphia Black Panther office, which questioned Newton's leadership abilities; accompanying it was a cover letter purportedly from an anonymous Party supporter accusing the Philadelphia chapter of "slandering its leaders in private." FBI headquarters, in approving this operation, noted that prior COINTELPRO action which "anonymously advised the national headquarters that food, clothing and drugs collected for BPP community programs were being stolen by BPP members" had resulted in criticism of the Philadelphia chapter by the national office, transfer of members, "and the national office has even considered closing the Philadelphia chapter." The memorandum concluded, "we want to keep this dissension going."

The Los Angeles FBI office suggested that a death threat against Newton be sent to Black Panther leader David Hilliard, purportedly from a contract killer. FBI headquarters stopped this action, however, in the belief that if Newton were to be murdered then, the letter might be traced to the bureau by postal authorities.

When Angela Davis, then one of the FBI's ten most wanted fugitives, was arrested in New York City in mid-October 1970 and charged with conspiracy in the Marin County Courthouse incident, the FBI falsely tried to cast Newton as the fingerman:

In view of the fact that there is suspicion in the Negro [*sic*] community that DAVIS was "set up," NYO suggests that HUEY NEWTON...be cast in the light as "fingerman." If such a ploy could be successfully carried out it might result in disruption in the Black Nationalist field as well as divorcing BPP from CPUSA and Militant New Left groups.

One handwritten letter was sent to *Ebony* magazine by the Chicago FBI field office, "mailed from a Negro [*sic*] as follows:

Dear Brothers and Sisters:

As of this writing, our lovely Sister Angela languishes in jail and her chances of freedom seem remote. She's got to pay the man, right? But the question I put to you is: Who did the money pay?

You know and I know the pigs can't come up with a Black in a Black community just by driving around the streets and hassling the Brothers. I tell you that Sister Davis would still be free if her capture was left to the federal pigs alone. Of course, it was not that way at all. There was bread—lots of pure cash rye—put into an eager Black hand which in turn twisted the knife of treachery in our Sister's back.

Now, the big question is who? Who was the cat who dishonored his skin and took the 30 pieces of silver?

Some of the west coast cats are looking hard at Brother Newton. Shit, you say, Huey would never sell out to pig country. He's a dedicated Nationalist leader of the of the Brothers and Sisters and a cat with real soul. Maybe it's bullshit, but let's look at Huey a little closer. He gets sprung from a stiff rap in August. The man suddenly turns kind and sets our Brother free. In that same month Sister Angela is among the missing as the result of a frame the pigs laid on her. What did Huey give for the sunlight and flowers? Or better still, what did the man give sweet Huey? How come Huey's size 12 mouth has been zippered since our Sister's bust? Nothing, he says. Absolutely nothing. Not one appeal for justice. No TV, no papers, no radio, no nothing. He got five grand, so the cats say. It's enough to make a man wonder. Wouldn't be surprised if Huey didn't split the scene soon. I, for one, will be most interested.

A Friend of Sister Angela

Another handwritten letter was mailed to the *Village Voice* newspaper by the New York FBI field office:

Sister Angela is in jail. Poindexter is free. Huey Newton is free. David P. is a dumb-head and a hop-head. Forget him. But Huey is smart. Gets along well with the MAN. The question is: Did this cat bank five big bills lately...as a gift from the federal pigs?

Concerned Brother

The bureau did not miss any chance to further its disinformation campaign. Later, in the fall of 1970, the San Francisco FBI field office sent an unsigned letter, purportedly from a "white revolutionary," to Newton criticizing the Party-sponsored Revolutionary People's Constitutional Convention: "You," the letter concluded, "must be held responsible for this fiasco and it is due to your total incompetence for selecting stupid lazy niggers to do the job and you and your whole party have set the revolution back five years." When the Howard University student newspaper printed a letter signed "Concerned Students of Howard University," which was critical of Huey Newton and the Party, the San Francisco FBI field office mailed Xerox copies to seventeen newspapers in northern California; the letter had been prepared and sent to the student newspaper in the first place by the Washington, D.C., FBI field office.

When Newton's conviction for allegedly shooting a policeman was reversed in 1970, FBI director J. Edgar Hoover immediately requested official authorization from Attorney General John Mitchell for "a microphone surveillance and a telephone surveillance at apartment 25A, 1200 Lakeshore, Oakland"—Huey Newton's new residence. Hoover considered it "likely that high-level party-conferences will be held at this location," and he reminded Mitchell "that existing telephone surveillance on certain Black Panther officers, all of which have been authorized by you, have provided extremely valuable information on Black Panther Party involvement in foreign matters and plans for violent acts against top officials of this country and foreign diplomatic personnel." (The ending clause, clumsily tacked on the sentence, was the requisite "national security" justification for covert action.) Hoover's request concluded with the observation that "trespass will be involved with respect to the microphone surveillance."

Mitchell approved the request, and San Francisco FBI agents paid

the building engineer, Roger DuClot, to accompany them in breaking into Newton's apartment to install the microphone in the wall.

But the FBI was not content with surveillance. On November 24,
1970, the San Francisco FBI field office proposed an additional COIN-
TELPRO operation concerning Newton's new apartment. The field
office proposed a media campaign which would characterize the apartment as a "luxurious lakeshore" penthouse, far more elegant than "the
ghetto-like BPP 'pads' and community centers" utilized by the Party.
However, the field office agreed to refrain "presently" from leaking "this
information to cooperative news sources" because of a "pending special investigative technique [i.e., the 'bug' and wiretaps]."

Once the installation of the surveillance devices had been completed,
the FBI gave the "plush penthouse" story to one of the bureau's key
media "assets," reporter Ed Montgomery of the *San Francisco Examiner*. Shortly, Montgomery's FBI-furnished article was featured on the
front page of the *Examiner*. Pleased with this quick success, the San
Francisco field office mailed copies of the feature article, anonymously,
to "all BPP offices across the United States and to three BPP contacts
in Europe." Additional copies were mailed to newspaper editors in all
cities where the BPP was active.

To bolster the innuendoes of lavish living and misuse of Party funds,
the FBI sent a fictitious letter from a national Black Panther Party officer to Party chapters in Baltimore, Boston, Chicago, Indianapolis, Los
Angeles, New Haven, New York, Philadelphia, and Washington, D.C.
The message, mailed from Oakland, read in part:

> Comrades:
> Too many of your leaders have now turned this movement into
> something to line their own pockets and have little regard for the man
> on the street selling "The Black Panther." Ask the members of your
> chapter coming to the national where the Comrade Commander and
> the Chief of Staff live. Huey Newton lives miles from another nig-
> ger and you'll never find him in National Headquarters.
> If you're lucky you can see him buying drinks for white freaks in
> Oakland supper clubs.

In addition, FBI Headquarters formulated a COINTELPRO plan
to "embarrass BPP leader Huey Newton through use of a fictitious bank

account, indicating misappropriations of BPP funds." This plan required that:

> a fictitious bank account record be created in the name of HUEY P. NEWTON through an appropriate bank which will cooperate with the Bureau confidentially. A photostat of a false ledger card could be prepared and mailed to national headquarters anonymously along with an appropriate letter condemning NEWTON. The account should show regular sizable deposits over a period of several years and have a sizable balance existing.

Beginning April 1, 1971, and for months thereafter, the FBI paid "$540 per month…for the rental of apartment 25B, 1200 Lakeshore, Oakland, California." In this apartment, adjacent to the one in which Newton was living, the FBI placed an undercover agent with instructions to keep Newton under physical surveillance, as well as monitoring the electronic eavesdropping devices. Subsequently, hardly a day passed when Newton was not followed or observed by a plainclothes agent on all of his travels to and from the apartment building.

One of the undercover agents placed in apartment 25B was Don Roberto Stinnette, who was described (in an FBI case report on Newton) as "involved with local drug traffic." Stinnette, who professed to be on parole from a California prison, remained in the apartment for several months while he spied on Newton, his associates, and guests.

On November 18, 1972, Newton's wife, Gwen Fountaine Newton, discovered several men burglarizing and ransacking their apartment when she returned unexpectedly:

> After leaving the apartment with Huey, I returned with Huey's niece, Deborah, because I had forgotten something. I entered to find three men robbing the apartment. They held me at gunpoint. Their pistols had silencers on them. Huey's documents and other papers were strewn about on the floor.

Files and records, along with clothes and heavy furniture, were taken by these men from the apartment—a closed, supposedly secure complex with a doorman and basement garage that could be entered only with the aid of an apartment-supplied electronic garage-door opener. How and why did these men enter this complex, burglarize the penthouse apartment, and leave undetected with so much stolen property? The Party believes that the stolen records and material were actually moved next door during the robbery to the apartment of the FBI agent or informant. Later, when it was convenient to go unnoticed, the materials were quietly but openly moved out in crates and boxes from an art exhibit supposedly held in this same agent's apartment.

Literally no tactic was too bizarre, unconscionable, or extreme for government intelligence officials. On Saturday morning, February 18, 1973, at 5.30 A.M., a squad of Oakland police officers conducted a raid on the twenty-fifth floor of Huey Newton's apartment building. For cover, they had obtained a warrant, "authorized for night service," for the arrest of Don Roberto Stinnette for unpaid traffic tickets. The police team proceeded to engage in a shootout with Stinnette, who was equipped with a semiautomatic rifle, in the hall outside Newton's apartment. Newton refused to take the bait to open his door. Surprisingly, neither Stinnette nor police were injured. Later, the media reported the news of gunfire at the "swank apartment...next door to Black Panther leader Huey Newton." But the press had missed what was perhaps the real story: that the police and undercover agent had staged the entire shootout in hopes that Newton could be drawn out of his apartment where he could be shot.

It is not difficult to divine the intended effect of these FBI actions, or just why the bureau felt they might, through the aggregate of activity, neutralize the Party's founder. In the words of one observer:

> Do you remember what it is like to have one friend mad at you, against you, or even an enemy, or someone out to get you as may have happened occasionally when you were a kid? But how many of us have this experience now? Occasionally someone may be after our job or promotion, but not our life or our freedom. We cannot even imagine what it is like to have one or all of the major investigatory agencies against us. To have phones always tapped. To have no one able to know you without that person also becoming a public enemy. To be watched for minute traffic violations every time you drive to the store. To be under constant observation. To never know who might be a paid informer or a fake next door neighbor. And in the midst of this, to have a developing community strained by the very pressures around you, around your friends, around a vision of the people which is unbearable to our present society.

In March 1970, the FBI zeroed in on Eldridge Cleaver, then in exile in Algiers after he had been told to leave Cuba. The bureau learned that the high-strung Cleaver had "accepted as bonafide" a fictitious letter "stating that BPP leaders in California were seeking to undercut his influence."

For the next year, FBI field offices supplied Cleaver with a steady stream of messages containing erroneous information about various Black Panther Party leaders and activities, especially about Huey Newton. After his release from prison in August 1970, Cleaver led a Black Panther Party–sponsored delegation of American activists to North Korea and North Vietnam. After the conclusion of the tour, "the Los Angeles FBI field office was asked to prepare an anonymous letter to Cleaver criticizing Newton for not aggressively obtaining BPP press coverage of the BPP's sponsorship of the trip."

In December 1970, with the adoption of the Key Black Extremist program, the FBI increased its COINTELPRO efforts to turn Cleaver against Newton. The Bureau issued instructions to:

> ...write numerous letters to Cleaver criticizing Newton for his lack of leadership. It is felt that, if Cleaver received a sufficient number of complaints regarding Newton it might...create dissension that later could be more fully exploited.

One letter to Cleaver, written to appear as if it had come from Connie Matthews, then Newton's personal secretary, read in part:

> I know you have not been told what has been happening lately.... Things around headquarters are dreadfully disorganized with the comrade commander not making proper decisions. The newspaper is in a shambles. No one knows who is in charge. The foreign department gets no support. Brothers and sisters are accused of all sorts of things.
>
> I am disturbed because I, myself, do not know which way to turn.... If only you were here to inject some strength into the movement, or to give some advice. One of two steps must be taken soon and both are drastic. We must either get rid of the supreme commander or get rid of the disloyal members.... Huey is really all we have right now and we can't let him down, regardless of how poorly he is acting, unless you feel otherwise.

More flattery came from "Algonquin J. Fuller, Youth Against War and Fascism, New York," supposedly one of Cleaver's white admirers:

> Let me tell you what has happened to our brothers in the Party since you have left and that "Pretty Nigger Newton" in his funky clothes has been running things....
>
> Brother Eldridge, to me as an outsider but one who believes in the revolution, it seems that the Panthers need a leader in America who will bring the Party back to the People.
>
> Brother Newton has failed you and the Party. The Panthers do not need a "day time revolutionary, a night time party goer and African fashion model as a leader." They need the leadership which only you can supply.

The New York FBI field office mailed another fictitious letter to Cleaver, supposedly from the "New York Panther 21," in order to "further aggravate the strained relationship between Newton and Cleaver":

> As you are aware, we of the Panther 21 have always been loyal to the Party and continue to feel a close allegiance to you and the ideology of the party which has been developed mainly through your efforts....
>
> We know that you have never let us down and have always inspired us through your participation in the vanguard party. As the leading theoretician of the party's philosophy and as brother among brother, we urge you to make your influence felt. We think that The Rage [i.e., Cleaver] is the only person strong enough to pull this factionalized party back together....
>
> You are our remaining hope in our struggle to fight oppression within and without the Party.

By late January 1971, the bureau's COINTELPRO campaign had begun to achieve favorable results. Cleaver was responding to the prompting of the disinformation campaign. One bureau memorandum reported that Cleaver considered one of the fictitious letters to contain "good information about the Party." Another COINTELPRO report ebulliently noted that "Cleaver has never previously disclosed to BPP officials the receipt of prior COINTELPRO letters."

Now was the time for the bureau to "more fully exploit" the dissension it had fostered. FBI headquarters directed the field office to intensify the campaign against the Black Panther Party:

> The present chaotic situation within the BPP must be exploited and recipients must maintain the present high level of counter-intelligence activity. You should each give this matter priority attention and immediately furnish Bureau recommendations...designated to further aggravate the dissension within BPP leadership.

On February 2, 1971, FBI headquarters directed each of twenty-nine field offices to submit within eight days a proposal to disrupt local Black Panther Party chapters and the Party's national headquarters in Oakland. The bureau command believed its four-year-long war against Huey Newton and the Black Panther Party was nearing victory. The situation, field office supervisors were reminded, "offers an exceptional opportunity to further disrupt, aggravate and *possibly neutralize* this organization through counter-intelligence. In light of above developments this program has been intensified...and selected offices should...increase measurably the pressure on the BPP and its leaders."

For three solid weeks, a barrage of anonymous letters flowed from FBI field offices in response to the urging from FBI headquarters. The messages became more and more vicious. On February 19, 1971, a false letter, allegedly from a Black Panther Party member in the Bay Area, was mailed to Don Cox, Cleaver's companion in Algiers. The letter intimated that the recent disappearance and presumed death of Black Panther leader Fred Bennett was the result of Party factionalism.

On February 24, an urgent teletype message from the FBI director authorized the most daring step in the campaign—a falsified message to Cleaver from a member of the Party's Central Committee. A letter over the forged signature of Elbert "Big Man" Howard, editor of *The Black Panther* newspaper, told Cleaver:

> Eldridge,
> John Seale told me Huey talked to you Friday and what he had to say. I am disgusted with things here and the fact that you are being ignored. I am loyal to the Party and it makes me mad to learn that Huey now has to lie to you. I am referring to his fancy apartment

which he refers to as the throne. I think you should know that he picked the place out himself, not the Central Committee, and the high rent is from Party funds and not paid by anyone else. Many of the others are upset about this waste of money. It is needed for other Party work here and also in Algeria. It seems the least Huey could do is furnish you the money and live with the rest of us. Since Huey will lie to you about this, you can see how it is with him. You would be amazed at what is actually happening.

I wish there was some way I could get in touch with you but in view of Huey's orders it is not possible. You should really know what's happening and statements made about you. I can't risk a call as it would mean certain expulsion. You should think a great deal before sending Kathleen. If I could talk to you I could tell you why I don't think you should.

Big Man

Eldridge Cleaver apparently believed the letter to be legitimate. Huey Newton telephoned Algiers to ask Cleaver to participate in a long-distance telephone hook-up on a San Francisco television talk show; Cleaver agreed to the plan. Three hours later, when the TV station's call to Algiers went through, Cleaver launched into a furious criticism of the Black Panther Party's Central Committee, and demanded that Panther Chief of Staff David Hilliard be removed from his post, and attacked the breakfast program as reformist.

Cleaver had regained his place in the spotlight, if only for a moment. When the Central Committee expelled him from the Black Panther Party for his behavior, Cleaver announced that the "real" Black Panther Party would thereafter be directed from Algiers. Like an ultra-left sorcerer's apprentice with a gift of verbal magic, Cleaver frenetically tried to coalesce his own followers with transatlantic exhortations for immediate guerrilla warfare.

FBI officials were elated. In mid-March, FBI headquarters declared its COINTELPRO operation aimed at "aggravating dissension" between Newton and Cleaver a success. New instructions for the field offices were promulgated:

> Since the differences between Newton and Cleaver now appear to be irreconcilable, no further counter-intelligence activity in this regard will be undertaken at this time and now new targets must be established.

David Hilliard and Egbert "Big Man" Howard of National Head-quarters and Bob Rush of Chicago B.P. Chapter are likely future targets....

Hilliard's key position at National Headquarters makes him an outstanding target. Howard and Rush are also key Panther func-tionaries...making them prime targets.

publication history

Portions of the *Huey P. Newton Reader* first appeared in *The Black Panther* newspaper between 1967 and 1980, while a variety of selections either were first published or subsequently published in the following books by Huey P. Newton:

Revolutionary Suicide. New York: Harcourt Brace Jovanovich, 1973. Scoring; Freedom; Bobby Seale; The Founding of the Black Panther Party; Patrolling; Sacramento and the "Panther Bill"; Crisis; Trial

To Die for the People: The Writings of Huey P. Newton. New York: Random House, 1972. Fear and Doubt; From "In Defense of Self-Defense" I; From "In Defense of Self-Defense" II; The Correct Handling of a Revolution; A Functional Definition of Politics; On the Peace Movement; The Women's Liberation and Gay Liberation Movement; Speech Delivered at Boston College; On the Defection of Eldridge Cleaver from the Black Panther Party and the Defection of the Black Panther Party from the Black Community; Statement; On the Relevance of the Church; Black Capitalism Re-analyzed I; Uniting Against a Common Enemy

In Search of Common Ground: Conversations with Erik H. Erikson and Huey P. Newton. New York: W. W. Norton & Company, 1973. Intercommunalism

War Against the Panthers: A Study of Repression in America. New York: Harlem River Press, 1996. Response of the Government to the Black Panther Party

selected bibliography

Blackstock, Nelson. *COINTELPRO: The FBI's Secret War on Political Freedom*. New York: The Anchor Foundation, 1975.

Brown, Elaine. *A Taste of Power: A Black Woman's Story*. New York: Pantheon Books, 1992.

Churchill, Ward and Jim Vander Wall. *Agents of Repression: The FBI's Secret Wars Against the Black Panther Party and the American Indian Movement*. Boston: South End Press, 1988.

————*The COINTELPRO Papers: Documents from the FBI's Secret War Against Domestic Dissent*. Boston: South End Press, 1990.

Cleaver, Eldridge. *Post-Prison Writings and Speeches*. New York: Vintage Books, 1970.

Davis, Angela. *Angela Davis: An Autobiography*. New York: Random House, 1974.

————*If They Come in the Morning: Voices of Resistance*. San Francisco: The National United Committee to Free Angela Davis (NUCFAD), 1971.

Dr. Huey P. Newton Foundation. *The Legacy of the Panthers*. Oakland: The Dr. Huey P. Newton Foundation, 1995.

Erikson, Erik H. and Huey P. Newton. *In Search of Common Ground: Conversations with Erik H. Erikson and Huey P. Newton*. New York: W. W. Norton & Company, 1973.

Fanon, Frantz. *The Wretched of the Earth*. New York: Weidenfeld/Grove Press, 1961.

Foner, Philip S., ed. *The Black Panthers Speak*. Philadelphia: Lippincott, 1970.

Freed, Donald. *Agony in New Haven: The Trial of Bobby Seale, Ericka Huggins, and the Black Panther Party*. New York: Simon & Schuster, 1973.

Genet, Jean. *Prisoner of Love*. Hanover, N.H.: Wesleyan University Press, 1992.

Heath, Louis, ed. *The Black Panther Leaders Speak: Huey P. Newton, Bobby Seale, Eldridge Cleaver, and Company Speak Out Through the Black Panther Party's Official Newspaper*. Metuchen, N.J.: Scarecrow Press, 1976.

————*Off the Pigs!: The History and Literature of the Black Panther Party*. Metuchen, N.J.: Scarecrow Press, 1976.

Hilliard, David and Lewis Cole. *This Side of Glory: The Autobiography of David Hilliard and the Story of the Black Panther Party*. Boston: Little, Brown and Company, 1993.

Jackson, George. *Blood in My Eye*. New York: Random House, 1972.

————*Soledad Brother: The Prison Letters of George Jackson*. New York: Random House, 1970.

Keating, Edward M. *Free Huey*. New York: Dell Publishing Company, 1970.

Kempton, Murray. *The Briar Patch: The People of the State of New York v Lumumba Shakur et al*. New York: Dell Publishing Company, 1973.

Lockwood, Lee. *Conversations with Eldridge Cleaver*. New York: Delta Books, 1970.

Malcolm X and Alex Haley. *The Autobiography of Malcolm X*. New York: Random House, 1965.

————*By Any Means Necessary: Speeches, Interviews, and a Letter*. New York: Pathfinder Press, 1970.

Mao Tse-tung. *Quotations from Chairman Mao Tse-tung*. Peking: Foreign Languages Press, 1972.

Marine, Gene. *The Black Panthers*. New York: Signet, 1969.

Moore, Gilbert. *A Special Rage*. New York: Harper & Row, 1971.

Newton, Huey P. *The Genius of Huey P. Newton: Minister of Defense of the Black Panther Party*. San Francisco: Black Panther Party, 1970.

———*Revolutionary Suicide*. New York: Harcourt Brace Jovanovich, 1973.

———*To Die for the People: The Writings of Huey P. Newton*. New York: Random House, 1972.

———*War Against the Panthers: A Study of Repression in America*. New York: Harlem River Press, 1996.

Newton, Huey P. and Ericka Huggins. *Insights and Poems*. San Francisco: City Lights Books, 1975.

O'Reilly, Kenneth. *"Racial Matters": The FBI's Secret File on Black America, 1960–1972*. New York: The Free Press, 1989.

Seale, Bobby. *A Lonely Rage: The Autobiography of Bobby Seale*. New York: Times Books, 1978.

———*Seize the Time: The Story of the Black Panther Party and Huey P. Newton*. New York: Random House, 1970.

Van Peebles, Mario, Ula Y. Taylor, and Tarika Lewis. *Panther: A Pictorial History of the Black Panthers and the Story Behind the Film*. New York: New Market Press, 1995.

Williams, Robert. *Negroes with Guns*. New York: Mazani and Munsell, 1962.

Beginning with his founding of the Black Panther Party in 1966, HUEY P. NEWTON (1942–89) set the political stage for events that would place him and the Panthers at the forefront of the African-American liberation movement for the next twenty years. Eldridge Cleaver, Bobby Seale, Angela Davis, Mumia Abu-Jamal, and Geronimo Pratt all came to prominence through Newton's groundbreaking political activism. Additionally, Newton served as the Party's chief intellectual engine, conversing with world leaders such as Yasser Arafat, Chinese Premier Chou En-lai, and Mozambique president Samora Moises Machel, among others.

Born in Monroe, Louisiana, Newton grew up in Oakland, California, where he and college classmate Bobby Seale created the Party. At first a local self-defense force against poverty and police abuse, the Black Panthers rose to international renown with Newton's arrest for the alleged murder of an Oakland police officer in 1967. The trial became a defining moment in radical left politics, and African-American history, leading to Newton's iconic status within social justice movements up to the present day.

DAVID HILLIARD is a founding member of the Black Panther Party and former chief of staff. He is the author of *This Side of Glory*, a Black Panther memoir that recounts his lifelong friendship with Newton. He also served as consultant on the Spike Lee production of Roger Guenveur Smith's acclaimed film *A Huey P. Newton Story*. As the Dr. Huey P. Newton Foundation's Executive Director, Mr. Hilliard also coordinates the Black Panther Legacy Tours (www.blackpanthertours.com). He teaches at New College in San Francisco and Merritt College in Oakland, and lectures internationally on Black Panther Party history.

DONALD WEISE is co-editor of *Black Like Us: A Century of Lesbian, Gay and Bisexual African American Fiction*. He also edited Gore Vidal's essay collection *Gore Vidal: Sexually Speaking*.

FREDRIKA NEWTON is president of the Dr. Huey P. Newton Foundation. She joined the Black Panther Party as a youth member in 1969, marrying Newton in 1981. Along with Mr. Hilliard, Ms. Newton was a consultant on *A Huey P. Newton Story*. She currently operates the Foundation's community-based programs, which include literacy, voter outreach, and health-related components.

The DR. HUEY P. NEWTON FOUNDATION is a community-based, non-profit organization devoted to disseminating the teachings of the Black Panther Party and its founder Huey P. Newton. Created in 1993 by Fredrika Newton, David Hilliard, and Elaine Brown, among others, the Foundation provides public speakers to classrooms, offers students access to the largest private collection of Party-related materials, and coordinates Black Panther Legacy Tours (www.blackpanthertours.com) in Oakland, California. Further information on the Foundation's programs, events, activities, and tours can be located at www.blackpanther.org.